LEAVE IT TO THE SPIRIT

LEAVE IT
TO THE SPIRIT

COMMITMENT AND FREEDOM IN THE NEW LITURGY

JOHN KILLINGER

SCM PRESS LTD

334 00890 5

First British edition 1971
Published by SCM Press Ltd
56 Bloomsbury Street London WC1

© John Killinger 1971

Printed in Great Britain by
Lowe & Brydone (Printers) Ltd London

This book is for Krister,
my golden-haired boy with the dancing eyes,
who lights our days with love and laughter

Contents

FOREWORD ix

INTRODUCTION xiii

FORMS 1

GAMES 15

DANCE 33

BODY 47

PERSONS 70

DRAMA 88

STORY 107

LANGUAGE 120

BLASPHEMY 143

SERMON 154

MUSIC 167

TIME / SPACE 189

METAWORSHIP 214

NOTES 225

Foreword

One critic recently remarked of the works of two other authors that they were "books written to be superseded." I gladly confess that the same is true of this book. It is really only a book on the way to becoming a book—or on the way to becoming *many* books.

It is the very nature of the material, or of what it is about, that requires its being published now, while it is still in the process of becoming something else.

We are in the midst of a far-reaching and profound cultural revolution which is just now beginning to make itself felt in the way Christians approach the matter of worship. So much is happening in liturgical innovation, and so many books and articles are being written about what is happening, that it is impossible to keep up with everything, much less assimilate it and correlate it. This is not a time for "finished" studies; it is a time for notes and tracts. Anything pretending to be more would be not only false but possibly harmful. It is important that the revolution continue.

It may be that liturgy, as the ritualistic center of what Christians believe and how they act, is the last area of traditional Western Christianity to be affected by the new cultural situation. The reluctance of many people to change their manner of worship is therefore understandable. This is a dangerous matter. But for that reason it is also fraught with the most incredible possibilities. Even the most calculating risk-taker should in this case be tempted by the odds of success.

The reader will probably note in the chapters to follow an occasional evidence of ambivalence in the author himself. Let me confess it at the outset. I am a child of the past as much as I am a man of the future. I know that the wholeness of man necessitates a backward glance or a posture of reflection as much as it does a forward look. We cannot live only on the surface of time and history, skimming along into all our tomorrows. We become schizophrenic and ill when we forget our origins.

Yet I am convinced that the major problem of worship today lies the other way around. It is not the problem of forgetting our past, but the problem of remembering and living in our present. If there is a nearly fatal lapse between the ancient and modern understandings of God, it is not because we have not perpetuated the old forms of worship but because we have not engaged in newer forms which would permit the full play of our contemporary sensibilities. We have, at the very heart of what we do as Christians, made it very difficult for God to be God in our midst. We have enshrined him in venerable liturgies when we should have freed him to assume new guises.

If I were more entirely the new man myself, the ambivalence would not have occurred. But I am not. I am amphibian, I suppose, now cherishing the aesthetic appeal of a Gregorian chant or a Gothic church, now daring to repudiate all that, if I must, to be a man of my own time in search of appropriate forms and symbols for religious belief today.

My students in seminars on worship at Vanderbilt Divinity School have been, for the most part, less divided than I. They are younger, and their sensibilities have not had to span the same gulfs as mine. I am hopelessly indebted to them, therefore, for what they have taught me. Their enthusiasm for the day in which they live has been totally contagious. They have stimulated me more than I can ever express, and have often helped to carry me, albeit sometimes screaming and kicking, into the final decades of the twentieth century.

For their sakes, if for no other reason, I am glad to offer this book as part of the "work in progress," or as a temporary stage along the way to a fuller understanding of what is required of Christian worship in our day.

Introduction

SOMETHING DRASTIC must surely happen to the church's worship during the next few years. Too much has happened to the world around us during the last half-century, and to the way we perceive reality, to permit the church to go on uninterruptedly conducting worship the way it has for the past three or four hundred years. Two global wars, nuclear fission, cybernetics, Freud, Stravinsky, Picasso, moon shots, wonder drugs, organ transplants, Telstar, ethnic revolutions, confrontation politics, the Beatles, nude theater, LSD—how many light-years are we away from the church that entered this century, the liturgy it brought with it, or even the kind of God it confessed to in its creeds?

What contempt the church shows for the world by going on, business as usual, as though nothing had happened, either outside its walls or in the consciousness of those who enter to worship! What gall is displayed by the numerous conciliar groups which begin their work of reforming the liturgy by turning to the past and trying to discover ever "purer" original forms instead of looking to the present or—heresy indeed!—even to the future, where they might descry modes of belief and action much more significant to contemporary man.

Significance is of far greater importance to aesthetics today than beauty, says critic Michael Kirby.[1] In fact, Kirby sees it as the most critical factor in determining what is art and what is not art in our time.

The same ought to be true, it seems, in liturgical matters. Granted, there is a certain muscularity about the Mass of the fifth century, or a mysticism of the Word about Luther's Communion service, or a limpid rhetorical quality about Cranmer's Eucharist in the Prayerbook. But how *significant* are they today? What do they really *signify* to a contemporary congregation of worshipers? Remember that they come from the eras of Byzantine triptychs, Breughels, and Dürers; of crossbows and armor and stone fortifications; of witches and Inquisitions, crusades and holy wars. What they signify, then, must inevitably be the theologies and religious opinions of their own epochs, much of them lost on persons who no longer share their contexts, either physically or philosophically. The significations are often, in that case, not even significant any more—at least not to men with a healthy sense of belonging to their own times.

It cannot really be argued, I think, that the old liturgies are utterly meaningless to any of us, or that they do not have a great deal of meaning to some persons who have determined to maintain rather set, traditional religious viewpoints against all odds in the world and all pressures to become contemporary in their outlooks. It is possible, after all, to "freeze" one's categories of speech and belief, and to exist reasonably well with those categories—at least among others who have agreed to do the same. As Professor Sten Stenson has shown in his book *Sense and Nonsense in Religion,* the language of Zion is truly meaningful to people inside the traditional church in the same way that the alogic of the pun is meaningful to persons who agree upon the terms of the pun and to their being used in an alogical way.

It must also be true, however, that the act of freezing categories, of halting further experimentation, exploration, and risk, carries its own doom inside it. We can feed positively on our discoveries or achievements only so long before we reach a point of inversion and begin to receive primarily negative value. It does not matter what area of human life we talk about —marriage, community, environment, religion—the same is always true. When we cease to grow and venture, the sources of our existence become stagnant and even toxic.

To talk of God's reinvesting the acts and language of traditional religion with his own life and power may be a kind of spiritual charlatanism designed to keep cultic leaders and manipulators in office. It clearly defies both our own theological insight that he has usually chosen not the established religionists but the disenfranchised and disaffiliated to do his work and the rather obvious historical information that he has constantly been engaged at new activities in our midst. What we believe about God does not lead us to think he would *withhold* his presence and meaning from our traditionalized rites and ceremonies. But what we know about traditionalized rites and ceremonies, on the other hand, inclines us to suspect that they themselves become less and less congenial to manifestations of spirit and originality, so that finally they divorce themselves from the possibility of divine infusion. They congeal and harden around a memory, and so refuse the present or the future. Their words become mere empty rhetoric, and the further their actual origin from the life-styles and situations of the persons using them, the less capable they are of becoming the receptacles of imparted meaning.

Liturgists who are charged with the continued use of old ceremonies must consequently become liturgiologists, explaining the *meaning* of phrases and actions grown occult through the years, in the attempt to resensitize participants and enable them to derive some semblance of value from them. They are confronted by the almost impossible task of reawakening spontaneity and immediacy in forms that have become habitual and "dead," so that they no longer resonate to contemporary rhythms. The pathos of this is obvious in Monsignor Ronald Knox's beautifully written little book *The Mass in Slow Motion,* which describes how priests become bored with their roles as celebrants and must continually invent games and fantasies to keep them awake while saying their offices.

Still, this is an accepted environment in the church, accepted because it has become the environment. Many faithful parishioners return without fail to the announced services, and do it year in and year out. If they are bored, as many of them will confess in private, they accept the responsibility of that themselves and don't blame the church. "There must be something wrong with me," they say. And continuing to go, to endure it, becomes a form of penance for them; like some bitter medicine, it *must* be good for them.

It would be difficult to overestimate the damage that has been done to the Christian religion by this lethargic kind of practice over the past half-century. One can hardly wonder at the fact that many persons feel an immediate, if somewhat reluctant, sympathy with the theologians who in recent years announced the "death" of God. It did not matter that the theologians were young and somewhat unskillful as practitioners of their discipline; what they had to say struck responsive chords deep inside many moderns who had experienced the withdrawal of the divine in an almost mystical or intuitive way. They did not care about philosophical arguments or metaphysical premises; what they understood was that they knew far better the hollowness of religious creedalism and ritualism than they did the excitement, or rumored excitement, of the presence of holiness. Nothing of the holiness was really communicated by the forms of worship they had known, because, contrary to what some theologians and ministers appear to believe, holiness can never be communicated outside of vitally secular and contemporary forms.

Henry Adams, scion of the famous early American Adamses, understood this already in the late nineteenth century, when he noted that the crowds of tourists in France no longer traipsed adoringly through the great medieval shrines to the Madonna but gathered excitedly instead before the new dynamo on exhibit at the Exposition in Paris. It would be simplistic to accuse them of worshiping the machine; what they were awed by was the *power* and the *relevance* of it, qualities obviously diminishing at the former shrines.

This is not to suggest that the church adopt a faddist approach to matters of faith and worship, always wetting a finger to the wind to see which way to veer. It is to say, on the other hand, that power and relevance are definitely related, and that the church is bound to find itself powerless in a society where its concerns and forms are of little obvious relevance.

We can sneer at the times if we like, and smugly draw our institutional robes more tightly around us, shutting out the chill. We can even congratulate ourselves on our perseverance and perdurance in a world which, if it is not actively hostile to our existence, is at least passively indifferent. After all, didn't Jesus promise that we would be hated by the world which hated him? It is easy to become self-righteous about failure.

But those who are still concerned for the world we live in will be uncomfortable with such an attitude. We suspect, even if we cannot prove it, that it is unfaithful to the mind and heart of Jesus. *He* did not shut himself off from people or adopt a priestly pose and identify himself with conservative religious practice. In fact, he daringly predicted to the traditionalists that their beloved Temple, which was the fixated center of their highly institutionalized religion, would be destroyed, and then where would they be? No, somehow we are convinced that there is some truth to Johannes Hoekendijk's observation that people have got it all wrong if they believe the proper order of God's evangelization program is GOD-CHURCH-WORLD, with the church standing self-importantly in the middle as a channel of grace and information to the world at large; that the real order is GOD-WORLD-CHURCH, with the church in fact receiving its life and style and information through the world and then becoming the M.C., the poet, the toastmaster, for celebrating the presence of God in all life.

What we need, perhaps, are more of what McLuhan calls "anti-environmentalists" in our midst, more people who have not been blinded by habit to the inadequacies and incongruities of Christian thinking and worshiping, who will honestly speak out and say so whenever they feel that there are radical discontinuities between the church and our period-style. In our fear, our hesitance, our insecurity, we tend to discourage such voices, if we do not actually squelch them. They unsettle and annoy us. But, more than we know, they may be the voices of God, warning us against pride in our fonts and phylacteries— or even in our creeds and liturgies!

LEAVE IT TO THE SPIRIT

Forms

FORM AND CONTENT, as the human mind perceives them, are invariably related to each other. McLuhan's famous dictum that "the medium is the message" is only another way of saying the same thing. The form of a thing cannot be altered without affecting, albeit even imperceptibly, the way we experience and understand its substance.

It is all the more remarkable, in the light of this, that there has occurred such a profound revolution in the arts during the last hundred years or so. We cannot but wonder at the enormous personal courage of men such as Stravinsky, Picasso, Klee, Artaud, Beckett, Godard, and Cage. They have actually dared to alter the way we perceive reality, the way we feel, the way we experience the world around us. Somehow, unconsciously, they must have been men of the deepest kind of faith possible. They hazarded the world as they knew it against the possibility that a new world, one which they could descry only dimly and uncertainly, would come to exist in its wake. There was no promise that the new world would support them—only the intuition that it was there, waiting to be discovered. And the way between the old and the new was fraught with as many perils as any uncharted journey ever is. Yet they felt compelled to risk it.

Think of the kinds of chances they took. Marcel Duchamp exhibited common artifacts such as a commode and a bottle rack as works of art. Hugo Ball and the Dadaists in Zurich recited entire poems composed of nonsense language or phonemes, sometimes doing them in antiphonal arrangements or to the accompaniment of music or noises. Franz Kafka wrote stories and novels which appeared to be mere transcriptions of dreams and the unconscious life. Dali and Buñuel made films combining startling, fantastic images with a shockingly Freudian interpretation of the human subconscious. Ionesco wrote a play comprised entirely of silly, inconsecutive speeches found in textbooks of grammar. Jackson Pollock developed huge canvases by dripping paint on them from above. Allan Kaprow made environmental art pieces which required the "viewer" to turn on lights, ring bells, work treadles, etc. John Cage recorded four minutes and thirty-three seconds of silence, allowing the various background noises, the nonmusical sounds, to become the only "music" in the piece.

In one sense, the whole history of contemporary art reads like the scenario for a Marx brothers film, with the emphasis on zaniness, discontinuity, and exhibition!

Michel Seuphor, a well-known artist and critic, has expressed amazement that so many famous figures from the first half of our century were willing to pay the price of such a revolution. He notes the fact that the many "little magazines" which sprang up all over Europe and bore an influence far out of proportion to their size or regularity or elegance were usually published just one step ahead of the bill collectors, and often folded after only a few issues. The astonishing experimentalism of those years went on at a time when there was practically no audience at all except the artists themselves to enjoy it and contribute to its maintenance. "Were there at that time," asks Seuphor, "even ten persons in the world who bought abstract art?"[1]

One can hardly forbear contrasting with this picture the almost paralyzing timidity which characterizes most Christian groups when faced with the problem of their outdated liturgies.

Imagine this scene in a local church where the council has been convened to consider revisions of the order of service which has been in use there longer than anyone can or cares to remember. The pastor lays the matter on the table: There have been suggestions from time to time that the old order is something less than a suitable vehicle for the worship of the present congregation, especially the under-thirty group. There are no specific recommendations, just a few expressions of discontent. Amidst some grumbling and a few giggles, discussion is undertaken. It has been delayed through three previous meetings, and there is not now any serious business whose consideration might delay it longer.

Elder *A* begins the discussion by stating that there is nothing wrong with the present order, which has served him and one generation before him and will surely serve any thoughtful generation that might follow his. "The trouble is not in the order," he says, "it's in people who don't want to worship any more."

Elder *B* agrees that the present order has been good and useful for many years, but says that he often trades for a new automobile before the old one is worn out, "just to keep in style." He would favor making "a few changes."

Mrs. *X*, who represents the women's group on the council, says that the prelude the week before was "simply awful, too bombastic for our little sanctuary," and wonders if the organist, old Mr. Primple, isn't becoming too senile for the responsibility he has borne so faithfully for over forty years.

The pastor confesses that he has considered abandoning the use of the Nicene Creed, which many of the folk attest they cannot repeat in its entirety without perjuring themselves. He can understand how there might be divergences of interpretation at certain points, and would prefer sacrificing "a grand old creed" to maintaining a stumbling block before any of the parishioners.

Elder *A* is temporarily incensed. Let the squeamish depart, if they wish, and find a creedless church more to their liking. He himself would leave before he would see that "dignified, ancient statement of belief" removed from the service.

And so it goes, our usual game of moving the furniture, of trying it on this wall and that, and of leaving it finally where it all stood in the first place. Even the persons who have the courage to make some changes are reluctant to make them at the expense of peace and good will in the congregation. And, as a group, we are far less daring than the artists of the world. We seem not to have the confidence required to reshape the liturgical environment in any drastic way. Perhaps we fear that if we retire our traditional forms and language, the God we knew will disappear with them, and we shall wake up bereft of everything.

It seldom occurs to us that our hesitance at this point says some rather distressing things about our theology—not the theology we say we hold, but the theology that actually informs our behavior and way of life. It suggests, for example, that we imagine God to be somehow dependent on our particular way of approaching him in worship, or at least that we expect him to react favorably only so long as we cleave to that particular way. God is reduced to the size and shape of *our* activities. We preserve his existence, or prolong it, by conforming to certain time-hallowed practices. If we don't rock the boat, neither of us gets into trouble.

What is the opposite of this viewpoint? That God is indeed God, and in no way at all depends on our patronage or conformity to particular rituals for either his existence or his mode of acting in the world. *We* are affected by what we do in worship; that much is obvious. But styles of worship—whether we use a threefold amen or a ninefold, whether we sing folk songs or a High Mass, whether we come draped in liturgical robes or in clown outfits—do not alter the nature and being of God. We can sing the Doxology standing on the pews, we can play hopscotch or Red Rover in the chancel, or, *in extremis*, we can even urinate in the font, and *God* will not be changed by it!

Genuine confidence in the deity, the kind of confidence the gospel of Christ is supposed to produce, frees us to do anything we choose in his presence without fear that it will upset him, prejudice him against us, or in any manner shake or undermine his existence. On the contrary, there is a sense in which the freedom to do absurd or foolish things, even to the point of introducing obscenities into the sanctuary, as has been done on occasion, is the surest sign of a true confidence in God's being and in his good will toward men. There are some things, depending on our individual pieties and sense of taste or propriety, which we shall not wish to do, and some things which we shall deem unproductive for common worship. What we do choose to do will depend largely on the gifts and backgrounds which we bring to the occasion. But, as a general thing, a reluctance to address ourselves to the stodginess and inadequacy of old forms of worship is evidence of hidden insecurities with regard to faith and theology; an unwillingness to venture, to explore, to take risks, is symptomatic of rather common disorders in the area of belief and commitment.

In order to establish a point of reference at the other end of the spectrum from the hesitant church council I described earlier, let us imagine the following synopsis of a service of worship devised by a liberally-oriented congregation accustomed to seeing contemporary theater and viewing the world through the eyes of recent artists.

A SCAPEGOAT SERVICE

The congregation enters in absolute silence and remains seated without speaking or looking around. After a few minutes of this, a man somewhere near the front of the congregation stands up and begins to remove his clothes. He may stop at his shorts or an athletic strap. Someone near him, who has been provided with a grease crayon, begins to write aggression or resentment phrases on him. Someone else joins the first writer. They, in turn, pass the crayons on to others and urge them to write on the man.

At this point, musical accompaniment may begin. It may be provided by a small combo or by stereo tapes. It should be primarily secular in nature, although an occasional hymn or Bach number may be included.

While people continue to write upon the first man, a woman in another part of the room rises and begins to disrobe. The same process is followed. Elsewhere, a third person rises and repeats the action; a fourth, a fifth, perhaps more.

The ministers, who may have been robed and seated facing the congregation in the beginning, must take part in these inscribing rites also.

When the graffiti-bearers are all marked up, they begin to race about the room crying and screaming. The music should at this time become tumultuous and cacophonous. Members of the congregation should likewise howl and scream, and some might even produce drums and castanets and begin to sound them.

During the melee a figure in white robes walks quietly down the center aisle to the altar and begins to disrobe, laying the pieces of clothing aside very carefully. He may be painted as a harlequin, either in very bright splotches of color or in black-and-white waves emanating and swirling outward from his navel; or he may be painted in black-and-white stripes like a prisoner. He stands on the altar and stretches as in a dream ballet.

Suddenly the music stops. The graffiti-bearers, heretofore unaware of the new figure, see him and fall silent. In ghastly silence, the altar-figure continues his dance.

The music bursts forth again, and the graffiti-bearers, immobile before, rush forward to the altar-figure. Seizing his limbs, they hold him aloft, circle the altar, lay him upon it, and pile upon him in a frenzy of writhing limbs. During the most hectic part of this, the music reaches its crescendo (it could be the "Hallelujah Chorus" from the soundtrack of *Bob and Carol and Ted and Alice*).

Then, with one deafening note from a bass drum, the music stops. Stillness. Exhaustion.

Quietly, after a moment, the graffiti-bearers return to their
original places in the congregation, replace their clothing, and are
seated again in prayerful attitudes, as if nothing had happened.
The women may even put on lipstick or adjust their coiffures, the
men comb their hair.

A woman or a child in the congregation stands and says, without
obvious emotion, "He was wounded for our transgressions, he was
bruised for our iniquities; the Lord has laid on him the iniquity of
us all."

The minister in the front stands and says, "Go home."

Admittedly this is a radical departure from customary forms of
worship. It is too daring in its conception and use of physical
action, too harsh in its compression and symbolism, for most of
us. I confess that it scares me; I should tremble at being named
a participant in such a service, or at being the minister in charge
of its staging and execution. But I suspect it is what we ought
to be doing, occasionally if not with some frequency. The reason
we are so frightened by it is that we have always ventured so
little. Worship has always been "safe." We have stayed close to
base and avoided the chance of offending or being offended.

We live in a Peter Max world of exciting colors and configurations. We listen to music that is produced both electronically
and atonally. We read novelists who write cryptically and
suggestively, so that we are forced to puzzle over their meanings or else despair of their having any meaning. We produce
and watch television shows and movies that are so weird or
imaginative as to defy our intelligence and appeal only to our
emotions. But for some reason we have not brought our everyday way of life into the sanctuary of the church. We have a
syncopated, rock-and-roll, electronic consciousness for most of
the week and a funereal, four-four attitude toward Sunday
morning. And what it means is that Sunday morning is where
least is happening in our lives.

Michael Kirby says that the important changes in man's history are "those more or less permanent ones in the state and

organization of consciousness"—the ones which actually bring
about an alteration in the structure and efficiency of consciousness, of the way man sees his world.[2] Kirby regards art as being
vastly important to man precisely because it changes his way of
viewing things, and thus, by extension, his entire being, his
self-conception, his mode of consciousness.

If worship is to exert the formative influence on man and
civilization in our day that we have been pleased to believe it
exerted in previous eras of the church's life, it must become as
inventive as the arts and as central to the modern consciousness
as the Mass was to men in the Middle Ages.

This is not to say that there is not today a great deal of residual
meaning in the Mass even as it was performed between the
Council of Trent and Vatican II. François Mauriac said in *What
I Believe* that he could no longer bear to go to Low Mass in his
old age because his emotions overwhelmed him so. W. H.
Auden once told a reporter that he was grieved by the church's
decision to abandon Latin in its worship; let the sermon be
timely and in the vernacular, he said, but let the Mass be timeless and in Latin. And Jean Genet, the French criminal turned
poet, playwright, and novelist, remarked in *The Thief's Journal*
that the Mass is the most dramatic form in all of Western history
and culture.

But this in no way controverts the need for new liturgies in
an imaginative contemporary mode. Old art continues to coex-
ist with the new. Men still weep before the works of Botticelli,
Michelangelo, and Rembrandt. Yet the sensibility of our time
has required a new vision, and the new vision has in turn influenced the sensibility. As one design for worship, the Mass has
certainly proved itself, and it is difficult to imagine that it will
ever be surpassed. Especially in its Latin form, it bears the
marks of irrationality, mystery, solemnity, irony, and contradiction which are so much a part of even the present-day mood
of absurdity and daring. It is only when we are limited to the
single form, when it is maintained as the exclusive mode of

worship or holy tradition, that it begins to seem heavy and
oppressive to the consciousness.

The theory implicit in the arts today is that reality is not, and
for that matter has never been, so precise and small and regular
as our fathers in earlier times believed. Confronted by enormous geographical problems, reality for them had to do with
recognizing physical barriers and limitations; their energies
could be poured into moving westward, acquiring new lands,
exploiting them, even defending them against new aggressors
or the return of the natives. But in an imploded world like ours
today the mind has many other things to consider. Reflection
begins to ricochet, and it becomes impossible to tell image from
reality. The images themselves, as a matter of fact, have an
obvious kind of reality all their own.

In this complex and multifaceted situation it is no longer
possible to deal comprehensively with human reality. The artist
"permits" reality to "break through" in his works; he becomes
a kind of enabler, manipulating colors or sounds or shapes with
a sensitivity to the moments when they suddenly reveal something, when they catch reality in flight; and he freezes that
split-second of reality, immobilizes it, so that it remains arrested
for others to see or hear it. But he cannot begin to capture all
reality or to express it in his work. He understands, more than
the artists of any age before him, how limited and humiliated
he really is.

But his sense of humiliation for his person and his work is
compensated for, on the other hand, by the supremest confidence in the world itself, in the reality which is to be revealed.
The artist has decreased, but his respect for reality has in-
creased. He feels like a poor, inarticulate priest serving at the
altar of truth; he never fully recognizes the presence when it
comes, or expresses very well what he does recognize; but he
is surer of its existence, and of its will to make itself known, than
he is even of his own being.

As a result of this kind of confidence, the artist is free to experiment, to try all kinds of new forms and techniques and approaches. Success is no longer measured in terms of quantity. A certain kind of glaze on a rock, a particular bobble in a single line transversing a canvas, a mere household item or piece of clothing affixed to a textured background or a vertical support, may bracket reality as definitively as a "David" or a "Mona Lisa" or a "Guernica." Pieces of thin glass suspended in a mobile may achieve it as purely as a fugue or a sonata or a symphony. As Kandinsky said, "Alles ist erlaubt"—everything is allowed!

This could well be taken as the motto for the arts in our time. It isn't always possible, of course, to tell the jokes from the serious works, the high jinks from the masterpieces. But there is a new reverence for the vastness of reality, for the depth of the mysteries in which we live, and for the possibility of communication between those mysteries and our lives. The more outlandish the medium which the artist attempts, the greater his success if he succeeds at all. The fresher his approach, the more he enriches us.

Most of us, unfortunately, seldom exercise our imaginative powers to their full capacity. Like an animal which keeps digging in the same hole even after it is apparent that what it seeks is not in that location, we continue to burrow down in the same spot long after we have mined most of the significance from it. What we ought to learn, contends Edward de Bono, is to forsake old mine shafts and sink new ones. Instead of always pursuing things vertically, we ought to pursue them laterally—move to the side and begin new explorations.[3]

In his recollections of the painter Fernand Leger, Michel Seuphor reflects on conversations he had with Leger concerning the work of Mondrian, who exerted an obvious influence on Leger. Leger, he recalls, would frequently conclude a conversation with some quip to the effect that "these Northerners always carry things too far." "I never contradicted him," says Seuphor. "But it has since become clear to me how important

it is to carry things too far. The world would stand still if no one
ventured beyond the limits of the familiar."[4]

The danger in our liturgical attempts is that we will not carry
things far enough. We will not think radically enough. Because
we are trying to serve paying constituencies (in some ways
equivalent to the patronage system in art), we are too liable to
provide for them only such compositions or arrangements as we
think they are prone to care for and readily accept. We pander
to former tastes and states of being, and thus do nothing to
prepare new tastes and states of being. By keeping just barely
up with the times, and reflecting only the mood people are
presently in, we are always slightly behind the times and never
truly contemporary. We do not lead the spirits of the worshipers, or challenge them.

Consequently our ideas of God are usually more neat and
precise than they ought to be. They are more comfortable than
they have a right to be. People are not put upon to reach or
stretch or reconceive anything. Their systems can handle things
very well, and they go on subconsciously believing that God can
really fit into the limited confines of their own existence. We are
only catering further to the supreme inversion which has occurred in Western theological life sometime during the past
millenium or two, whereby God depends upon man for his
validity and not man upon God. It is no wonder, given the ways
by which we try to worship God, that we have finally begun to
suspect that he is dead, or just not up to the modern sense of
reality.

"Audiences know what to expect," says a character in the
play *Rosencrantz and Guildenstern Are Dead*, "and that is all
they are prepared to believe in."[5]

Isn't it the same in the church? Don't we begin too modestly
and expect too little of worshipers? How are they to respond to
the wildness of God with a liturgy which, chances are, represents a three- or four-hundred-year-old religious mentality,
brought up to date only by occasional minor linguistic revision,

such as changing "thee" and "thy" to "you" and "your"? Whoever said it was not wrong: that if the body of the deceased God is ever found, the silver dagger sticking in his back will belong to the church.

There is much we could learn from Aaron Copland, who has complained of the "universal preponderance of old music on concert programs," and how this practice stifles both creative listening among audiences and creative composition among artists.

This unhealthy state of affairs [he says], this obsession with old music, tends to make all music listening sage and unadventurous since it deals so largely in the works of the accepted masters. Filling our halls with familiar sounds induces a sense of security in our audiences; they are gradually losing all need to exercise freely their own musical judgment. Over and over again the same limited number of bona fide, guaranteed masterpieces are on display; by inference, therefore, it is mainly these works that are worth our notice. This narrows considerably in the minds of a broad public the very conception of how varied musical experience may be, and puts all lesser works in a false light. It conventionalizes programs, obviously, and overemphasizes the interpreter's role, for only through seeking out new "readings" is it possible to repeat the same works year after year. Most pernicious of all, it leaves a bare minimum of wall space for the showing of the works of new composers, without which the supply for future writers of masterworks is certain to dry up.[6]

Copland is right, of course. In a conventionalized situation the interpreter's role does become immense. It has done so in Christianity. It has become so important, in fact, that the interpreter has been institutionalized, and we sometimes wonder whether there will ever again be a sense of immediacy in our faith. We are even distrustful of immediacy. We no longer believe in the kind of spontaneity which was once the very hallmark of Christian belief. Everything is programed and controlled by old masters. We are afraid of novelty. We discourage invention. We live in the past.

We could likewise learn from Antonin Artaud, the speculative dramatist whose writings, principally in *The Theater and Its Double,* have so greatly influenced the thought of writers and directors in the theater of the last twenty years. Artaud was alarmed by the same kind of practice in the theater that Copland was alarmed about in the concert hall. Everybody played Shakespeare or Ibsen or Shaw. Even the new plays echoed the old ones. There was no originality in the theater. When people came to the theater, they saw neat little vignettes out of their own lives encapsulated in a play and set on the stage before them. They were entertained, but they were not changed.

Away with this kind of theater! cried Artaud. It does no one any good. It only reflects our own opinions back to us. Let us see instead visions of the unknown, phantoms from the subconscious mind, shapes out of the imagination. Stop the old speeches! Use the words as missiles, projectiles. Hurl them at us without mercy! Make us want to stop our ears against them. Turn the lights in our eyes. Blind us! Forget about sequences of action. We know all we need to know about sequences of action. Show us instead fantasies, nonsequiturs, impromptu behavior. Let the theater become a whirlwind of higher forces, filled with updraughts and downdraughts of spirit capable of upending a man and disorienting him completely to life as he knew it. His old way of seeing things was worn out, anyway. This may be his only hope of salvation. Show him no mercy.

Artaud was not generally respected in his own day, and he died a lonely suicide. But the theater—and the movies as well —will never be the same again because of him. The present-day renaissance in both forms of art is largely indebted to the idea for which he stood, namely, that it is the duty of the arts not to comfort men with palliating visions of the realities confronting them but to disturb them, to get them off their duffs, to sear their imaginations in such a way that they can never forget to think and feel again.

The church ought to be ashamed of itself. It has identified itself too thoroughly with conservatism, hesitance, and tradition. It has tended too often to support old ideas, old doctrines, old ways of conceiving things, when, with its word of creativity and grace, it ought to have been setting fire to the old and giving birth to the new!

"There are too many signs," said Artaud, "that everything that used to sustain our lives no longer does so, that we are all mad, desperate, and sick."[7]

It is time we dug some new holes. What the world needs today, says Harvey Cox in *The Feast of Fools*, what it *must* have, is a "meta-institution" which exists to link together the worlds of fact and fantasy, which is in touch with the most advanced artistic movement of the day and with both historical and transhistorical images of the future. But the church has thus far turned down its opportunity to become this meta-institution, because it has been unwilling to risk its propertied status in Caesar's society. "The sad truth is that the church *cannot* be the meta-institution our world needs to instruct us in festivity, to open us to fantasy, to call us to tomorrow, or to enlarge our petty definitions of reality. It cannot for only one reason: the church is not the church."[8] It is time we rediscovered our vocation in the world, and with it the sense with which to fulfill it.

Games

ONE CAN HARDLY help being struck, when he sees films or descriptions of various primitive forms of worship, by how unsedentary they are. They usually involve rhythm, movement, dancing, even frenzy, before they are over.

The picture of religion as largely sedentary, as sitting and listening, is rather peculiar to Western Christianity, and particularly to post-Reformation developments in Protestantism. "That bitch Reason," as Luther called it, finally managed to crowd out other elements from the time of worship and to establish what amounted nearly to a death grip over the behavior of Christians assembled for liturgical purposes.

The liturgy of the church is *zwecklos aber doch sinnvoll,* says Romano Guardini in *The Spirit of the Liturgy*—"pointless but still significant." But Protestantism, arising coevally with rationalism, was determined that it should not be pointless. God had given man a mind with which to surmount his passions and his environment, and the most godlike thing men could do in worshiping him was to exercise the mind in understanding God and his will for the world. Thus were we betrayed into what D. H. Lawrence once called "the *cul de sac* of mind-consciousness," and so learned to give ourselves, in a liturgical setting, to "interpreting" the scriptures, solving problems, and thinking God's thoughts after him.

The paradigm of this kind of worship is the Puritan worship

service in old New England, which clearly valued the acts of the mind over the acts of the body, and enforced a dreadful seriousness on the whole business of praising God. There was nothing in the churches to delight the eye or any other of the bodily senses. The body was to be kept in utter submission while the mind fed upon divine matters.

The Puritan meetinghouses were plain, unadorned pine buildings, with no hint of comfort about them. The only velvet or leather "cooshooning" in most of them was on the lectern, where the great Bible sat—not on any of the pews. The pews were usually made of split logs, hand-riven, with spraddled legs under them, like long milking benches. They had no backs. Even when pew boxes became fashionable, with floors a little higher than the floor of the aisle and with doors that could be latched and shut after the occupants were in, the backs of the boxes rose perpendicularly from the rear of the seats, so that they offered support but little comfort.

In this abstemious setting, freezing in winter and suffering from the heat in summer, the Puritans normally sat for two and three hours through a single sermon, and sometimes more. No minister was considered worth his pay who did not pray for at least an hour in the meetings. Cotton Mather recorded that he prayed for an hour and a quarter at his own ordination, and then preached for another hour and three quarters. A tithingman, descendant of the English beadle, was equipped with a long pole for keeping sleepers awake. It had a knob on one end, with which he rapped the heads of men and boys, and a rabbit's foot or a squirrel's tail on the other end, with which he tickled the faces of women and girls until they had quite recovered a sense of where they were. The tithingman also had the duty of turning the hourglass which sat at the front of the building, but the minister rarely took notice of it, his sermon usually running to "twenty-seventhly" or "twenty-eighthly" or beyond.

At noon, after a full morning of listening to prayers and sermon (what little music there was appears to have been small relief, amounting to what the *Bay Psalm-Book* described as "Squeaking above and Grumbling below"), the people repaired to their homes, if they were near enough, or to the tavern, or in some cases to what was called a "Noon-house," where they ate their lunches, visited, and gossiped. Then they returned, after the lapse of an hour or sometimes two, for another service not unlike the one they had endured in the morning.

It is no wonder that children often stared at the thin rod supporting the heavy sounding board above the minister's head and hoped that it might snap, "putting out" the minister, or that they often got into trouble out of sheer boredom.

This was the protoform of American Protestant worship. It was the disciplined handmaiden of the rationalistic movement in Western philosophy. In later meetinghouses, the ones with pew boxes, there were often swing-shelves installed in the front of the boxes to be used as writing desks for the worshipers, who were expected to copy out the main divisions of the sermon, take home their notes, and continue "reasoning together with the Lord" there. Even the men of the community who were illiterate often made a great show of doodling on their note paper, for they were unwilling to be outdone in holiness. And this emphasis on propriety and order, reason and thoughtfulness, has persisted right down to the church on Main Street in our own time. The setting may be more comfortable; there are sometimes cushions on the pews, and buildings are usually centrally heated and air-conditioned. And the services may be briefer; they rarely exceed an hour or an hour and a quarter on Sunday morning. But the notion that worship consists primarily of singing, praying, and instruction or exhortation, that it is sedentary, done primarily with the mouth and the mind, is nearly as strong today as it ever was.

The world outside the meetinghouse has changed a great deal, however. There have begun to be enormous reservations about the power and place of rationality in human existence. Freud and the psychologists have undermined its position as the absolutely preeminent human faculty. The Dadaists and Surrealists injected a spirit of fun into the arts, and made the creative persons in the world aware of the significance of the insignificant, wild, and unpredictable elements in human existence. Valéry as an old man repudiated the stodginess of Monsieur Teste, the man who was all mind and science, whom Valéry the young man had created. Beckett designed *Krapp's Last Tape* as a satire on Proust and Joyce and other giants of thought who endeavored to fix or freeze human reality by an act of the intellect. Philosophy and theology have been humbled. Feelings are in resurgence. Man has found that he cannot live by thought alone, even the thoughts proceeding out of the mouth of the man of God. He requires more.

As Sam Keen explains it in *Apology for Wonder,* there is something wrong with any culture that leans too exclusively toward Apollonianism, doing everything with decency and order, or toward Dionysianism, living always in heat and frenzy. There must be a healthy balance between the two. And it often happens, when a society has been oriented too long in one direction, that it will overreact in the other.

I could not fail to remark, in a recent documentary film about Eskimo life, the innate sense of balance in Eskimo rituals. There is a climate of excitement and rejoicing about them which compensates for the normally austere existence of the people. The Eskimo hunts, fishes, skins animals for clothing, collects ice for drinking water, and spends much of his time in relative inactivity, sequestered in his small home against the blizzards of a long winter. When he does emerge from this retirement, then, he dons his best garments and undertakes the ritual acts of the tribe or community with great enthusiasm. First there are dances to the gods in gratitude for food and safety and in appeasement for any offenses committed. During these dances, the participants wear appropriate holy masks, sing, and clap their hands. As the ritual proceeds, the dancing becomes more spirited, until finally the holy masks are laid aside and the dancers put on other masks which are caricatures of individuals in the village. Then things really become frenzied. No one is spared in these last dances. It is an occasion of great merriment. Men are put in their proper places after homage has been paid to the deities, and it is all done with an obvious *élan* and sense of joy.

How many Christians, I thought as I glanced around the theater in front of me, must secretly wish that their religion were so profoundly simple and joyous! Yet they will return to their churches on Sunday with the same sense of gravity and decorum that has marked their religious observance for the last several centuries, and restrain themselves long enough to say a few prayers and sing a few hymns and listen to a sermon. They will probably never articulate to themselves the dissatisfaction they feel with the latter way, or connect it in any meaningful manner to the performance by the Eskimos they have witnessed. Some of them will quietly and gradually defect from the churches. But they will not realize it could have been as much fun in church as it was for the Eskimos.

It is at this point that more Christians need to become acquainted with the thought of Robert Neale, who has developed an anthropology of play.[1] Man is by nature a player, says Neale, not a worker. It is a distortion of his true nature when he sees work as his most important objective in life. Then he enslaves himself, and his spirit of adventure begins to diminish. He cannot respond to his environment with his full potential. He utilizes only those energies necessary to the discharging of certain functions, and represses others which would become immediately evident if he were able to relax and enjoy life. He makes certain gestures toward playing, but even his gestures smack of contrivance and performance. He finally loses the ability to respond totally, the way a child does.

There had been notable studies of play before. The most famous were perhaps Johan Huizinga's *Homo Ludens* and Roger Caillois' *Man, Play, and Games*. But Neale's is the first to conceive of the entire life-style in terms of play. Huizinga defined it as "a significant function" of man; Neale sees it as a normative state from which all other states are merely derivative or to which they are related. Maturation in the individual, he declares, is growing from a state of playfulness in infancy to full play in adulthood. And full play, he says, is what religion is.

There is thus a connection between gracefulness, or the ease with which people move through life, and grace, or the state of the soul.

> Full movement is always graceful and awkward action is always inhibited action. An easy way to discover the worker is to look for awkwardness, awkwardness of body, mind, and spirit. To discover the adventurer, the one who plays the game, look for the gift of gracefulness. It can be perceived on the pingpong table and checkerboard, and on any other field of human activity. Play sets boundaries that cut across those set by the work world.[2]

Neale distinguishes between "partial play" and "full play." The twelve-year-old child playing a game of checkers is only partially at play; he is not employing the characteristic bodily energies of a child of twelve. An old man of seventy-seven, on the other hand, may very well be at full play when he is engaged at a game of checkers. It is not necessary that we be at full play all of the time; indeed it is probably impossible for anyone to be so engrossed in play. Work and partial play are also required. But it is important that we be at full play at least part of the time, that we be able to throw ourselves into some things, to lose ourselves in the game. Otherwise we never discharge the energies we have, and fail to live full and well-expended lives.

What is wrong with most of our religion, says Neale, is that it does not permit us to play at it fully. It has too few moments when it sweeps us out and away from ourselves, when it takes all of our faculties into tension with itself, and uses them. It tends to concentrate on our need for design, for knowing the order of things, and not enough on our need for discharge, for release, for ecstatic deliverance. It is long on *story* and short on *game*.

This is precisely the criticism we feel instinctively about Puritan worship. It is too verbal, too design-oriented, too given to knowledge and thought about life. It lacks movement, spontaneity, joy, ecstasy, grace. It does not offer the necessary opportunity to discharge energy, to dance, to celebrate.

The need to discharge energy cannot always be repressed, however, and the revivalistic outbreaks among the Puritans are one evidence of this. The inventive subconscious discovered in the revival a mode of release which the church could not fail to sanction. Descriptions of a New England meeting in which people screamed and writhed on the floor and ran wildly about the church house remind us of the vengeance often wrought by long starved and neglected desires to dance and revel before the Lord.

This need is more often met among sectarian groups than in the established churches even in the present era. Anyone who has been to a Holy Roller meeting in a courthouse auditorium or read John Sherrill's *They Speak with Other Tongues* knows something about the freedom in the sect meetings to surrender to the urge to shake or shout or run around the room or give testimony to the spirit that is "moving" in the meeting. Sherrill, who was an Episcopalian when he undertook an assignment to write a book about the glossolalia phenomenon, became so impressed by the extraordinary demonstrations of spirit and delight among tongues-speakers that he finally surrendered to the movement and had an experience of "seizure" himself. There is nothing cheaply journalistic about his descriptions of the holiness movement. There is, in fact, a sense of joy and healthiness about them.

Sherrill describes in the introduction of his book a kind of analogy for understanding what happens when people are "in the spirit." He says he was sitting across from a big bass voice in the choir one night at choir practice and noticed that he sang better than he ever had before. He "resonated" to the voice across from him. Afterwards he spoke to the possessor of the voice about it. The man said, in effect, "If you thought that was something, try sitting in front of me next week." Sherrill did. Midway through a song, the man said to him, "Lean into me." Puzzled, Sherrill leaned back until he was touching the man's chest. Suddenly, he said, the music seemed to pour through him. It originated in the big bass voice behind him, but it swelled through him and caught up his own voice as it went, bearing it up with unusual force.

People who are able to "swing" religiously, who can "lean into" the spirit, are caught up in it, caught up and carried beyond themselves. The movement of the spirit becomes the vehicle for projecting what was theretofore hidden or secreted in them. They do more than they thought they could, the way a golfer or a swimmer or a runner sometimes does more than he thought he could do.

I remember an occasion when Dr. Carlyle Marney was preaching at the American Baptist Theological Seminary, a black institution in Nashville. Dr. Charles ("Chuck") Boddie, the president of the school, was the liturgist for the service and also the director of the choir. When the time on the schedule came for the choir to sing a special number, he said that he had been out of town for two or three weeks and unable to rehearse the number with them, so they would not perform at that time but would sing at a later service. Then Marney preached. The great, affable bear of a man stood there, the musical phrases rolling off his lips in deep, resonant tones, the cadence varying, now swift, now slow and deliberate, the volume rising and falling, with "Amens" and "That's how it is, brother" sounding around the room. When Marney was through, there wasn't a person in the room who hadn't had the experience of Dilsey, in Faulkner's novel, of seeing the Beginning and the End, the Alpha and the Omega. Suddenly Chuck Boddie jumped up, waved the choir to their feet, and said, "Let's sing it now!" They did. The song rolled up to the roof and got thicker and thicker and louder and louder and more and more joyous until you almost couldn't breathe in the room. And when it was over Boddie smiled meekly and said, "We couldn't have done that before."

That is the point, of course. They couldn't have. Not until they were drawn into the game. Not until they had felt their pulses racing and their hearts beating in their throats. Then nothing could stop them. Once they joined the game, they couldn't be beaten.

Blacks in our country generally know a lot more about playful religion than whites. Ever since they were allowed to have separate meetings from the whites, their services have been theaters for release and ecstasy. As William Brink and Louis Harris observed in *The Negro Revolution in America,* the Negro church has been the one refuge where blacks could be themselves, where they could sing their agonies and dance their joys without interference from the white man. As we know from description of Negro church meetings in Faulkner's *The Sound and the Fury,* Ralph Ellison's *Invisible Man,* and James Baldwin's *Go Tell It on the Mountain,* even if we do not know it from firsthand experience, such meetings are characterized by a high degree of spontaneity, physical movement, and congregational participation. There is clapping, swaying, shouting, repartee, even dancing and hugging. The minister is a kind of leader of the game. He initiates the fun and gradually invites the group to join. The group responds slowly at first, then more and more quickly, until all are joined in full play, using their bodies as well as their minds. Worship becomes an act of integration and wholeness.

The average white Protestant is liable to complain that there is an escapism about such practice. The Negro forgets the realities of the world he lives in. He behaves like a child, forgetting that the piper must be paid. The incandescence of the worship hour is soon smothered by the cold ashes of the workaday world outside, by poverty and labor and sickness and other forms of stress or distress. The ecstasy doesn't last.

Or does it?

Admittedly, there is something illusory about such an experience. But is the illusion ever fully useless? Is it ever fully dissipated? Suppose it isn't. Suppose the flavor of it lingers in the mind long after the time has ended. Suppose it becomes a spice for life, imparting a different character even to the so-called realities of existence. Is it so unreal if it does that? Is it useless if it helps a man to live gracefully under even the worst of circumstances?

We have usually been prone to think of play as having an unreality about it, as being wholly illusory. We say to a child, "Stop playing and concentrate on what you are doing," as though the playing were of a different realm from the doing. We call people back from playing, as though playing really served no function aside from entertainment.

But think, now. Remember, in the midst of a period of concentration and work in your life, some moment of playing, of becoming intensely relaxed and open to the world. It was a time for the opposite of concentration, the opposite of being narrow and restricted. It was a time for exposing the self, for being wide enough to receive the world and its messages. Maybe it was a vacation in the sunshine by a glittering lake. Maybe it was a trip to the mountains. Maybe it was a time of reading and lounging and talking to someone you found very engaging and exciting. When it ended, when you went back to your concentration and narrowness, was the playtime utterly nullified? Was it as if it had never existed? Or did you not carry something new with you into the concentration and work, something invigorating and nourishing, upon which you continued to feed, in inner feeding grounds, long after the actual vacation itself had ended?

As Harvey Cox points out in *The Feast of Fools,* fact and

fantasy are not really so distinct and separable. There is a fantastical quality about factuality and a factuality about fantasy that cannot be divided neatly and easily. Man tends to use his times of fantasy as his *design* times. That is, he reorders his life through fantasy. And this surely carries over into his world of normal realities. If there were no moments of fantasy, man would be utterly at the mercy of contingencies in the world. He would merely submit to whatever happened to him, and to whatever state of affairs happened to be in existence.

One of the problems with contemporary life is that there has been too little fantasizing to go along with a great deal of scientific and factual development. Consequently we are now faced by tremendous advances in the methods by which we can exist and act in the world, but lack commensurate resolutions about the value of the ends to which those methods can lead. During the Middle Ages the monks, the retired saints, served the function of fantasizing for the Western world. They dreamed about what kind of world men should live in, and culture generally turned in that direction. But with the breakdown of the monastic system and the onset of modern scientific method, men began to look condescendingly upon fantasy. "Dreaming" became an opprobrious word, often connected with the modifier "idle." The engine, which performs its function without a mind, became the real model for human emulation. The model is still prevalent today. People speak of their "horsepower," their "input" and "output," their "fuel consumption," their "efficiency," and their "machinery," as if they were little more than rather defective pieces of mechanism. The modern world is starved for fantasy. If there are more erratic attempts at the fantastic in our age than men have seen for centuries, there may be a compensating factor at work, for it has been neglected for a long time. And the church is as guilty of the neglect as anyone.

A student who was greatly attracted to the work of John Cage put in my hands some time ago this passage from something Cage wrote:

Morris Graves used to have an old Ford in Seattle. He had removed all the seats and put in a table and chairs so that the car was like a small furnished room with books, a vase and flowers, and so forth. One day he drove up to a luncheonette, parked, opened the door on the street side, and unrolled a red carpet across the sidewalk. Then he walked on the carpet, went in and ordered a hamburger. Meanwhile, a crowd gathered, expecting something strange to happen. However, all Graves did was eat the hamburger, pay his bill, get back in the car, roll up the carpet, and drive off.

The student was attracted by the irrationality of the act described. One does not normally expect a man to roll out a red carpet and walk across it merely to secure a hamburger from a diner. There is an element of surprise in such an action. But there is also something strangely compelling about the picture. Why shouldn't a man roll out a red carpet when he is going to buy a hamburger? Why shouldn't he have a car furnished with the objects he likes to have around him? Although these things defy our sense of expectancy, they actually fantasize about the way life might be, perhaps ought to be. There is something remarkably human about the man in the story—much more so than about a man who merely submits to life with its usual boundaries and definitions.

Is fantasy in this case unreal? Or does it not in fact lead to more reality than we should have known under normal circumstances? If fantasy does in fact affect our designs for reality, it can hardly be accused of being useless.

Besides, it is a moot point whether illusion is or is not meaningfully real.

The child's fantasy world, whatever the adult thinks of it, is real to him. When he crouches under a soft pillow breaching two armchairs and says, "I'm pretending this is a fort," it *is* a fort to him. It will not withstand shelling from a cannon, it is true; it will not even withstand a playful whack from the capricious adult. But when the whack comes, if it does, it is not just a blow by an arm or fist: it is the enemy forces dumping all they've got upon the roof of the fort. There is still a reality to what the child is pretending, a reality which he is able to extend into contingent events. To him, at least, it is a more important reality—because it is an inner reality—than the more precise scientific view of things, or outer reality.

The adult easily dismisses such realities: they do not stand up under the mere blow of a fist.

But it is ironic that the adult, who was once a child and believed in such forts, still takes shelter under illusions of his own which differ in quality but not in kind from those of the child. He now believes in the security of bank accounts and jobs with reputable business firms. He values social status, a professional education, and a house on a quiet street in a good neighborhood. He helps to uphold a certain form of government and joins in the support of a particular church. And he resents any radical or liberal voice that insinuates to him that these things are not to be greatly valued. They are, after all, his fort, and he cherishes them. The world would fall on him if he did not have them over his head.

Perhaps there are several reasons for the superiority of his illusions over those of a child, but one of them, at least, is the fact that adults are in control of the world and can say to the children that their play-forts are only illusory.

The point is, of course, that none of us is without illusions. They are part of the sum and substance of our being. The scientific mind would like to banish them, but the thought of doing so is itself only another illusion. The important thing is to be aware of the nature of illusion, and of our universal susceptibility to it, and then to be concerned as much as possible for the management of the *right kind* of illusion. It is at this point that the matter or content of religious faith enters the picture, for the content of the faith is what controls the illusions of those who adhere to the faith, and so, in consequence, designs their world. I shall address myself to this in a later chapter, but for now we must concentrate a little longer on the fact or reality of illusion and the importance of surrendering to it more completely. If we do not surrender to it as totally as possible, it stands little chance of modifying our existence, of entering our "real world" as design, and so remains next to useless for us.

Neale makes the point that making-believe is no different for the child, the primitive, or the saint. Each abandons himself to his illusion so completely that the question of reality ceases to be of significance to him. "A story cannot be participated in," says Neale, "and manipulated at the same time. It can either be enjoyed or used, but not both."[3] That is, if the player wishes to remain in control of his illusions, and to recognize them always as illusions, he cannot really play; he disqualifies himself. Only as he commits himself, abandons himself, resigns himself, and is willing to take the consequences, is he borne out and away from the shore of his old anchoring place and given a chance at newness.

Some of the saddest figures one ever knows are those persons who have been so disillusioned as to be unable to abandon themselves any more, and are condemned to remain forever on shore while others are setting sail. Miguel de Unamuno once wrote a very pathetic little story, called "Saint Emmanuel the Good, Martyr," about a priest who had lost the power to believe and who watched the humble villagers with sadness and envy because they still carried away comfort and hope from his words.

It is true that agreeing to play, to enter the illusion, bears a great element of risk with it. One abandons his old safeties completely. Every forest becomes an enchanted forest. There are all kinds of hazards, some physical, some emotional. The more engrossed the participant, the more dangerous the game. The child who really slides for home with no thought for his safety may come up with skinned knees. The teen-ager who abandons caution in a drag race may careen his car into a utility pole. The businessman who enters the spirit of a touch football game on the weekend may easily sprain an ankle or a wrist.

Similarly, anyone who really gives himself to the liturgy as an illusion-structure runs the risk of losing control of himself. If the illusion-structure is good enough, he may actually make a fool of himself before he knows what he is doing. He may get carried away and say or do things he would not ordinarily do.

But again, this is precisely the point of engaging in illusion-structures in the first place. We do it in order to get beyond ourselves. There is no real humility without it. As long as we are effectually in control of ourselves, we are still playing god. Only when we have given up the controls, and lost ourselves in the illusion in process, have we surrendered ourselves spiritually and won a chance to be renewed.

The old testimonial meeting offered an opportunity for approximating humility, when a man could stand up before the other members of his community and say, in effect, "I am a fool." There was something basically cathartic about such an act if it was approached sincerely and in good faith. It cleansed the slate and permitted the person offering confession to begin again.

A properly conceived liturgical opportunity in the contemporary church should offer the worshiper a similar chance to play the fool without actually saying so in so many words. If its games or rituals are engrossing enough to allow self-forgetfulness during participation, then the participant has basically achieved the level of "foolishness." He has hazarded his dignity, his status, his worth in the community, in an act of faith. He has made his confession in the liturgy itself.

Such a hazarding of everything is not forgotten, either, when the worshiper returns to the secular side of his existence. Complete acts never are. They linger in the mind and heart like all important memories, and influence both the individual's behavior and the way he receives information from the world around him. I remember a professor of mathematics who sustained a broken rib in a football game between the faculty and the students of a certain college: he wore that broken rib as if it had been the Queen's own pennant. He had behaved enthusiastically, foolishly, daringly, and the memory of his actions pervaded him with an aura of pride and triumph for weeks afterwards. I sat in a box at the Folies Bergère once and saw three bald-headed little men brought up onto the stage by lovely showgirls. The girls enticed the men into rolling up their pantlegs, putting on frilly aprons, and dancing the cancan with them. Afterwards they rewarded them with kisses on their perspiring pates, and had difficulty getting them off the stage. Probably the same men under ordinary circumstances were quite diffident. But once they had got caught up in the act and had surrendered their composure, they loved it. They very likely think of it occasionally when their wives are berating them or when they are afluster in a salon full of chattering women, and throw their shoulders back with a sense of pride. Such moments *do* carry over into our more mundane existence, and continue to have their effect.

The sects, as I have said, provide for this sort of daring or foolishness more regularly than do the more established churches with their more sedate liturgies. But all liturgies, at whatever level of sophistication, should be designed with such opportunities in mind. We desperately need a chance to play, to be our inner, hidden selves in sympathetic public situations.

One word of caution: everything that looks like play is not play. As Huizinga says, "Civilization today is no longer played, and even where it still seems to play it is false play."[4] We are so conditioned to think work instead of play that we easily deceive ourselves by contriving work that is got up to look like play. And we are especially susceptible to this delusion in the church. It is so hard to get away from the Puritanical, manipulative approach to worship, of doing everything for a particular, limited end, that we can unwittingly substitute gamelike appurtenances for worklike items on the liturgical agenda, failing to realize that we are not really playing at all, but working toward the same old ends by new methods.

For example, a graduate student of mine in a seminar in experimental worship proudly brought to the group one day several copies of a multiple-media liturgy which he had recently used with a church he was serving as pastor. It was an interesting liturgy in that it employed a number of recent folk songs and some rather jazzy mottoes and prayers, all of which gave it an air of contemporaneity. And at the end of the service there was a spectacular moment in which the minister and the ushers provided colored balloons to all of the congregation, with various words describing the church's multiple ministries ("words like jail ministry, Sunday School, counseling, food service, etc.") painted in white on them, and mimeographed material on those aspects of the church's work tied to them with string. The balloons were filled with helium, and the members of the congregation were instructed to release them outside the church so they would float over the city and apprise people of the work of their church.

At first glance, this appeared to be a new way to worship, with lots of dash and color. Surely the people had fun participating in it.

But reconsideration prompted other reflections. It was really only a traditional liturgy with some recent trappings—an old garment with some shiny new buttons. The folk songs lent an aura of contemporaneity, but were betrayed by the traditional prayers which followed them, interpreted them, and gave official approval to them. And the balloons were nothing more than a gimmick to propagate the crassest kind of institutional information service. They were only a clever way of getting people to pass out tracts. There was not really a spirit of play at work in the service at all. Playfulness, perhaps, or cuteness; but not play. There was not the kind of reconstruction of liturgy which would have permitted grown men and women to enter into a newly illusioned world and act out new roles as mature and responsible persons in a setting of love and permissiveness. People could not lose themselves in this liturgy. They could give only surface approval to it—indulgence or patronage.

It was another case of the Puritan hang-up. The end result, calculated in advance, was still in view, only half-hidden by the camouflage of a few folk songs and several dozen colored balloons.

The true liturgy for the new age will have to be more than that. It will need to be as daring for its time as the simple Liturgy of the Table was for the first Christians, who were often swept up into the spirit of it and later lost their lives because of it. It must offer worshipers a real adventure with God, one in which they can actually lose control of the illusions.

Dance

ROBERT NEALE HAS observed that man never quite gets away
from the idea of the holy. Even in the secular age, he is "continually plagued by a quasi-religious response to the sacred in
spite of himself. No longer knowing that he fundamentally
desires awareness and acceptance of the sacred, he falls into
minor forms of worship."[1] These "minor forms" include
"camouflaged myths" and "degenerated rituals" in films and
literature, the "various forms of merrymaking that accompany
the New Year and other holidays," little festivities related to
marriage and other personal events, the cults and occultism
that flourish in some parts of the country, and all the competing
ideologies of the age.

They also include the dance.

Dancing originated of course as a sacral activity. The body is
the primary instrument of expression. Children "speak" with
their hands, postures, and facial gestures before they ever learn
to imitate vocal speech. There is no doubt that the first "language" of worshiping man was body-language, which, when it
became the least bit standardized or repetitive, was equivalent
to ritualistic dancing. Possibly some of the first religious dances
were done in imitation of certain animal dances, rhythmic
movements still discernible among some bears, foxes, rams,
monkeys, horses, peacocks, and cranes. Or they may have mi-
micked the branches of trees tossed in the storm, or flames

dancing in a crackling fire, or water leaping in a brook. But regardless of the mode of origin, dancing was a natural activity for primitive man, and instinctively it became a form of prayer and worship. As Jane Harrison and R. R. Marett have pointed out, and later Huizinga, such dancing was not only *mimetic*, imitating the rhythms of nature and the gods, it was *methetic*, participating in the rhythms and helping to produce them.[2]

The dance appears to have been at one time almost universally accepted as a major form of worship. The Hindu god Siva is pictured as a dancing god who pours his spirit into mortals and makes them dance as well; his rhythms are the reciprocal motions of creation and destruction in the world, and those who imitate him in the dance become part of the natural harmony of the spheres. The Greeks considered disapproval of the dance as constituting blasphemy, for dancing was the basis of all the mystery religions. Even the Hebrews danced their religion at times—much more regularly, says Oesterley, than the Old Testament itself would indicate. What we have, he says, is a situation where dancing was such an accepted form of religious expression that writers simply made no point of recording instances of it. The few references we have—such as Exod. 32:6, Judges 16:25, 2 Sam. 6:14-16, and Ps. 48:13-14—are casual and unselfconscious ones.[3]

Oesterley enumerates and elaborates upon at least eight varieties of dance which he was able to discern in the Old Testament: (1) processional dancing; (2) encircling sacred objects; (3) ecstatic dancing; (4) dancing at agricultural festivals; (5) victory dances; (6) dancing for circumcisions; (7) dancing at weddings; and (8) dancing for burial rites.

There is some evidence that dancing was not unknown among the early Christians, and that they had at least choral performances by dancing groups during their times of assembly.

At what point dancing began to fall into disrepute among Christians is difficult to say. It may have had something to do

with the Gnostic controversy in the early church, for some of
the Gnostics are known to have favored ecstatic dancing. Or it
may have been related to the withdrawal of Christians from the
Roman theatrical performances as lewd and unchaste.

Even after the disdain arose, however, dancing appears to
have maintained a rather popular hold on the religious mind.
Throughout the Middle Ages there are references to the godly
life as a dance and to Christ as a dancing master. Sydney Carter's well-known hymn "The Lord of the Dance" often strikes
people as a medieval borrowing, for the imagery of it is to be
found in numerous hymns and devotional writings from that
period. The secular dances which flourished outside the church
in survivals of pagan ceremonies, such as dancing around the
Maypole, doubtless found their way occasionally into the sanctuary, particularly during eras when the mystery and morality
plays were permitted to be performed in the church buildings.
A restrained and sublimated form of dancing, the processional,
sometimes with several steps forward and a few steps backward, has continued in the church till the present day. The
Cathedral of Seville, in Spain, has never lost its special dispensa-
tion to enjoy a religious dance before the high altar on three
occasions per year. And it was still the practice in Germany
until the eighteenth century for the professors in theological
faculties to do a dance around the candidate who had just been
awarded his Doctor of Theology degree!

But these are exceptions. The more typical Christian attitude
toward the body has been one of fear and distrust. In true
dualistic and rationalistic spirit, the church has viewed the mind
as good and the body or the flesh as evil. Hence the rigidly
disciplined physical attitudes of worshipers in the Puritan tradition, and the steadfast resistance of what William Birmingham
calls "the eroticization of liturgy."[4] The flesh must be kept in
strict obedience to the intellect, which is the part of ourselves
most like God.

As Gerardus van der Leeuw says, "The dance, once *the*

religious art in the strictest sense of the word, is today scarcely conceivable as an expression of the holy. The Church speaks, sings, paints, and builds, but it does not dance; or at least it does so no longer. Once it did dance, and occasionally, in some hidden corner, it still does. But its dance is a 'relic' and reminds us of the fact that the Christian Church is not only a church, but also a superb museum."[5]

Consequently, according to Robert Neale's theory that sacred actions find secular outlets if they are thwarted from finding their proper religious expressions, the dance lives primarily today in the youth culture or subculture, alternating between the more Apollonian forms (rhythmic movement, acrobatic dancing, ballroom dancing, dancing "cheek to cheek") and Dionysian ecstasy (jitterbugging, rock, and their more intoxicating subforms). Participants in such dances generally feel enraptured, "groovy," "with it," all of which expressions are reminiscent of the sacred purposes to which the dance was once put.

The urge to dance is an elemental or fundamental part of the human constitution. Rhythmic movement is instinctive: we all tend to nod our heads at symphony performances, pat our feet to the drumbeat at parades, and twitch or jerk to the patterns of jazz. We speak of "dancing to another tune" and "dancing for joy." A friend of mine who had just shot his first deer yelled and danced and turned somersaults for hours. We associate dancing with marriage and jocularly promise friends, "I'll dance at your wedding." Another friend of mine, who has an ulcerated intestine and is not permitted to drink alcoholic beverages, made a point of drinking himself drunk and dancing at his daughter's wedding reception. We also associate dancing with success or victory. I once saw a college graduate dance all the way back to his seat after receiving his diploma. Student bodies sometimes celebrate football or basketball victories with snake dances through the campus or college town. We speak of "dancing on the grave" of an enemy or someone who has been particularly odious or hostile to us. Zorba, in Kazantzakis's novel, said that he had to dance when his little son died or he could not have borne the sorrow, and he danced when his rigging for carrying logs down the mountainside collapsed.

For the church to deny men the right to dance their emotions in worship has been to deny them one of the most vital and fundamental means of communication at their disposal. It is no wonder that many persons sense something innately unreal about the "illusioning" that goes on in the sacred precincts. It is because they are not able to enter the game as fully as possible, to experience its real abandon, its ecstasy, its wildness. Nothing happens to alter the quality of their vision of life. Intellectual reordering is not enough. They require that the new vision get into their bloodstreams, into the marrow of their bones. They need to become new persons. And they cannot do this with their bodies in shackles and stocks. That is to deny the very assertions of worship, that man is to "lose" himself in God.

Of course there are problems inherent in the freedom to become ecstatic, just as there are problems in any freedom. As Harvey Cox says, "It is a mistake to try to defend jazz and modern dance by pretending that they are not sensuous and that therefore it is perfectly safe to allow them in church. They *are* sensuous and they are *not* 'safe.' "[6]

But the problems apparent in refusing the freedom are greater than the problems involved in granting it.

For one thing, it permits the existence of a populace which, as it grows older, dances less and less. In secular culture, it is the young who dance. Their bodies, attuned to rhythm and movement, seek outlets, sometimes excessively. Some young people would rather dance than eat. Even while sitting in classrooms they must be drumming their pencils, patting their feet, or jerking to some inaudible beat in their heads. But they tend, as they get married and become involved in professional life and the raising of children and the responsibility for the community, to dance less frequently. The wife is pictured as complaining to the husband, "We never go dancing any more." As their

own children come along and begin to dance, they sit on the
sidelines and "remember when." Even when coaxed onto the
dance floor, they feel awkward and out of tune with the times.
They want to "leave the dancing to the children." They remi-
nisce about the "good old days" and the dances they used to do.
"Those were the days, when dances were dances!"

There is something wrong with a populace which is thus
unable to sustain forms of rhythmic motion beyond the period
of youth. It means that the culture itself must defer to the
young, that it must value youth more than it does age and
maturity. A cultural inversion occurs. It is no longer necessary
to kill off the aged "fisher kings"—they all atrophy after thirty
anyway.

Religion as an adventure likewise dies after thirty. However
untrue the death of God may be as a philosophical or theological
statement, it is dramatically true as a statement of the emotional life of the older generations in the church. Intellectualism
simply cannot sustain the truth about God. If God cannot be felt
in the body, in the entire psychosomatic unity of the person,
then he cannot really be said to have an efficacious existence in
the life of the person. And the sheer physical restrictions placed
upon worshiping congregations in most religious traditions of
the last few hundred years have finally done their work and
crowded out many people's sensitivity to the divine as belonging to anything more than the intellectual or problem-solving
realm of their being.

The fixed pew in Protestant church buildings has become a
symbol of the gaol–like imprisonment of worshipers, so that,
contrary to the Protestant insistence on liberty of conscience
among individual believers, they are finally restrained from
taking liberties and becoming intoxicated with the holy. As a
result of such practice, there is probably more feeling for the
numinous in "The Electric Circus" or in most similar discothèques than there is in the average church service. A professor
of English in a church-related college told me once that he had

had his only confrontation with the mystery of God in a discothèque in Los Angeles, where the beat of the music, the psychedelic effect of the lights, and the swaying of dancers' bodies
ultimately combined to induce what he was convinced, in the
light of his own experience as a Christian, was a beatific vision.

The musical style of the present-day youth culture is of course
largely an outgrowth of the Negro culture that has existed in
this country, sometimes under cover, since the arrival of the
first slaves from Africa. Now that culture is emerging and domi-
nating the entire Western world. Even the Kremlin is unable
to keep it away from the Russian young people.

LeRoi Jones recalls in *Blues People* how the more conscien-
tious ministers among the colonial slaves endeavored to get the
blacks to give up "all dem hedun ways," including dancing, but
were largely unsuccessful. The Negroes simply incorporated
their dances into Christian ritual, and continued them under
the guise of "ring shouts" and "shuffle shouts" or movements
like the "rocking Daniel" dances or the "Flower Dance."[7] The
so-called "sanctified" black Protestant churches still retain
some of these "steps" or "moo-mens" today and continue, as
then, to use drums and tambourines in their services.

There is evidence today that the vitality of Negro religious
culture is making some inroad into white Protestant worship,
principally through the so-called "Jazz Mass." The first time I
participated in such a Mass, it was held on a Sunday afternoon
in the chapel of the University of Chicago. I arrived about
fifteen minutes prior to the time announced for the service, and
was astonished to find the chapel nearly filled already, with only
a few scattered seats remaining near the back of the sanctuary.
This proved to be a marvelous vantage point, however, for
observing the effect of the Mass on the congregation at worship.
The combo which played for the Mass was located in the balcony in the rear of the sanctuary. The first hymn of the service
was a majestic one from the past, "All Creatures of Our God and
King." But the effect of hearing it and singing it in syncopated

time was something new. People instinctively twitched and jerked as they sang. At first they looked at each other rather sheepishly, as if they were almost ashamed to be enjoying themselves so much; then they abandoned themselves to the movement and sang and swayed rapturously. This seemed to be the principle effect of the entire service: people felt a freedom to participate maximally, with their whole selves. There was not actually any dancing, of course; no one entered the aisles and gave way to exaggerated movement. But the truncated movements were definitely related to dance: they were dance with a fixed base.

The appeal of this rediscovered dimension in worship was obvious when Duke Ellington played his famous Jazz Mass at Fifth Avenue Presbyterian Church in New York City. People who normally never go to church at all—boys off the street, nightclub performers, even persons of the Jewish faith—appeared in droves in the swanky pseudo-Calvinistic sanctuary. Their presence even led to grumbling on the part of some of the church's members that "all the riffraff" had been let in.

This "different" musical experience in the modern church has in turn resulted in a higher degree of openness and permissiveness toward other "experimental" forms of musical worship. Liturgical dance groups have appeared here and there in various churches and particularly in connection with worship services on college and university campuses. Normally such groups "interpret" a theme such as love, anguish, forgiveness, humility, or a combination of such themes under the rubric of a "parable" or a "rhythmic sermon."

One minister in Louisiana told me about a service conducted in his parish during Lent, in which participants were fenced off from one another by card tables erected in a checkerboard fashion throughout the room. While they were thus cut off, the worshipers spoke their confession of sin and drank a cup of bitter herbs, symbolizing their anguish as individuals. Then some dancers interpreted the sufferings of Christ, following which the tables were removed, overcoming the isolation, and the participants were joined in a circle to have Communion together.

Risk magazine, in its special issue devoted to liturgical style (vol. V, no. 1, 1969), provided photographs of a jazz dance entitled "The Wise and Foolish Virgins" done in a large church in Stockholm to the music of Sven-Erik Bäck, and of an Indian student, Ronnie Sequiera, dancing the Lord's Prayer at a Mass in Neerland, Holland.

There is value to this kind of performance, of course. It is almost unthinkable that Christians could live in the age of Martha Graham, Isadora Duncan, Doris Humphrey, Mary Wigman, Merce Cunningham, and José Limon and not regard the human body as perhaps the most dramatic and responsive means of interpretation in the world.

But there are also obvious shortcomings, especially if solo or group performances are as far as it goes.

For one thing, we are still at the "interpretative" stage of Christianity, the stage occupied by the lesson and the sermon and the creed and the didactic hymn. We are still operating thematically, and according to an intellectual theme at that.

For another thing, most persons have been so culturally deprived when it comes to the dance that they are ill equipped to appreciate or understand a dance interpretation when they see one. This is a sad commentary on the cultural life of a people, but it is true. Even in Western Europe, ballet has become a neglected art, and the numerous folk dances are relegated more and more to performance at special festivals or in nightclubs where the prices are too high for the average citizen to pay. American television, which is not subsidized as the B.B.C. is, rarely concedes prime showing time to any serious program of dance; the viewers would deluge the station switchboards with complaints about "that long-haired stuff" that appeared in the slot where their favorite slapstick hour should have been.

Still more important, people need to engage in the dance themselves, not just watch other persons performing it. This is the complaint that liturgiologists have been making about worship in general for several years now: that it must somehow come to involve all the people in its actions, not just the ministers and celebrants and choirs. The complaint holds good for the dance as well. Unless Christianity is to exist mainly as a "spectator sport," with people witnessing a service and then returning to their workaday world with their lives largely untouched and unchanged, we must figure out some way of increasing their amount of active participation in the worship, of assigning them parts and causing them to be swept into the very vortex of passion and concern in the service.

This was no problem in the Negro service. It was no problem for the Quakers and Shakers. It is a problem for us because our liturgical dancing is still primarily token dancing, dancing done to show our liberality of spirit, our liturgical sophistication. And the problem will not begin to be solved until we have taken the risk that Cox spoke of, and pushed back the seats and had music with a strong beat and allowed maximal freedom to parishioners to move about and dance their religious feelings. The problem will not finally be solved until we have gone further and provided choreography for the myths and stories which are determined to be most essential to the lives and faith of the people, so that they can really *do* the rituals, so that they can *believe the creed with their bodies.*

There have been a few attempts at this. The mime entitled *A Man Dies,* which was first produced in a Presbyterian church in Bristol, England, has had a fair amount of success in several places where it has been used. Combining slide projections, beat music, some narration, and congregational dancing, it helps to contemporize the events of Holy Week and Easter. Colin Hodgetts, a young minister in England who began by directing a production of *A Man Dies,* went on from there to do the Christmas story in poetry and dance. Again, slides were

used and the dances were carefully rehearsed. The climax of
the performance was reached by using slides of a real birth
against a crescendo of drumbeats to which the dancers jerked
and writhed.[8]

But these are still special occasions. Much remains to be done
in terms of the regular worship routines in the churches—so
much, in fact, that one hardly knows where to attack the matter. We are hampered by the fact that the entire culture, or the
members of it over thirty, at least, has forgotten how to dance.
Can they be taught in the church to do what they do not know
to do in everyday life? Perhaps a beginning can be made in
terms of rhythmical movement, especially movement in which
persons act in unity, even having some form of bodily contact.
Until this occurs, people are fearful of exposing themselves
before others, of making fools of themselves.

I remember the first time a square dance was held by the
Couples Club of a church to which I belonged. The persons who
had gathered for the dance were somewhat timid, even though
most of them were acquainted with each other in at least a
casual manner. Many of them had not been in the church for
a long time, and they felt a natural social diffidence before each
other. But the music and the calling were good, and before very
long everyone was absorbed in the dancing. People who had
never danced before swung wildly and happily back and forth
in the patterns of the games. There was a oneness about the
group that few of us had felt before.

The experience proved to be a meaningful one in the life of
the church. As Huizinga observes, "A play-community generally tends to become permanent even after the game is over."[9]
The men especially, some of whom had not been inside the
church for years, carried over a sense of enthusiasm from the
occasion. The dance had been held on Saturday night. On Sunday morning, every single one of them was in the worship
service, and all of them were in a notably joyous, exuberant
mood. Significantly the church entered a new period of life and

growth at that time which was to last for several years.

I remember also the roller-skating and ice-skating parties we enjoyed in that church on subsequent occasions. There was something valuable about the experience of playing crack-the-whip on a frozen pond under a full moon—holding hands and skating in an unbroken line, then "snapping" the end person off and sending him flying down the ice into a distant cove or inlet. People felt an uncommon bond among themselves after an activity like that. They felt something undergirding them, something deep, something like confidence in God.

What I am trying to suggest is that something approximating these experiences ought to be brought into the sanctuary itself. If communion is what we are hoping for in the church, if it is the one aim behind everything we do, then why deprive ourselves always of the activities and modes of behavior which do most to induce a spirit of communion in the secular world?

The fact of bodily contact is important. For a beginning in church we might try locking arms and swaying to music. This could be done even in buildings where the pews are still rigidly fixed to the floor. People in alternate pews might swing in alternate directions, 1-3-5-7 to the left, 2-4-6-8 to the right, and so on. Frazer described agricultural rites among the Oraons and Mundas of Bengal in which young people of both sexes planted a Karma tree, linked arm-in-arm, and then danced in a great circle around the tree.[10] This simple act of joining arms is highly expressive of unity, and could, if properly included in the design for worship, help to induce a spirit of true communion.

A rabbi who was formerly a leader in the Hillel Foundation at Stanford University, Harry S. May, has told me of worship experiences with students in which everybody sat on the floor in a circle and clapped and swayed rhythmically to the music. Among the Bedouin Arabs, dancing is almost always thought of as rhythmical movement while remaining fixed in a single spot. These students were practicing dance according to the same notion. They also ate nuts and raisins, as they worshiped, from bowls set in front of them.

Even rhythmic clapping can produce a kind of intoxicating effect in an audience or congregation. At a service at Baylor University in Texas, students played a prelude of popular instrumental music while flashing pictures of contemporary world events, social problems, and scenes of beauty and love on the curtain of the stage at the front of their large chapel. The writer then spoke to the congregation on the topic, "The Lord of the Dance," emphasizing the theme of celebration and love in the gospel. At the conclusion of the sermon, I suggested that the person who really listens for the music of God can begin to hear it. Very faintly, a deliberate, methodic rhythm began to filter through the public address system. As it gradually built in intensity, the spotlight which had bathed the pulpit moved to the center of the stage, and a lovely young dancer stepped into it. Clad in the garb of a Greek peasant girl, barefooted, and with long chains of jewelry jangling at every move, she began a sinuous dance to the beat of the music. A few minutes later the music stopped, then began again very rapidly and exultantly. A troupe of dancers swept out of the shadows of the wings, shouting and screaming as they came. Together with the original dancer, they did the wild, exuberant dance which constitutes a climactic moment in the stage show *Zorba*. The congregation, caught up in the enthusiasm, began to clap in rhythm with the music and dancing. A sense of delirium engulfed the entire room. When the dance was over, and the service (*sans* benediction or other traditional paraphernalia of worship), people were weeping and hugging each other. Everybody seemed to want to touch everybody else. It was a genuinely moving experience. The musical beat, and the movement of human bodies in resonance with it, had created a sense of unity which drew people out of themselves and made them want, more than some of them had in a long time, to be part of one another.

The next morning I was having breakfast with the minister

c

of a campus church. He said: "My wife was there last night. She said it was the most tremendous experience she had ever had in a worship service."

How we are to accomplish something like this on a more regular basis in the church is more than I can say. Individual congregations will have to discover the means within themselves for such expressions. But it needs to be done—sorely. Corita Kent, in *Footnotes and Headlines,* quoted Jerome Murphy: "If we left it to the Spirit, there would be nothing in the churches but Jesus and dancing." I think that is true. It speaks of a purity and intensity of emotion which ought to characterize our life in the church. It describes what it would be like if we played the game seriously and not just in a halfhearted way.

Body

THERE IS A definite correlation, says Alexander Lowen in *The Betrayal of the Body,* between being in touch with the world around us and knowing who we are. People who have forgotten how to feel, how to receive continuous sensory impressions from their environments, have lost track of themselves. They don't go around asking, "Who am I?"—because they once knew who they were and assume that they still do. But the assumption is false, because they have been silently and unwittingly drifting away from the persons they were, until there is now a considerable gulf between who they were and who they have become. It would be difficult to overestimate, says Dr. Lowen, the extent of this kind of schizophrenia in the world today.[1]

The conditions under which men live in a highly technological, highly mobile society undoubtedly contribute to such a schizophrenia. People often forsake their places of origin rather abruptly and definitely, thus dissolving their identities into vast, fluid, and relatively amorphous entities. The society becomes one without roots, without a feeling for history, without an intimate knowledge of its own past. The sickness of not knowing who one is, of not being in touch with the self, becomes general and widespread.

The church has not been extremely helpful at this point. Its acceptance of the idea of a body-spirit dualism and its puritanical interdiction on the sensual life have only helped to enforce the split in the modern consciousness. One often encounters among Christians the belief that the enjoyment of this world is somehow for them an illicit love affair. Their ability to accept the world as a gift of the Creator and to celebrate it as an arena of presence is diminished by medieval teachings of self-denial and castigation of the flesh. Shrove Tuesday, with its dancing and abandon, is associated with sinfulness and indulgence; Ash Wednesday, the day of the hangover and prayers and repentance, with spirituality and godliness. It is almost as if God hated the world and expected the Christian to hate it too.

Intellectually, we are beginning to understand today that this kind of dualism was really a perversion of the religion of Jesus, that the "abundant life" of which he spoke was not some etherealized existence riding piggyback on the end of this one, but a new dimension of life here and now. We see what Father Zossima meant when he said to the saintly Alyosha, in Dostoevsky's novel, "Kiss the earth, and love it with a consuming passion." In whatever sense the kingdom had an extendedness in time, surmounting death and the grave, it had nevertheless an immediacy, and produced a sense of immediacy, so that the early followers of Jesus did not wait to be ushered into some Jewish Valhalla, but were translated into a new being at once.

As Professor Arthur McGill has pointed out in his book *Celebration of Flesh*, the "world" and the "flesh" which the first Christians were at such pains to avoid were not the world and the flesh *per se*, but life shut up to itself without a passage to God, without any sensitivity to the way all things cohere in him.

The New Testament keeps two points always yoked together, without letting either compromise the other. Men find their life in God alone, as He gives himself to them in Jesus Christ, but they have this life as concrete fleshy creatures, embedded in this world. The "I" that stands before God and lives in God is the "I" engaged with food and wars, with other people's bodies and other people's voices. Nowhere is a man disengaged from the realm of immediate experience, that is, from his body. That is where God's act in

Christ touches him anew each day for judgment and mercy. That is where God's word works anew each day to produce the fruit of repentance and charity in him. That is where he is called anew each day to the service of his neighbor's concrete needs. Members of the Christian community always exist as flesh, as perceptually engaged with the things around them. Their call to be Christians is a call for them to be exactly where they are, because exactly where they are is the place in which God shares his eternal life with them through Jesus Christ.[2]

Intellectually, I say, we are beginning to accept this. We talk about it in the church; ministers preach about it. But otherworldliness is a habit of mind hard to break. We have real difficulty *enacting* our belief in the sanctity of the world. We still suffer from what Amos Wilder once called "hangovers in old-fashioned modes of transcendence." It is hard for us who have concentrated so long on the transcendence of God to accept now in any full sense his immanence, his participation in the earth.

But we will not be healthy until we have discovered the earth again, and our sense of belonging in it. We will not recover from the spiritual vertigo with which we have suffered so long until we feel *terra firma* under our feet again. The only cure for our docetic consciousness is a reimmersion in things, objects, facts. There is a real sense in which our way to God in this time must be through a closed door. We must encounter him again in the facticity of an objective world, a world of color and texture and form, a world of sensory impressions. These must become part of our liturgical experience again. Worship must put us in touch with the world again. It is the only way we can be in touch with ourselves and with God. It is the only way we can be real men and women again. It is the only way we can help to cure the schizophrenia of the society we live in.

For centuries, the sense of reality in worship has been diminishing in proportion to the way attention to man's sensory environment has been permitted to languish. The church has confused the preservation of doctrine with the preservation of identity, and has succeeded in saving the one while losing the other. Now the doctrine seems irrelevant and our sense of identity is just as imperiled as that of all the other people in the modern world. It is true that we have the sacraments and that they keep us at least slightly in touch with the world of things. But their ability to do this has been greatly impaired by the way we have reduced them to the barest of forms. When we exchanged an actual cup of wine, with which there was still some risk of intoxication, and a loaf of bread, still capable of feeding a hungry man, for those diminutive glasses of juice and niblets of pastry we are pleased to call the Communion today, we took a long step from reality. And when baptism which was an immersion in a living stream, a near-drowning in the name of a symbolic drowning, was attenuated into a few drops of perfumed water, *toilet water,* sprinkled on the pate of a person, it was effectually reduced to a nothing, to a zero in the consciousness of the baptized as well as in the consciousness of the witnessing community. And those are all we have—those and a musty old flag, some battered songbooks, a wheezing organ, and some tasteless glass windows—to keep us in touch with the ground of our experience in the world. I am exaggerating of course; but sometimes it seems that bad.

It is imperative that we now make serious efforts in the church to bring into the liturgical life of the body of Christ a renewed sense of the body of the worshiper. We must help the Christian to be sensitive to his identity by reminding him of the things of the world over against which he maintains an identity. The church has got to do more to bring the sensory world into its midst, and in celebrating that, to discover the meaning and value of life, the glory of human sentience, and the intimate presence of God in creation.

"A person experiences the reality of the world only through his body," says Dr. Lowen.[3] Most of us, however, stop experiencing the world once we have some acquaintance with it.

We think of childhood as the period during which a person should learn to perceive his environment and of adulthood as a time for other things. But the problem with this attitude is that the growing person experiences things differently at each new stage of development. To forsake the life of the senses once one has learned the names of the animals and trees and cities is essentially to forsake existence. New ways of organizing experience must always have new experience to organize, or the organism, the organizing entity, is dead. Thinking we have solved the matter of our relationship to the world around us, we have only abandoned the solution.

Experiments in sensory deprivation indicate that massive disruption of sensory relationships leads to the total breakdown of organic functioning. In one instance, an insulated cubicle was suspended inside a soundproofed room, and twenty volunteers entered the cubicle through a series of soundproof doors. The volunteers were dressed in heavy clothing and padded gloves and socks designed to reduce tactile sensation to a minimum. Their eyes were covered with translucent goggles to obscure normal visibility. They were to remain in the cubicle as long as possible, knowing they could terminate the experiment at any time they needed to. Some were able to stand the isolation only six hours. The longest anyone could bear it was ninety-two hours. All suffered various forms of discomfort during the period. Several experienced distortion of the body-image, and complained of limbs becoming too heavy to carry any more, or of their heads spinning away. The heaviest damage was to their ability to think. They discovered that their minds had become highly disorganized, so that they were unable to establish thought-sequences. Panic ordinarily ensued, and attacks of anxiety.[4]

If an individual is deprived of sensory stimulation for very long, says Lowen, he will begin to hallucinate. The severe reduction in external stimulus gives him a sense of unreality in his body. When he loses touch with his body, he begins to fade out.[5]

This is the same thing psychologist William Schutz of the Esalen Institute in California is talking about when he says that joy is the feeling that comes from the fulfillment of one's potential, and that one fulfills his potential only to the degree that he is physically responsive to the world around him.[6] When one shuts off the channels of communication with the outside world, through lethargy or indifference, he automatically projects himself into a state of depression or despair. Joy is the emotion of being alive, of functioning as a receiving center for all the signals being sent by one's environment.

Think of the signals today. The cinema, discotheques, even suburban shopping centers, are vibrant with colors and images. Peter Max art has exploded off the pages of magazine advertisements into haberdashery, tableware, and household furniture. And the drug culture, if reports are reliable, has opened a whole new world of violent sensual experience. Some acid-droppers undergo such heightened awareness on a trip that they find ordinary life almost unbearable by comparison. As one user expressed it, LSD causes him to experience everything in terms of **more**:

> Looking at a thing one sees **more** of its color, **more** of its detail, **more** of its form.
>
> Touching a thing, one touches **more**. Hearing a sound, one hears **more**. Moving, one is **more** aware of movement. Smelling, one smells **more**.
>
> The mind is able to contain, at any given moment, **more**. Within consciousness, **more** simultaneous mental processes operate without any one of them interfering with the awareness of the others. Awareness has **more** levels, is many-dimensioned. Awareness is of **more** shades of meaning contained in words and ideas.
>
> One feels, or responds emotionally with **more** intensity, **more** depth, **more** comprehensiveness.
>
> There is **more** of time, or within any clock-measured unit of time, vastly **more** occurs than can under normal conditions.
>
> There is **more** empathy, **more** unity with people and things.

There is **more** insight into oneself, **more** self-knowledge.

There are **more** alternatives when a particular problem is considered, **more** choices available when a particular decision is to be made. There are **more** ways of "looking" at a thing, an idea, or a person. . . .[7]

Other users report hearing music as though the music were inside their bodies, seeing colors as if they actually participated in the colors, feeling ordinarily smooth surfaces as if they were heavily grained or ridged, and feeling the breeze as if it were entering the very pores of the body and blowing through it.

This state of acute awareness does not really require the use of chemical stimulants or drugs, of course. One recalls the words of Rainer Maria Rilke, in *The Notebooks of Malte Laurids Brigge*, "I am learning to see. I don't know why it is, but everything penetrates more deeply into me and does not stop at the place where until now it always used to finish."[8] Or of Henry Miller, in *The Wisdom of the Heart:* "I acquire more and more the gift of immediacy. I am developing the ability to perceive, apprehend, analyze, synthesize, categorize, inform, articulate —all at once."[9] Persons are capable of this vivid apprehension of life and the world through the discipline of the senses to receive it. It is a matter of recovering the ability which most of us had as children but failed to develop or even keep alive, the ability to perceive our environments directly and without artificial constructs which no longer serve their purpose. And it is in this state of unofficial sensibility that we know the real experience of joy and stand in a basically friendly relationship to other men in the world.

The effort ought to be made, in liturgical design, to sharpen men's senses in such a way that they reach this high point of inner development in the worship of God, and realize, with a pungency they have perhaps not felt before, the real connectedness between God and their existence in the world. Unless it is made, and fairly successfully, there will continue to be a rupture between what is done in the church and what is done in the world, and the worshiper will continue to experience the sense of depletion and listlessness which is a result of his schizophrenia.

For a beginning, the worshiper may be simply resensitized to the world of the inorganic which he tends to take for granted. He may be asked to grip the rounded back of a pew in front of him during a prayer, or to kneel and put his hands on a stone or carpeted floor, feeling the texture beneath his fingers. He may be reminded verbally, or with colorful slides projected on a screen, of his feeling for such sensuous objects as

> a green watermelon just lifted out of a cold spring
> the rough-smooth bark of a giant pine tree
> a soft, lovely quilt in the summertime
> huge, near-to-bursting blackberries
> damp moss under bare feet
> the silky, sticky ears of young corn
> a worn leather billfold

or of his taste for

> hard-boiled eggs
> tender young shrimp
> cool milk
> peanuts
> fried chicken and gravy
> hot coffee
> after-dinner mints
> bits of orange peel
> a chocolate bar

The gift of these things may be celebrated in a prayer or a litany or even a song. The congregation might even be asked to clap its approval for being so richly endowed with feelings of appreciation.

The church ought to make much more use of bright colors than it presently does. What if Corita Kent were let loose in all the gloomy little cathedrals of Protestantism? Religion might blossom like Alice in Wonderland, with pews of yellow and blue and pink, and with pulpits of chartreuse or atomic red! Or what if we followed the lead of Henri Matisse, and designed our robes and chasubles with brilliant flowers and geometrical figures on them? Or what if we hung great banners from all the pillars and decorated the chancel and the nave with balloons and paper streamers? Christ the harlequin might return to our midst, and we might remember the Resurrection in new ways for our time.

Light itself offers endless possibilities. Strobe lights, spotlights, flickering lights, alternating lights, colored lights—it is a wonder that the larger churches have not developed ministers of technology, on the analogy of the ministers of music and education, to bring into the service of the congregation the kind of expertise in this area that is available to the lowliest discothèque or cheapest nightclub. And *sound!* With contemporary audio techniques at our disposal, there is no limit to what we might achieve with various sounds or combinations of sounds in the sanctuary. We could bring the whole world—chirping crickets, honking ducks, whizzing traffic, lonely footfalls, the voices of men in other lands—all of it, into our midst in the congregation.

When the Rev. Jack Myers was a student at Vanderbilt University he developed a unique Light Show on the theme of the crucifixion and resurrection of Christ. Slides of great crucifixion paintings, bullfight pictures, and photographs of human misery were projected in staggering sequence onto a screen which virtually wrapped around the audience. An extraordinary electronic sound track was used to accompany the pictures. When the crucifixion was finally at its climax, the sound stopped abruptly, and the audience sat in silence and darkness for several seconds, or perhaps a minute. Then a sound recording of an atomic blast—an actual one, I was told—began to rumble through the speakers. A contemporary portrait of a rough, laughing Christ began to flash to alternate positions around the screen. The roar was almost deafening as it reached its crescendo. The mocking face of Christ was everywhere. The effect, to put it inadequately, was galvanizing; everyone who saw it was captivated by it.

The mention of moments of silence reminds us too that there is a sensuality about silence itself which most Protestant groups exploit too seldom. Many persons do not like silence in worship because it means confrontation between the self and the void and therefore seems threatening to them. They complain that it is awkward, that they do not know what to do with their eyes or their hands or their minds in such intervals. But the confrontation with nothingness can be extremely creative if they are coached in how to approach it, what to listen for with the inner ear, and how to respond when various emotions arise. In the Upanishads, men are advised to meditate upon their bodies, to consider the length of their inhaling and exhaling, the "feel" of their blood, phlegm, bones, marrow, bile, flesh, sinews—even their excretum. The meditative one thus passes through his body as through a portal to become one with Brahman. Perhaps similar devotional efforts would reward Christian worshipers with a new sense of the reality of their bodies, and thereby of their identities as persons and sons of God.

The sense of smell is also neglected in most Protestant congregations. We respond quite readily to most smells. If they are pleasant, the effect is positive; if unpleasant, it is immediately negative. One remembers the smell of preserves cooking in the kitchen, of perfume on a woman who walked by in the street, of spicy candles burning in a little boutique, and wishes to experience it again. There is every reason for Christians to employ various scents to make the experience of worship more memorable and evocative. The releasing of incense at the time of the gospel lesson, for example, enforces the lesson at a more

ˈsensual level, so that the worshiper experiences it almost physically, and certainly psychically, as well as mentally.

Part of what is aimed at in all of this is the element of surprise: making the worshiper recognize what he has seen and heard and taken for granted but has not deeply experienced. It is what Camus in *The Myth of Sisyphus* spoke of as "learning all over again to see, to be attentive, to focus consciousness . . . turning every idea and every image into a privileged moment."[10] The problem is that people think they know how to see and be attentive, while the truth is that they have become habituated to the most common things around them and don't see or feel them at all. They would recognize their absence if the things were removed, or at least feel some undefined disturbance about the loss, but they have really learned *not* to see or be attentive to them. If they can be made aware again, their ability to worship will be enhanced. The selves they present to God will be more total than they were in their lethargy. Absentee selves, those abstracted entities which no longer know their bodies, are not much to offer. They have no joy. They are heavy and colorless. They will not rise to converge with spirit. Worship which helps to overcome the divorce between the self and the body stands a much better chance of succeeding as real worship.

As the church is at base an aggregate of persons, the problem of sensory awareness inevitably merges into the problem of recognizing the presence of others. This means receiving them physically as well as mentally or spiritually. And we are suddenly at the heart of the objection which some church members have to admitting *any* sensuality to worship: it is so hard to draw the line between the smallest emphasis on the body and its responses, on one hand, and libertinism or riotous sexuality on the other. Yet the question of sexuality in worship must be broached and some consensus reached about it, for it is too obviously central to human existence to be routinely dismissed from discussions of liturgy.

In the book *Multi-Media Worship* there is a description of a kind of worship experience that iş beginning to become more common in the United States. This particular service took place at the University of Michigan's Canterbury House in a large room where the participants were seated cross-legged on the floor. Its structure was basically that of the Anglican prayer book, culminating in Holy Communion. The uniqueness of the service consisted mainly in the casualness of the minister and what happened between the lines of the traditional order. After the minister had read the gospel lesson, he paused for a minute. Then he said, "You can hardly avoid it, but touch each other." When no one moved, he said it again: "Come on, touch each other." A university student, reporting the result, said, "Two hundred and fifty people sat on the floor and the stage, leaned against walls and railings, hand in hand. Communication became fellowship—the message was the people, and, if only for a few moments or a few hours, the message was lived."[11]

It is interesting that the minister had to urge the congregation a second time, even though by most standards it was a rather unusual congregation. What is it about Christians that makes them so fearful of touching other persons? It is the same reluctance shown by worshipers who do not wish to participate in the Passing of the Peace. Do we sense that others do not wish to be touched, and so hesitate to intrude upon their privacy? Does the act of touching flesh remind us that our own flesh is somehow foreign to us, unknown, and so make us uncomfortable about our lack of self-acquaintance? Do we naturally associate the flesh with sensuality, and that in turn with lust and evil? Are *all* of these things involved?

Certainly it is impossible to avoid the presence of the human body in contemporary culture. Pictures of nudes adorn all the weekly news magazines and daily papers. Since *Hair* and *Che!* and *Oh! Calcutta!* there is hardly any length to which exposure of the torso cannot go on stage and screen. Fashion designers have transferred seminudity for the masses from the beaches to the market place and from the dressing room to the salon and the dining table. Some older persons, especially churchmen with puritanical backgrounds, cringe at the thought of what is happening to the world; they cannot help identifying this superexposure of flesh with the utter decadence of natural man and the approach of an hour of cosmic retribution.

Something that we haven't very often considered, apparently, is the high degree of interrelatedness between sexuality and religion, and the way the church has nearly always made an effective use of sublimated forms of sexuality in the pursuit of its own spiritual goals. The full force of this realization struck me one day in a chapel service at which a group of teen-aged boys and girls were performing a folk-rock musical. The youngsters were extremely radiant and cheerful, and appeared to have been fed all their lives on a lot of milk and to have spent much of their time scrubbing their hands and faces. They smiled and glowed and bubbled with energy. Those of us in the congregation responded enthusiastically and joyfully. Then it occurred to me that here was a group of young people singing songs about the spiritual vision, about Jesus and the Christian life, and we were all intent on their presence because they were young and vibrant and lovely. I looked around the chapel at the professors and students. The adoration on their faces was unmistakable. Their innate sensuality could not be separated from the religious fervor of the occasion. I began to think about other things. I thought about some highly successful pastors and ministers of music and education I had known: there was a kind of animal magnetism about them that attracted people, even though they were inept in their jobs and confused in their own personal lives. I thought about the rakish Elmer Gantry in Sinclair Lewis's novel, and how churches not only endured but prospered under his unconscionable pastoral leadership. I thought about a woman I had once overheard saying, "That Bishop Sheen is just about the sexiest thing in the Catholic church!" And I realized that we Christians are not fundamen-

tally so different from the old Greeks at Corinth who erected
a temple to Aphrodite and considered it an honor for their
daughters to become sacred prostitutes. Our fears of the body
and the sexual act have led to modification of the extent to
which we permit such things to go, but the underlying principle
is surely the same.

Wherever we derived our prudery about admitting the interrelatedness of sex and religion, it certainly was not from the
Bible. There is no denying the witness of the anthropological
scholars that Yahweh or Jehovah, whatever else his propensities
were, was at one time considered an erotic deity. The use of
circumcision as a symbol of religious commitment, especially to
a God who was frequently memorialized by phallic-shaped pillars and referred to among the Hebrews as "the Rock that begat
thee" (Deut. 32:18), indicates that the Jews accepted with little
question the primitive concept of the deity as the ultimate and
indispensable agent of fertility in the world. The Hebrew fathers swore their oaths with their hands on the "thighs"—
"thighs" being a euphemism introduced into translated versions for "privates" or "genitals." Goldberg further argues that
the Tree of Knowledge in the creation story was by legend a fig
tree—ficus or sycamore—and not an apple tree, as we cus-
tomarily think of it.[12] It was a *fig* that Eve is represented as
offering to Adam—the symbol of the virgin's yoni or pudenda.
And it was fig leaves she was supposed to have sewn together
to cover their nakedness. The serpent, moreover, has from prehistoric time been connected symbolically with the male organ.
And it will be recalled that the serpent in the Genesis account
walked *erect* before God cursed him and commanded that he
should spend the rest of his days crawling upon the earth. Goldberg also thinks that there is a suggestion in Ezekiel to the effect
that there was a large image of the lingam, or phallus, in the
Holy of Holies in the Temple, and insists that the description of
the bronze stands for lavers in the Temple (I Kings 7:27-39),
which has suffered numerous corruptions and mistranslations,

actually speaks of images of the lingam and yoni in union.[13] It is less wonder, then, when we consider the social climate in which they lived, that Abraham and Samson and David and Solomon appear to have been so liberal in their sexual attitudes. As Karl Barth once warned us in *The Word of God and the Word of Man*, we cannot begin to understand "the strange new world of the Bible" if we insist always on making innocent little boy scouts of all the great heroes who stride through it.

Admittedly there are signs of troubled sexual consciousness in the New Testament. The Apostle Paul appears to have held rather strict views about male and female behavior. It has been generally theorized that he had had unhappy or at least less than satisfying encounters with persons of the opposite sex. This would not account, however, for the commendations of some of the women, friends of his, in various churches to which he wrote. It is more likely, I think, that he tended, out of his broad experience with devotees of the Greek mystery religions, for whom sex was so vital a part of any ritual, to react against sex as a hallmark of non-Christian groups, wishing to intensify as much as possible the sense of separateness and exclusiveness among the early Christians. Certainly there was no such prohibition against sexuality in the life and teachings of Jesus himself. Respect for the law and a healthy kind of monogamy, yes; but injunction against the flesh and sexuality, no. He seems always to have been around women, and not ladies of the court either, but women who were known to be prostitutes. And, interestingly, little is made of this fact. It is noted almost in passing, the same way it is noted that some of the disciples had been fishermen and others had followed other trades. It is principally in the pulpits of later Christendom that a lurid interest is taken in the moral character of the women with whom Jesus consorted. Iconography and hierography indicate, moreover, that the Christian virgins of the early church often carried amulets and idols of sexual significance in their processions, and that the cakes which the worshipers ate, the forerunners of the hot cross buns associated with Holy Week and Easter, were for a long time actually in the shape of lingams.

It is also obvious, from any study of the adoration of the Virgin or of Christ during the Middle Ages, that one of the principal roles played by these figures for the medieval saints was that of sex deity. It was not uncommon for male mystics to pledge marriage to Mary, or for female counterparts to do likewise to Jesus. Henry Suzo, a fourteenth-century Dominican, for example, wrote passionate love letters to Mary as "the Queen of my heart," idolizing her as a young maiden with lovely hair, and promising her that his consummate adoration for her made all the treasures of earth seem as nothing to him in comparison. And it is said of the famous Bernard of Clairvaux that sometimes when he was celebrating Mass to the Virgin he would be so overcome with passion that his very soul would seem to leave his body and go to her. There is little doubt, I think, that there were significant relationships between the great traditions of courtly love in the later Middle Ages, which celebrated in song and codification the glories of sensual passion, and the nearly universal practice of Mariolatry. The adoration of the Maiden who bore the Lord of Christendom out of union with the spirit of God was transferred to the more secularized interplay of the sexes, and so did much to elevate the place of women in a romantic way.

If one wishes cruder evidence of the carry-over of pagan sexual notions into Christianity, he may consider the fact that until fairly recent years there were at least twelve Holy Fore-skins of Jesus to be found in European churches as treasured relics, and that at least one of them, at the Abbey Church of Coulomb, in the diocese of Chartres, France, was believed to possess miraculous powers for making sterile women fruitful and relieving the pain of childbirth. And, on the psychological level, one is asked to consider the subconscious implications of kissing the cruciform, which has always had phallic significance, or kissing the ring of a prelate, which possesses the opposite, or yonistic, meaning.

The truth is that all religions in earlier eras, even the Christian religion, made no fundamental distinction between sexuality and holiness, but recognized that man's sexuality, which was thought to be the primal part of him, the seat of his regenerative power, must be somehow utilized in achieving a union between him and his gods. The suspicion that the flesh is somehow inclined to sin and disobedience is by no means new, having been voiced by Paul and incorporated in numerous Body/Soul dialogues extant from medieval times. But the treatment of the body as conspiratorial and subversive, relegating it to immobility and nonparticipation in worship, is of rather modern origin and smacks much more of Protestant pietism than of anything else.

The effect of this prolonged, unnatural repression of the body and of sexual tendencies during the act of worship has already been, in the opinion of some psychologists, a loss of the sense of reality associated with worship. Instructed by habit and tradition, the worshiper restrains himself from any overt discussion of or movement toward the sensual, and so further alienates his religious sensibility from the fact of his corporeal existence. When he does behave sexually, then, he invariably identifies such behavior as wrong, and incurs a sense of guilt about it. He goes to church to get rid of his guilt, and, whatever he *hears* about forgiveness and absolution with his ears, subliminally absorbs the notion that he is even guiltier than he realized. Unable to get off the whirling merry-go-round, he polarizes his emotions more and more, taking a stronger and stronger illicit pleasure in sex while he prays more and more fervently for deliverance from it.

I am not recommending that we convert our services suddenly into orgiastic sexual happenings, or that we show nudie films in the church parlor on Sunday evenings, but it does seem to me that we must relax our extremely repressive attitudes toward the body and begin to use it for what it is, one of the major vehicles we have for communicating and receiving information. Until we do, worship in the fullest dimension will be impossible, and we shall continue to sense something unreal and remote about our liturgies.

We can begin merely by recognizing the latent sexuality already existent in our services—our attraction to certain ministers, musicians, and other persons prominent in the group, our use of both phallic and womb symbolism (cross, spire, cup, font, baptistery, etc.), and the sexual imagery in our language about love, union with God, salvation, etc. There is something liberating about the realization that one inevitably employs sensuality in worship, even though he tends to mask it from himself because of the cultural pressure not to admit it. It is the same principle that is at work in psychotherapy. If we can get our involvement in sexuality out in the open, where it can be faced and admitted, we can make more redemptive and creative use of it.

Then we can begin to explore the very natural socially acceptable forms of relating to others physically—the handshake, the touch, the linked arms, the closeness, and so on. I remember one Methodist minister's comment about a meeting he attended and the joy he felt in a service when the bishop who was presiding at Communion gave him the wafer. "He actually looked me in the eye and touched my hand when he put the wafer in it," said the minister. "That sounds simple and commonplace, but I mean it. He really touched my hand. Touched it so that something passed from him to me. It's crazy, I guess, but that's the first time a thing like that ever happened to me." How many times had he received Communion before? Hundreds, doubtless. Yet it was the first time. We have generally been afraid of making real contact with the body, even when we shook hands or received Communion. It isn't really necessary, in order to rediscover the meaning of our bodies, to go all the way and employ thermal baths enjoyed bisexually in the

nude, as some Western sensitivity training groups have done.
There are worlds of meaning to be communicated through a
mere touching of hands, provided we are sensitive to our bodies
as agents of communication.

W. H. McGaw, Jr., an Episcopal layman on the staff of the
Western Behavioral Sciences Institute in La Jolla, California,
has experimented for several years now in the use of modest
sensual experience as a basis for Christian worship. When the
World Council of Churches met in Uppsala, Sweden, in the
summer of 1968, he conducted a famous "touch-and-tell" service there in which participants were encouraged to reach out
and touch the faces of fellow participants and then say something nice about the faces they were touching. Reactions were
various, but included a comment by one disgusted clergyman
to the effect that if he wanted to neck he could go somewhere
besides church to do it. A Presbyterian minister who has
worked with McGaw in Southern California, Mikel Taxer, explains that some persons are simply threatened by experimental methods: "People who show little emotion at home where
there is not much touching may consider it an invasion of
privacy. And persons who feel 'chaotic' tend to regard a church
as the one place where they know what will happen, as far as
worship is concerned."[14]

But McGaw and most of the ministers working with him have
reported considerable success with their small group experiments, and the "touch-and-tell" methods have spread widely.
Often they involve the congregation's breaking up into groups
of six or eight persons, who are asked to stand in a circle, their
arms around each other, and talk or laugh or behave naturally
in that position of partial intimacy.

In an "Experiential Worship Service" which McGaw conducted at a National Liturgical Conference in 1967, the participants were seated in circles of six. McGaw began by saying, "I
would like for you to join hands; bow your heads; close your
eyes; and meditate, pray, or just be together." After two min-

utes, he said "Amen" and asked the participants to share with each other what those moments had meant to them. Next he spoke briefly about loneliness, and asked them to imagine that they were really shut off from other persons. They were to attempt to communicate with the others in the circle by the means of handclaps. Eye contact was permissible, but no noise except the handclaps. Again, they were to discuss their feelings about this afterward.

After another brief sermon, this time about love, the participants were invited to go and stand before others in their circle. The others were to stand in response, and they were to touch each other in some natural way. "For thirty seconds or so," said McGaw, "attempt to convey to that person what you can love, admire, understand, and accept in him. The person who is receiving this love, acceptance, and understanding should not reply at this moment. Instead, I suggest that he or she listen intently and do everything possible to receive and believe and internalize the affection coming forth. He will have his own opportunity to go around his circle and to give in turn." At the conclusion of this act, experiences were again shared verbally among the participants.

Then each group did an exercise in which the participants, one by one, stood in the center with the other participants close to him, dropped his arms close to his side, and just sort of fell back and allowed himself to be passed from individual to individual around the group. The intention was to let each one feel the love and support of the others physically and not just verbally.

After a brief time of holding hands again and expressing their prayers and concerns to each other, everybody was asked to stand, put the chairs aside, and back away from the circle as far as possible without infringing on the other groups in the room. Then they were to move slowly toward the centers of their groups again, getting as close as possible before returning to their original positions.

Finally, to close the service, they were to move slowly once more to the center of their groups and say good-by to each other in any way they wished to.

The response among some participants, both on this occasion and in other instances where variations of the service have been attempted, was spontaneous embracing and kissing, a sign of genuine love and emotion.

The difference between this service and the "participatory" experiments of little theater groups in which people hold hands and pass each other around the room from hand to hand is primarily in the little sermonettes about loneliness and love, which have the effect of focalizing the experiences of the group in the Christian tradition because they speak of Jesus' touching and healing people and of his followers' concern for one another.[15]

The secular forms of therapy of course have a validity of their own. But there is a historical and spiritual quality, a dimension in time and depth, imparted to the experiences by grounding them in the acts and ministry of Christ. The believer is linked, in only barely definable ways, with all believers everywhere, in every age. The particularity of his experiences is overcome in a sense of their universality, and he actually feels himself becoming part of the body of Christ.

Additional suggestions for simple touch-rituals may be found in Bernard Gunther's book *Sense Relaxation Below Your Mind*,[16] which is a repository of materials Gunther has gleaned through the years as a teacher at the Esalen Institute. Most of these suggestions are for two persons, but can be adapted for use in small groups as well. One is called "Back Talk." Two persons slap each other's backs as prelude, then stand back to back with their eyes closed, communicating through movement. One "listens" while the other "talks." They carry on a nonverbal conversation. They may even feign anger and then make up. Eventually they become quiet and slowly separate, each experiencing his back, how it feels. Another exercise is called "Head Knowing," and involves gently and thoroughly exploring and massaging the other's head, becoming more and more aware of the feeling of the head as it is done. Yet another, "Foot Washing," primarily calls for washing each other's feet in warm, soapy water, rubbing wet salt over them, rinsing them, and then massaging them with oil. Sensitivity is emphasized in each of the exercises. Both participants should emerge with new feeling for their own and each other's physical being.

It will be recalled, of course, that foot washing is practiced as a sacramental act by certain sectarian groups in Protestantism. One cannot help suspecting that this survival of the ancient custom of anointing a guest has been a fortunate one among the minor groups where it is still observed. It is a much more total kind of preparation for the act of Communion than either a prayer of confession or the Kiss of Peace, and anchors the eating of bread and drinking of wine in Christ's name to something inexpressibly real and tangible.

In the end of our discussion, we are brought back to the observation of Lowen, that modern man is getting more and more schizophrenic because he has lost touch with his body in his increasingly nonrhythmical and artificial environment. Liturgy is not the only place where this illness can and must be addressed, but it is impossible to have true liturgy if it is not addressed somewhere. Conceivably persons sensitized to themselves and their environments in various secular settings could enter into a rather formal and traditional kind of religious service on Sunday morning and really feel "vibrations" in it. But if they are not being sensitized in therapy groups or in their secular existences it is hopeless to try to "do" liturgy without quickening their senses in the service itself. Their wholeness and health depend on their reconceiving their bodies in new ways, in feeling their relatedness to the redemption of the world and the well-being of their psyches. They must be made fully "alive" in the worship; and this requires that they be led to communicate with more than their minds and their mouths. They must feel with their hands, taste with their tongues, smell with their noses. They must exist as persons at full potential. Only in this manner can worship be sacramental and deeply meaningful, not just in an intellectual sense, but in a life-sense.

Persons

"I SAW YOU in church yesterday," said one secretary to another.

"Yes, I've seen you there before," replied the other.

"Oh," said the first, "I didn't know you went there. How do you like it?"

"Pretty well," said the other. "Only it's very impersonal. I've been going there about four months now, and I don't think a single person has ever asked my name."

"Yes," admitted the first, "it is a bit that way. But Tom and I still think it has the best worship service in town."

This conversation, overheard in a busy office building, underscores what has become increasingly a problem in a time of urbanization and large, semitransitory congregations: many persons feel totally overlooked. They come to church lonely and go away lonely. They come thinking that the church will put them in touch with other people, and they leave just as isolated as ever. Somehow they expect that the church will bring off a miracle for them, that it will produce "instant relationship" for them. And it rarely does. Itself victimized by the fragmentariness of modern life, it can hardly cure the plight of individuals.

Or can it?

That is the question which needs to be faced and faced squarely. Is the church as it was once known, as a fellowship of believers, doomed in the modern city? Must it be contented to be only a kind of impersonal theater, where ministers who do not really know the parishioners perform certain holy acts and voice acceptable religious thoughts before them, while the parishioners themselves look on or take part in a direct line of spectator-actor relationship to the leaders, but never really become involved with other people beside them or along the line?

That is pretty much where it is today. Is it condemned to remain that way? Or can the church discover new ways of eliciting human response in worship and helping worshipers to feel that something has happened to them in the liturgy to make them more alive and hopeful as persons? We know there are numerous ways of achieving this in small groups and classes in the total life of the church, but are there ways of injecting a new personalism into worship? Many persons who attend public worship and find it unsatisfying never bother to inquire further into the program of the church. They assume that worship is the showcase, that it is what the ministers and the congregation do best, and that if it isn't worthwhile then there is no reason to look behind it and join a Seeker's Class or a Mixed Adults Group or some other segment of the congregational life. What can be done to meet their personal needs in the liturgical setting itself?

The first thing, of course, is to gain some understanding of what those needs are.

William Schutz in a chapter in his book *Joy,* entitled "Interpersonal Relations," defines them according to three basic areas: *inclusion, control,* and *affection.*[1]

Inclusion means inclusion in the group, acceptance, being a part of things. It means having an identity to others in the group, being recognized for something distinctive, being truly seen and known. Even some persons who are thoroughly accepted by the group have an inclusion problem, because it seems to them that others in the group look right through them. Their presence doesn't mean anything to the group. If they were absent, they would not be missed. The child who thinks he does not receive enough attention in the home may feel excluded from the inner circle of the family. He may even become rebellious or difficult in order to attract attention and feel included. Similarly, grown persons may appear particularly quarrelsome or intractable for identical reasons: they do not really feel included and so must attract attention in a special way in order to have assurance of their value to the group. All persons, regardless of how they manifest it, deeply want and need to be included in the group. This is an essential part of functioning as a human being.

Control refers to whether the individual has any effect on what the group does. It has to do with decision-making, with policy and direction and authority. As Schutz points out, the need for control or influence varies widely, on a continuum from excessive need—autocracy, tyranny, dictatorship—to its opposite, where people feel the need to relinquish control, to let others do it, to leave the decisions to someone else. It is possible for persons who have a high need for acceptance to have a low need for control. The clown or joker, for example, requires the attention of others and so exhibits the need for inclusion; but he is quite happy to have others make the decisions and shape the policy of the group. Or, conversely, the person who has a high degree of control, possibly by virtue of his office or social status, may also have a great need for assurance that he is really accepted by the others for himself, that they really care about him and not just what he represents in terms of power. On the whole, persons with excessive need for control tend to have consuming secret need for inclusion.

Affection refers to close personal emotional feelings between people, such as love, hate, or indifference. Love and hate are not true opposites in this case, but love/hate and indifference are. Schutz sees affection as a dyadic relationship, that is, as one occurring only between two persons, but it need not be confined to that. It is possible for an individual to feel affection for a group, as for a school class, a club, or a fraternity, and for the group to have a special feeling for the individual.

Of the three needs, Schutz says that inclusion is undoubtedly the greatest, because the greatest fear of man is exclusion. This is probably true. The great myths, legends, and dramas of mankind have always represented banishment as the worst fate that could befall a human being. The successful person, on the other hand, has been seen as one taken into the hearts of the people, carried on their shoulders, toasted as a jolly good fellow, and generally celebrated as a valued member of society.

The emphasis of the Christian evangelical has usually been on all three needs *as they relate to God.* The psychology of evangelicalism, in both song and sermon, has been unerring in that respect. The hearer of the gospel is assured of *inclusion* in God's plan:

"For God so loved the world that he gave his only Son, that *whoever* believes in him should not perish but have eternal life."

> *Jesus included me,*
> *Yes, he included me,*
> *When the Lord said "Whosoever,"*
> *He included me.*

He is assured of *control:*

"Truly, I say to you, whoever says to this mountain, 'Be taken up and cast into the sea,' and does not doubt in his heart, but believes that what he says will come to pass, it will be done for him."

"Ask, and it will be given you; seek, and you will find; knock, and it will be opened to you."

"With God all things are possible."

> *There are some rivers that seem to be uncrossable,*
> *There are some mountains you cannot tunnel through.*
> *God specializes in things that seem impossible,*
> *He knows a thousand ways to make a way for you.*

And he is assured of *affection:*

"God so loved the world . . . ."

> *Jesus loves me, this I know,* [etc.]
>
> *Jesus, lover of my soul,*
> *Let me to thy bosom fly,* [etc.]
>
> *I come to the garden alone,*
> *While the dew is still on the roses,*
> *And he walks with me, and talks with me,*
> *And tells me I am his own.*

It is easy to see, under this schema, why evangelicalism has always been so phenomenally successful with the masses, and especially among adolescents and neurotics. It feeds upon the very innermost needs of the person, enabling him to sublimate those needs into spiritual or transcendent emotions and to live with effectiveness in a world where those same needs are not being met on an interpersonal basis. It is even able to take advantage of the individual's failure at interpersonal relations by reminding him of Jesus' promise that the world would hate him if he did the work of Jesus, just as it hated and crucified Jesus himself. Thus rejection by men instead of acceptance, and neglect instead of control, and indifference instead of affection, become badges of honor and can even motivate the person improperly to seek the opposite of what he most inwardly desires. God becomes a refuge from human affairs and dealing with human beings.

While not all the effects of evangelicalism have been negative and undesirable, some of the personal and psychological effects have. For one thing, men have been able to attach the name of Jesus to persecution and oppression of groups and races unlike themselves, perverting the real nature of Christ and his way of relating to other men. For another thing, the religion of the Incarnation has been often and again deincarnated by it, so that union with God is glorified while union with other men is given only minimal attention. Now, in an era which has lost the sense of the transcendent or the holy, and which is trying to discover the meaning of human unity, there is a consequent and inevitable divorce between the worship of God and natural human relationships.

It is this divorce which must somehow be overcome in the new liturgical designs. Christian worship must do more to fulfill the needs of persons for inclusion, control, and affection on a purely human basis, and help worshipers to understand that God is to be experienced in beneficent interpersonal relationships as well as in more privatistic or mystical ways. Until this is done, we will use God, not worship him, and leaders of worship will manipulate the congregations for their own ends and purposes, not those of the congregations.

Manipulation is a subject which ought to be faced at some point in our consideration of worship. If we have true respect for the persons who are engaged in worship, we do not want to be guilty of manipulating them according to our own hidden agendas. But how can we give any design or shape to liturgy without unconsciously tending to influence the minds and reactions of those who participate in it? A seminar group with which I was present once spent an entire afternoon addressing itself to this problem. There was real concern about it, especially among the more freethinking participants, lest those who design worship merely transfer to other persons their own special concerns or hang-ups. The group arrived at the inevitable conclusion that there is no way in which persons can prepare an act or procedure of worship for other persons without in some way, even unconsciously, prejudicing the other persons toward a certain way of believing or a certain mode of behavior. Manipulation is a fact of life. It cannot be avoided even in Christian worship. The best thing, then, is to recognize this fact and to focus instead upon the question of which are the most legitimate aims of manipulation in Christian worship. The group decided upon four aims which it felt were bona fide aims within the Christian fellowship.

One, to free the individual from all forms of destructive servitude;

Two, to render more acute his powers of observation, so that he sees with less and less blindness;

Three, to sharpen his awareness of the underlying unity between himself and the rest of creation, including all men in the world;

Four, to help him to feel and express love.

It should be noticeable immediately that the manner of expressing these aims is highly secular and not necessarily theological. Members of the group felt that the use of theological language might of itself introduce certain dogmatic prejudices into the considerations, and so confined themselves to more humanistic expressions. But it was felt by the group that this manner of stating the matter did not preclude the possibility of interpreting it in terms of the more traditional announcement of the gospel and man's response to it. The important thing about the list was that it defined the aims of manipulation according to the individual's own personal needs instead of according to the control needs of some particular religious group or spiritualist mentality.

The attention of this seminar group to such a question as manipulation is perhaps indicative of the very thing that must be communicated through the liturgy itself: the feeling that someone really *cares* about the worshiper for himself and not for some vague or otherworldly end to which his energies may be put. This is after all the real message of the gospel of Christ. If it is a manipulative gospel, it is so in terms of a manipulation to freedom, to a bondage *chosen,* not one bestowed. I saw a sign recently on a motel between Nashville and Birmingham which said in bold letters, "We care." That is what must come through in the liturgy. Worship must itself breathe an air of pastoral care, or else the pastoral care of the church becomes diffuse and unrelated to the highest acts of the congregation.

The needs of inclusion, control, and affection may not all be met in the liturgy, or met uniformly for all persons. Still, there must be the assurance, in the things that are attempted, that the fellowship of believers is trying to face these needs and to deal with them in constructive, helpful ways. The demands in a technological era for assurances of humanity are tremendous. The liturgy, whether or not it succeeds in meeting the demands completely, must at least proclaim, "We care."

There are three general ways in which planned worship should always contribute to the meaningfulness of personal human experience.

First, it should always help people to be sensitive to their own personhood—to their value as persons, their ambiguities as persons, their potential as persons, their uniqueness as persons. The worshiper should be awakened to things about himself that he has either forgotten or never known. The romance of the self should be rekindled each time he participates in the liturgy. He should be reminded of the privilege it is to be a person, the joy it is, the adventure it is. Even if it is painful to him, it can be a joy. He should know that God means for him to be *alive* and *growing*.

The very language of the prayers and responses in a service should have a high quotient of sensitivity to persons about it. It should be easily internalized by worshipers, easily adapted to their own emotional tempers and needs. Consider this recent litany, for example:

L: Jesus died for me.
R: Jesus died to help me to be free and to realize myself. It is tragic if I do not respond to what he has done . . . if I remain in my prison . . . if I do not conceive of myself as a free person . . . if I do not realize myself.
L: Jesus meant for me to act freely.
R: He meant for me to discover who I am.
  He meant for me not to be afraid.
  He meant for me to know love.
L: It is a pity if I choose death rather than life.

D

R: I want to live. I really do. God help me to be more aware
of my own value. Then God help me to share myself with
others.

L: That way I shall be free.

R: That way I shall be serving God at the same time that I am
growing as a person. He will know that I am a serious disciple
because I am taking myself seriously. I am glad to be a Christian.

The language has to do with a personal response to the intention of Christ, a personal unfolding before that intention, a
blossoming of the self to become more aware of the world and
more responsible for it. The content of belief is there—Christ's
death, our coming to life, our sharing the effect of Christ with
others, etc.—but it is not stated creedally. It is implicit in what
is said, not explicit. Creed is subservient to persons, not the
other way around.

Harry Emerson Fosdick did much to help us to realize the
importance of this approach in worship. His own experience
was that being a minister was tedious and difficult until he
discovered how to release people's own hidden impetus and
ability to worship. In the beginning, he tried it the way we all
do it. He did the religious shaman act, saying the proper thing
in prayers and preaching sermons about doctrinal matters and
theological concerns. Then he dropped that act and began
treating his prayers and sermons as pastoral counseling opportunities, reflecting the concerns he knew people to have about
their day-to-day living and dying. Suddenly things came alive!
People responded to the prayers and sermons. Fosdick discovered an electrifying reciprocity between what happened in
church on Sunday morning and what happened in the counseling room on Monday morning. For the rest of his life he was to
speak of preaching as "counseling *en masse,*" and his prayers
were to become models of human interest, holding the concerns of real people before God. The hundreds of thousands of
persons who worshiped at Riverside Church through the years

came and went with the feeling that someone there cared about
them, that the God who was worshiped there cared, that being
the persons *they* were was a valuable thing in the world.

It is this high personality-quotient that accounts more than
anything else for the appeal of the kind of "intimacy prayers"
published by Malcolm Boyd and Michel Quoist. They take seriously the most incidental moments in the individual's daily
routine. They value the frivolous and the discrete and the un-
repeatable. They have a feeling for what Salinger in *Franny
and Zooey* called "consecrated chicken soup." They see the
possibilities for the numinous, the holy, in the most outra-
geously secular and profane areas of human existence, and they
never hesitate to celebrate these possibilities.

All worship should sensitize people in this fashion.

A Texas minister, Deryl Fleming, of the Lake Shore Baptist
Church in Waco, has apparently had a remarkable effect on his
congregation in this manner. Quietly and deliberately, he has
led in the designing of worship experiences which interpret and
hallow the individual and personal qualities of those who participate in them. Worshipers are encouraged to share prayers,
poems, and reflections of their own composition with others in
the congregation. Recently a collection of these items by persons in the church was published, noncommercially, under the
title *A Time for Everything.* It is a delightful collection, full of
little surprises and tender moments, some of them caught by
children, some by adults. Here is a contribution from a young
mother, Mrs. Donna McMullen, entitled "Early Morning."

> Phillip is five, every inch alive, running, climbing, rolling, yelling.
> After a rain he watched birds bathing and saw the leap of a
> furry-tailed squirrel. "What are you doing, Phillip?" "Just looking
> at things, just loving the world."[2]

Another mother, Mrs. Carolyn Henson, reflected on the sanctity of motherhood in a prose meditation called "Being a
Mother Is."

BEING A MOTHER IS

loving one man so completely that you long to be the mother of his child.

going through childbirth with anticipation, patience, and a sense of miracle.

remembering that unique sense of love and oneness with God which husband and wife share at the birth of their child.

holding your newborn for the first time with the assurance that GOD IS.

going home—to sleepless nights, formula, diapers, routine, responsibility.

letting the house go so you can take time. Time to play and teach pat-a-cake, time to rock and sing, time to hold a sleeping baby, time to grow and become.

being a wife and lover so that your children will know that the love between their parents is special, tolerant, respectful and secure.

teaching a child—how to say "Da-da," how to wave bye-bye, how to smile, what to touch and what to leave alone. Teaching love, hostility, approval, rejection, friendliness, optimism, pessimism, moodiness through mother-child osmosis.

keeping up—keeping up with a toddler in the garbage can, with a six-year-old down the street, with new styles; it is staying alert and keeping up with the news so that your child can be proud of you.

assuring your child of your love for her, of her worth, of the security of her home.

a bad day—when you've yelled at the kids, burned the supper, accomplished nothing and lost your perspective.

asking your child to forgive you when you have been "on her" all day unjustly, and loving her when she says she understands.

taking care of a child day in and day out during the preschool years to the point that you are dependent on her laughter and chatter.

taking your child to school on the very first day with smiles and good wishes while inside you experience the agony of "letting go."

pushing your child into the world and teaching her to be independent while keeping a listening ear and open arms.

helping your child to grow up, and all the while wishing she wouldn't.

being there—when there is excitement over a caterpillar, when there is fear over a bad dream, when she falls off a bike, when a disappointment comes, when friends ridicule, when Santa Claus comes.

an honor and an occupation, a frustration and a reward, failure and success, always and just once.

a gift and a calling from God.[3]

A deacon, Jim Dolby, contributed this prayer.

Here we are again—we're really a motley crew—thanks for loving us. We rushed from home with the Sunday paper only partly read and we've already yelled at the kids to hurry up so that we could get here fairly close to the starting time for Sunday School. The breakfast was cereal and toast, as usual, and the party last night lasted a little long and we're only part here—and that part that's here wants to play golf or go home and curl up for another quick nap. Already our stomach is growling and we're tired of sitting. We just sat through a Sunday School class which was less than exciting. Here we are—we're not much ready to meet with the God of all creation.

These people sitting on our row are really something. A lawyer, an ex-mayor of the city, a big-wig at the University, a college professor, a big business tycoon, a football coach, a well-known woman in these parts—some really sharp people—I hear we've even got seventeen Ph.D.'s in this church—this is bound to be the zingiest church in town. Oops—there we go again—we forgot

these people aren't significant because they are important in our
eyes; it's because they are just like us all—human beings and they
need to be loved like we do. I think if we saw things like you do
we probably would see that what they need is a warm handshake
and even perhaps a hug. We all need to know what it is to experience love from a fellow human being and from a person who, like
us, is committed to Jesus the Christ.

Remind us that he's not *just* a lawyer or a barber, and she's not
just a mother, grandmother, or teacher, but that we're all fellow
compatriots in life and that a tear shared together as loving
friends is more sacred than all of the praise of a detached world.
In our need to be loved help us not to forget that our command
from you is to love.

Lord, we would like to give our sons and daughters a big hug
—but we seldom do it. We want to put our arm around that
person who has helped us but we just never get around to it. We
want to cry when we're touched by beauty or yourself but we
can't do it before others.

You said that people would be able to pick out a Christ—one in
a crowd because he is a person who loves another. I'm afraid that
isn't the keynote of your church through the world or of us here
today. Well—we're here—in a way which is uniquely and divinely
yours, melt the coldness of our hearts, break through the fences
which separate us from you and our neighbors, and make us
sensitive to people—the people you died for. Lord, here we are.
Penetrate into our private world—Please!! Amen.[4]

One can *feel* the vitality of this congregation through such
things as these. The language of the church is *people*. Linger-
ing, thoughtful attention is paid to human individualities, to the
distinctiveness of the participants, to their most intimate needs
and joys. The worship of God, under such conditions, is not
mere worship-in-general; it is worship with a sense of reality,
worship anchored in the day-to-day existence of the congregation.

Second, worship should always help people to be sensitive to the personhood of others—to their rights, desires, fears, beliefs, hopes, ambitions, strengths, weaknesses, joys.

I heard a chaplain in the city of Boston say once that a group of interns working with him had spent an entire summer together before they could finally get over the ethnic and denominational differences that divided them when they first assembled. In one sense, the summer had been a loss. They had spent so much time just trying to relate to one another that they had covered very little ground in psychological studies and clinical training. But they learned one very important thing, the chaplain said, perhaps more meaningful to them than anything else they might have learned that summer. They learned that "the truly spiritual man is the one who sees the spirit in other men."

This is basically what Martin Buber meant when he said in *I and Thou* that "all real living is meeting."

Community is important in worship because persons are somehow closer to Christ when they are closer to each other, because there is something like the experience of God in the experience of other persons. The motion that carries us outside ourselves to the neighbor carries us on to God. The direction is the same, and the impetus from one serves the other.

What can be done, then, to sensitize worshipers to their fellow worshipers? There are many small things. The wording of prayers like the one by the deacon cited above, or the wording of responses, may call attention to the feelings of others who are present. People may be asked to concentrate on the persons directly in front of them, or to their right or left, and to care for them during the hour, to pray for them, to wish to pick up their burdens for them, assume their anxieties. The use of bodily contact, as suggested in a previous chapter, may greatly increase awareness of who the other person is, how he feels, how he reacts.

Coffee hours before or after church are often more successful in terms of human relationships than the worship services themselves. There people have a chance to visit, something as meaningful today in cities as it was in the days when pioneer farmers congregated after a week apart. Would there be anything wrong in providing for such a time, perhaps in a modified way, within the worship hour itself? Provost Ernest Southcott of Southwark Cathedral in London, England, says that worshipers in the cathedral have sometimes been served their coffee and doughnuts right in the pews, from little pushcarts in the aisles, instead of standing up in some little hall in another part of the building. This act of fellowship thus became a kind of crypto-Communion, with less of the formalism and ritual usually associated with the Eucharist.

Speaking of Communion, would anything other than mere tradition be offended if the bread and wine were actually served by one's neighbor in the pew instead of by some presiding officer or funereal bearer of the trays? It was my pleasure to officiate at a wedding once where the bride and groom served the consecrated elements to each other and then to the wedding party, and the wedding party served the guests in the pews. There was something touching and meaningful in the act, especially in the exchange between the bride and groom. What if we were to serve each other, side by side, in the pews? Wouldn't it heighten eye-contact, touch-response, and so on? Wouldn't it make a greater social reality of the act of Communion?

The aim is to see the other person, to become aware of him as a living, breathing, responsive organism, with his own problems and fears about life, with his own contributions and offerings to make. Yet we typify persons, we treat them as objects, things, aggregates. Somehow we must get beyond this facile method of handling persons and really effect a meeting.

William Schutz tells in *Joy* about a priest who came to a sensitivity training group at the Esalen Institute. He was not in his clerical clothes, and as one of the rules of such groups is not to deal in specific identification, the others did not know he was a priest. When the group was engaged at choosing its own new names for the participants, the others decided that the priest looked and acted like a pixie, so they called him "Pix." He was greatly pleased by this, and became more and more lively as the week went on, expanding to fulfill the role in which they had imagined him. Finally the rumor started that he was a priest, and someone asked him to confirm or deny it. By this time, however, he was so totally accepted by the group that this role identification did not impair communication. When the session was over, the others hugged and kissed their friend Pix, and he wept for the openness and honesty with which he had been treated, something he had not experienced during his thirty-five years in the priesthood. He went back to his parish determined to do more to promote interpersonal relations in the services and activities of his congregation.

This is probably not an unusual story. Most priests and ministers would testify that they are treated as objects by their congregations. And unfortunately many of them doubtless treat their parishioners as objects too.

This problem could be partially countered by designing into the liturgy more confrontation between worshiper and worshiper as persons, so that the awareness of human dependency which is to characterize the Christian's life *beyond* the sanctuary actually begins within the sanctuary. If it does not begin there, it is not likely to succeed in any measure elsewhere.

Third, worship should reinforce the sense of personal relation between the worshiper and God. This is the final step. It cements the other personal relationships dealt with. In a sense, it is also the foundation for the others, so that it must be conceived of as being prior to the others as well as sequential to them. It transmutes the various personal relationships into a unity for the worshiper, into a feeling for the whole of life. It is like breath to the body, and helps it to function as a unit despite its complexity. It is very obviously related to what the New Testament called the Holy Spirit.

There are clearly problems in our minds today with a personal God and a personal relationship to him. We are so greatly aware of our psyches and how they work that we are prone to agree with Freud that God is simply a grand illusion, a super father-figure man has invented in order to satisfy his subconscious need for a father who will not die. We tend to find the anthropomorphic descriptions of God in primitive Old Testament passages distasteful or meaningless today. Our mature minds wish to reject the "childishness" of that kind of religion, and hold on only to the more sophisticated teachings, which are partially validated to us by philosophy and apologetics.

We are really caught between matters. On one hand we are too modern and adult to entertain with any sense of reality the fantasies of an earlier age and engage fully in anthropomorphic, humanized language about God; and on the other hand we are total organisms and cannot abstract ourselves so completely from the merely human situation as to think of God only philosophically or scientifically. As a result, we generally try to do both, perhaps not at the same time, but darting back and forth, and so become schizoid, never quite knowing how we feel or believe. The debilitation of the worship experience in this manner was captured beautifully in the joke that made the rounds a few years ago about the benediction supposed to have been said at a religious gathering which featured both Billy Graham and Paul Tillich: "May the Ground of All Being bless you all real good." That is tragically where many Christians are in terms of their worship experience.

Perhaps what we must rehabilitate in people's minds is an understanding that is implicit in the gospel, namely that God, whatever or whoever he is, *bends himself to us* in our relationship with him. That is, he may be more than personal in the sense that we are personal, but if personhood is the epitome of our natures, if it is the highest, most unified sense of who we are, then he meets us as person. There may be as much anthropomorphism in our attempt, in a philosophical age, to conceive of him as mind or evolving spirit or whatever as there was, in more primitive times, in conceiving of him as a supernomad or a strong right arm. The safest, surest, and most rewarding approach is to meet God in terms of what is highest in us, our persons. This does not mean abdication of our mental powers at all. It means that we project ourselves toward God in the most central, vital way we can, with all the power of being mustered behind our human identities; and we trust that we will be met where we are by God, which means that we will experience him as person too.

With this understanding, the language of worship, at the same time that it should be more personalized with regard to ourselves and our fellow worshipers, must be more personalized toward God. This need not be done in a sentimental fashion, and it need not be done in Old English forms of address. It can be done with soberness and dignity, yet with warmth and feeling. I remember the prayers of the young assistant minister who had just come to a church where I worshiped for a year. He always addressed God as "Dear God, you . . ." and put special emphasis on the "you." For a while my sensibilities were bothered by this. I still had a "reverence hangover" and preferred to hear the deity addressed as "Thou." But now I am grateful for what the persistent use of that vocative did for me. It made me much more conscious of God as a contemporary force and a personalized force. It cut through a lot of haziness in my thinking about God and left me with a clean, muscular feeling.

There is really no beginning and no end of this matter. Whether one starts with personal language about the self or sensitivity to others or personal language about God, it is all part of the same ball of twine. We simply must do more to personalize worship, to take it out of the abstract, formalistic routines it so often falls into and make it dynamic, serving as a catalyst for intra- and extrapersonal understanding and integration. Only when we do can we begin to appreciate the full meaning of love as the context for Christian growth and maturation, and as the arena in which worship becomes a happening.

Drama

OUR WORD *person* is derived from the Latin *persona,* which means "mask." This appears contradictory to us at first, because we are accustomed to think of a real person as one who is *not* wearing a mask. "He is not just playing a role," we say. "He is sincere, honest, straightforward." But the contradiction is easily explained. When men put on masks in the ancient theater they assumed the fixed identities that went with them. They were no longer subject to the changing, illusory nature of real life. Their personhood was assured, even though everything else was in flux around them.

Dealing with the sense of illusion has been a special problem in every epoch of human existence when there have been large-scale, extremely noticeable shifts in the values and beliefs by which men live. These have been the great eras of creativity in both the theater and religion, because they have invariably reflected the attempts of man to come to terms with his environment in new ways. In such moments the "original un-reason," as Richard Sewall calls it, "the terror of the irrational,"[1] seems to come back in force, and individuals feel metaphysically naked, alone, and unaccommodated. They no longer know for sure what is real, fixed, or solid in their universe. All the landmarks by which they steered their course have shifted, and all the stories by which they comforted themselves have become false and irrelevant. Somehow they must find new landmarks and new stories. They must reestablish their relationship to the universe in terms that are meaningful to them in their particular moment of history. They must "illusion" themselves again, and find the masks that give them identity for the time in which they live.

There is no doubt that ours is one of those unusual periods of change and creativity when the feeling of illusoriness is everywhere. The erosion of traditional values was under way well before the end of the last century. A gallery of names such as Nietzsche, Melville, Dostoevsky, Freud, Picasso, and Einstein reminds us instantly of the great brilliance of the era—of the staggering, almost incredible distance we have traveled in a mere hundred years. The world of our grandfathers is no more. We are bound to feel confused, disoriented, uprooted, as though we lived in a vaporous landscape where the configurations never remain fixed long enough to become familiar and comforting.

The theme of illusion has itself been one of the most constant references in contemporary writing. Ibsen, Strindberg, Pirandello, O'Neill, Miller, Brecht, Genet, Beckett, have all been haunted by it. "You must now go home," says a character at the end of Genet's *The Balcony*, after a madcap evening of tricks and deceptions on the stage. "You must now go home, where everything—you can be quite sure—will be even falser than here."

And the character is right. This is an age of dissolving realities and aberrant understandings. Everything we had believed or thought about the universe and ourselves appears at times to be only a trick of the mind, an hallucination, a nightmare that has no end.

What *can* a man believe in a time like ours? What can he be sure of, even in church? *Especially* in church—for maybe Freud was right; maybe religion is all a gigantic hoax, the *super* illusion which we have conjured up to replace the father and the world we never had. We never seem to shake the suspicion.

The underside of all our creeds and all our devotion is blighted by doubt and reservation. More than any generation of men before us, we are aware of ourselves being religious, aware of ourselves being pious, aware of ourselves at worship. We are haunted by a double image of ourselves, one participating and the other holding back, afraid that it's all a trick or a mistake. We feel desperate to be whole, but don't know how. We think we are doomed to a double-consciousness—that mankind is doomed—for the rest of human history, however long or short that may be. Most of the time we think it will be short, because the sense of the eschaton—of the approaching end of all things —usually appears to accompany anxieties about illusoriness.

Thus far, in this particular period of flux and distress, neither the secular theater nor the religious culture has sufficiently answered the entropy of the age. For all its fascinating metaphors and innovations in style, the theater has not managed to present us with the kinds of images and rituals required to galvanize our fragmented, disarranged situation; it has explored instead—and brilliantly—aspects of our brokenness, our dementia, our awareness of illusion. It has only mirrored our wasteland, in other words; it has not provided a force field for reunifying us and setting us off in new directions. And the religious culture, needless to say, has done no better: it has lacked the imagination and the daring to dump its institutional and traditional baggage, and has thus spent most of its energies in the vain attempt to rearrange these encumbrances to best advantage. More often than not, it has appeared to be endeavoring to evade the cataclysmic nature of the modern upheaval and to engage in a mere holding action, as though it hoped the storm would soon pass and we could return to business as usual. The artists of the age have at least had the courage to kiss yesterday good-by; they know it is gone for good.

Part of our anguish in the modern situation, of course, stems from the fact that the theater and the church have become so polarized into opposite camps that each is denied a part of its vital nature. Theater had its inception in religion. In the beginning it was almost pure ritual, performed for totally religious purposes. Its genius has therefore always lain in its ability to put people into touch with their own mythological levels again, to reinstate the sense of mystery and unity in the universe we inhabit. Now its rituals are diminutive, isolated, truncated, ineffective; like the inchoate rites of *Waiting for Godot*, they never link up and become overpowering or salvific; they remain macaronic and irrelevant, only taunting and mocking the needs of the characters.

The church, on the other hand, has largely lost its sense of drama. Its liturgy no longer enspells or enraptures, catching men up into new cosmic visions or attitudes. There is not even much excitement any more about the Eucharist, which is essentially a dramatic reenactment of Christ's incarnation and sacrifice. The feeling for the divine struggle, with worshipers taking part in the action, has given way in the main to a prosaic repetition of doctrines and words. The sermon is more generally equated with worship than the ritual, and people choose their churches on the basis of the preachers' merits.

What must happen in the church, what has got to happen if the church is to recover its vitality and sense of direction, is that people must learn how to play again in the church, how to enter into the drama of salvation and wholeness. They must learn to risk everything in *full* play. The "illusion" of Christ must become so real and compelling again that it obliterates the double consciousness, the shadow-image, and reunifies men in their depths. Somehow our structures must provide opportunities for people to get beyond the world of fragments and into a sense of themselves and God that will enable them to live as whole men in a broken environment. Their illusions must be good again—and lasting. And this means that they must be consonant with what men know about themselves and their world; they must proceed with that kind of inner verification which has always separated good drama from poor drama.

How do we get there from where we are? That is of course
the big question. Our immediate temptation is to want to produce better liturgies of the kind we already have—to design
better litanies, turn better phrases, sharpen the imagery. And
this might be helpful. We are also tempted to cast about for
good contemporary plays or movies, like Rod Steiger's overpowering film *The Pawnbroker*, and introduce them into worship settings with the hope that they will reinvest our rituals
and formalities with substantive meaning which has been missing from them. This too can be helpful. But what we must
ultimately consider in the church are ways of *personalizing*
worship, of involving the worshipers in more than a spectacle-
spectator relationship. There is nothing particularly invalid
about older liturgical and dramatic forms; given certain conditions, and performed well, they still function very much as they
always did. But if McLuhan is right, that this is a "low defini-
tion" era, so that most of the people born since 1940 require a
maximal freedom to respond to stimuli in their own way and
not according to any controlled or prearranged plan, then we
should give primary consideration to designs for worship which
have a high participational ratio. We should be increasingly
concerned to discover rituals and liturgical acts which provide
beginnings, or points of initiation, but do not require standard
reactions or procedures all the way to the end.

This is something like what Sam Keen said in *To a Dancing
God:* "If I am to rediscover the holy, it must be in *my* biography
and not in the history of Israel."[2] He was not ruling out the
history of Israel; his biography *included* the history of Israel. As
a boy of six in a map-covered Sunday-School room in Tennessee,
he had walked the dusty roads of Galilee and Judea with Jesus;
he knew far more about Israel than he did about Tennessee. But
now, trying to get beyond the recent past—beyond the death
of God and beyond the death of his own childhood—he had to
begin at a radical starting point: his own feelings and experiences. And the same is true for most of our contemporaries:

history is bunk until they rediscover it in their own inner life.

Therefore worship must somehow provide forms capable of initiating the discovery process without dictating the literal route which it must follow. There must be ritual for reenacting myth which, at the same time that it suggests the myth to be reenacted, does not control the acting, but permits it to become the acting of the individual worshiper himself. In the end, perhaps the worshiper will realize that he is always acting out myths, and can find ways of bringing his existence into conformity with the more fruitful, helpful myths. That is, he may learn which roles or *personae* permit him maximal freedom of action as an individual, and which ones provide maximal return on the action investment.[3]

One form of contemporary drama which appears to offer possibilities for the construction of liturgies is the *happening,* which lies somewhere between the spectator and participational varieties of theater, inclining sometimes toward one and sometimes toward the other. Strictly conceived, the happening is designed as a spectator experience.[4] But the participational factor seems higher than in conventional drama because the spectator is usually surrounded by the happening and has a sense of being in the middle of the action. And often, during the performance of a happening, a spectator simply forgets to be passive and enters into the performance without any invitation to do so.

Happenings are usually not dramatic in the traditional sense. They merely involve the designed use of space and time by a group of people, with certain "actors" appointed to go through prearranged motions. They often depend upon the use of shock technique to produce new or unusual sensations in the viewers. In Carolee Schneemann's *Meat Joy,* for example, several actors move about the scene with dead chickens' heads in their mouths and the chickens hanging down, while some scantily clad girls obscenely caress the carcasses of dead animals. In Wolf Vostell's *You* the performers cavort in a swimming pool while the spectators shoot colored water on them from water pistols; the atmosphere is reminiscent of Nazi death camps, and the spectators are made to feel that they are playing the roles of persecutors.

What the happening has done, in one sense, is to go one step further with the confrontation theater of Brecht and Genet, which was designed to assault the audience, to oppose its normal way of seeing existence, and to force it to modify or break up that way of seeing. In the happening, the audience is almost unavoidably involved. It can resist by refusing to take part; but the resistance itself becomes an act, so that the resister is made aware of where he stands.

In a brilliant essay entitled "On the Necessity of Violation," Jean-Jacques Lebel, a leading French proponent of happenings, speculates that the bystander at a happening is catapulted, by means of the bizarre sights and actions around him, into the very arena of myth and fantasy, and is forced to test himself and his way of perceiving life against a total rearrangement of his perceptory modes.

> The Happening interpolates actual experience directly into a mythical context. The Happening is not content merely with interpreting life; it takes part in its development within reality. This postulates a deep link between the actual and the hallucinatory, between real and imaginary. It is precisely the awareness of this link that the enemies of the Happening cannot tolerate, for it might threaten their defense mechanisms. When Merleau-Ponty decrees that "the phenomenon of hallucination is not part of the world, and is not accessible," he is saying that art, considered as a language of hallucination, has no place in that "normal life" we are expected to tolerate. The extremely limited space assigned to art in society in no way corresponds to its mythical volume. To pass from one to the other—at the risk of breaking the law—is the primordial function of the Happening.[5]

The happening liberates "latent myths" in people, says Lebel; "it transfigures us and changes our conception of life."

There is no doubt that this is threatening to most of us. But that may be precisely the reason we cannot dismiss it. We may need to be disoriented, upended, mocked, threatened. As Hansen implies in his discussion,[6] our lives are actually filled with sights, sounds, occurrences, etc., which are irreducible to systems, categories, and particular ways of experiencing them. Happenings reopen our imaginations to the wonder and variety around us. They break up our preconceptions and routines, and make it possible to see again. When we view a drama or a movie, what we see is removed from life; it may even seem bigger than life. Then when it is over we turn back to our disordered world, where things do not proceed according to plot. Why not a theater where things do not appear to go according to plot, where their order in relationship to all the other things cannot be perceived because there is no order? Then we would go out to a world like the one we had seen, and would be able to function in it because of the training we had received under simulated conditions.

Roger Ortmayer, of the National Council of Churches' Department of Church and Culture, describes a worship service in a college chapel which employed a rock combo, an actor reading scripture for the entire time of the service, and "fifteen dollars' worth of streamers, balloons, and noisemakers."[7] As people arrived for the service, they were met at the door and divided into groups of seven, with six persons carrying the seventh in above their heads. The musicians were ten minutes late, but everybody seemed to think it was planned that way. The reader read, and Ortmayer blew up balloons and let them sail around the chapel as the air rushed out. Helpers in the balcony sailed paper plates over the heads of the people below. Each plate had a news clipping on it with instructions for the person catching it to stand and read it aloud, whatever else was going on. Some persons were throwing paper streamers; others were wrapping themselves or their neighbors in them. Everything was in bedlam. The combo played, the reader read, Ortmayer stood and preached a sermon, people read news items—all simultaneously. Students began a snake dance through the aisles. Two professors shouted "Blasphemy!" and left.

There was something of the happening about this service. It brought the confusion of Times Square or Piccadilly into the sanctuary, so that worship, if it occurred, had indeed to occur despite the confusion. And if the professors were upset by what Ortmayer was doing, they should be introduced to a proposal by Lawrence Ferlinghetti.

Ferlinghetti suggests in *Routines* that a new organization called BORE (Brotherhood of Radical Enlightenment) be established and dedicated to opposing "fatuousness, general stupidity, innocuousness, or whatever else offensive to the open mind & spirit." He offers this "Bore-in" as an example of the kind of protest or demonstration that BORE-members should stage:

> The scene: a large church or cathedral of one of the established medieval faiths. Enter Chief Bore (a thin man in loincloth) carrying a water pistol. He fills it at Holy Water fount and proceeds to baptize statues and worshipers with Holy Water from his holy gun. Bores in the pews chant and sing: "We want God! We want God! We want God!" (Anything may be substituted for the word "God," depending on what one has in mind for eternity: love, life, Enovid or enlightenment.) Chief Bore mounts to pulpit and begins sermon: "Brethren, we take our text today from the Old Testament itself. Repeat after me. If God is not dead, let Him now come down at last. We have waited and waited long enough. Let there be light at last! Why this eternal gloom? Unstain the glass! Lift off the gargoyle roof and let Him come down!" (etc., etc.) . . . Priests and police come running. Chief Bore holds them off with Holy Water but in the end they crucify him.[8]

It is admittedly difficult to think of this as worship. Our tradition has always been much more positively structured, and has employed neither irony nor negativism to accomplish its aims. Yet —and this is the point modern artists have tried again and again to make—there are times when the old structures and old methods become oppressively dull and routine, and at such times an apparently blasphemous antistructure may be required to break the hold of tradition. It is impossible to imagine that this kind of wild, nihilistic happening would ever replace the more sedate order in the majority of Christian churches around the world, but, on the other hand, it does train the liturgical designer to think more freely and creatively, and to import greater spontaneity and impulsiveness into religious services.

Here, for example, is a happening planned with a Christian congregation in mind.

Each person is handed a scrap of colored paper as he enters, and must find a seat where there is a matching piece of colored paper. Traditional church music emerges from a speaker in one section of the room, and instrumental rock music from a speaker in an opposite section. Strobe lights rake the dimly lit room, illuminating various objects such as a garden rake, a bird bath, a crucifix, a pot of flowers, and sometimes remaining momentarily focused on someone's head and face.

A man and a woman dressed in what appear to be garments of leaves pass through the congregation with a basket of apples, handing out apples to everybody. (The current Cranapple juice ad, featuring a sexy girl who says, "Hello. I'm Eve. This is a garden . . . ," could be shown simultaneously on a screen, or the sound track could be played.)

Spotlights focus on a scene at the front, left, with a table, a doctor, and two nurses. A very old man and woman hobble down the aisle. As they reach the light, it is obvious that the old woman is pregnant. Amidst groans and imprecations, she is helped onto the table. The others gather around her and a sheet is thrown over her, so that she is hidden from view. Loud groans, perhaps some expletives. The medical team straightens, rejoicing, and holds up a doll by one leg.

A noise is heard in the rear again. This time a chain of persons winds its way in and out through the room, intersecting the congregation wherever possible. The first person in the chain flashes a light on and off, and they all make sounds like a train in motion. Electronically produced noises of whistles, air brakes, screeching on tracks, etc., may accompany this part. A trolley bell may be substituted, or used in addition.

Two men walk down the center aisle or across the front, one very old, the other wearing a splendid-looking coat. Suddenly three or four other persons rush out of hiding, apprehend the man with the coat, take it from him, turn it inside out, and put it back on him and flee. The two continue walking as before.

There is the noise of an ambulance siren. Several persons in white come racing down the aisle bearing another person, a woman, aloft; the ones in front may flash a red light. It is an emergency case. The woman, younger than the earlier one, is also pregnant. She is put on the table and surrounded by the same medical team. The sheet; feverish operations. At last, triumph; the interns hold up a cross to which the woman has just given birth. It is carried to the other side of the room, where a light focuses on an oversized picture of a hippie or a Nazi or an Oriental, and dramatically nailed over the picture, essentially covering the human being on the portrait. Paper bags are passed out to the congregation. Everyone inflates one and pops it. Confetti is thrown around the room. The music is speeded up to double or triple time. There is a screech and the lights go out.

There are covert references in this happening to several biblical stories and motifs—the temptation and fall of man, the birth of Isaac, the coat which Jacob gave to Joseph, the coming of Christ—but they are forced on no one. Each person is free to respond to all kinds of subliminal signals, so that the references are in effect multivalent.

Here is a more explicit happening, designed around the Parable of the Sower and the types of ground:

As the minister rises and begins to read the parable, someone comes down the aisle scattering seed on the congregation. The minister is soon overtaken and drowned out by another version of the parable being fed through the public address system. The new version is repetitious and elaborative, and is read slowly and with sonorous gravity: "A sower, a so-so so-and-so sower went forth to sow—went third went fourth went fifth went forth to sow went the so-and-so sower the so-so sower to sow, etc." As the voice speaks of stony ground, someone in the congregation rises and loudly accuses someone else, "That's the kind of ground YOU are!" Similarly when other kinds of ground are introduced. Once the minister breaks in to confess that he is really stony ground himself—that he has brought forth some life which has since withered and died. His faith is now shallow and unproductive. He envies and despises other persons.

When the repetitious version of the parable has been read once or twice and is being repeated yet another time, a plowman appears, dressed in cutaway coat and tails. His plow, an ordinary garden plow mounted on wheels, is pulled by several girls wearing bikinis. If possible, they criss-cross the congregation, plowing up the ground; at least they move up and down all the available aisles.

A black then pulls a cart down the aisle while another black strews wretched-smelling manure around the pews or seats. The voice on the loudspeaker indicates that the manure is composed of various things: the decaying flesh of the persons they have despised; the excrement of thieves and successful businessmen; the ashes from the ovens at Auschwitz; flesh burned by napalm; etc., etc. ·

The sower comes through scattering seed again.

Then a wine cart is pushed down the center aisle, and the plow-girls pop out the corks on the bottles and serve the bottles to the people; each person drinks and passes the bottle on. The voice on the loudspeaker rehearses a piece about watering the seed with the blood of Christ and the blood of the saints in all the ages.

Finally the minister says, "Go, and be fruitful."

On the analogy of the Theater of Assault—*Hair,* Living Theater, Theater of Dionysus, etc.—this could be called Liturgy of Assault. Its style is harsh, strident, aggressive. It actively *confronts* the congregation. Herbert Blau, of the Actor's Workshop in San Francisco, once wrote that he was determined "that

nobody be able to take shelter in our theater."[9] The same could
be said of this kind of liturgy—nobody will find shelter in it. It
is designed to provoke, harass, offend, prod, probe. It is never
comfortable, even at best. It keeps men on edge. And it is
unlikely, for this reason, to find many supporters in the rank and
file of the church. Its main chance for existence in unadul-
terated form lies with small avant-garde fellowships and youth
groups looking for new experiences.

The important thing, however, is that the radical mood reflected by such liturgy will inevitably filter down into the main-
stream of liturgical practice, producing *some* innovation and
reorientation of spirit there. A number of congregations across
the country, for example, have already followed the lead of
New York's St. Clement's Church in producing *masked* liturgies, in which members of the congregation are given paper
bags to put over their heads until after the Confession of Sin and
the Words of Absolution, at which time they are invited to
remove them if they wish.[10] Others have become accustomed
to troupes of dancers with tambourines mingling with the worshipers, young persons draping the worshipers' necks with flowers and paper necklaces, and the use of weird, unnatural-sound-
ing electronic music.

The mention of masked liturgies prompts recollections of the
effective way some dramatists have used masks in recent years.
Genet, for example, put white masks on the black jury in his
play *The Blacks,* and wanted to put white masks on any blacks
who happened to be in the audience, in order to raise to a fever
pitch the tension between Caucasians and Negroes during the
performance. What if congregations were provided with various kinds of masks for role-playing in the liturgy? There could
be black masks for whites, white masks for blacks, Oriental
masks for Westerners, Western masks for Orientals, youth
masks for the elderly, elderly masks for the youths, poverty masks for the affluent, affluent masks for the poor—even
death masks for the living and living masks for the living-dead.

Part of the function of drama and liturgy is to confront us with reality in guises other than the ones we are accustomed to recognizing, thereby sensitizing us to our own roles or *dis*guises and helping us to discern relationships between the drama of our own existences and the dramas of history, nature, and the supernatural. Eventually, in other words, if theater and liturgy are to be successful, the drama of the self must be seen as converging upon and becoming united with the drama of the universe; this is the only means of catharsis in the theater and the only means of redemption in the liturgy; it is the only means, in either, of getting beyond the sense of flux and illusion to a feeling for what is permanently valuable.

The form of secular therapy known as *psychodrama* has of course tried to employ this understanding in helping to return persons to fuller, more enjoyable living, and has met with considerable success, particularly in its more recent derivative forms such as sensitivity training and the encounter group. It is quite possible that its insights, as formulated by Dr. J. L. Moreno of the Psychodramatic Institute of New York and others, could prove useful to designers of liturgy who wish to increase the personal "input" of worshipers themselves during the period of worship.

The usual procedure in psychodrama is for an "actor" (i.e., person undergoing therapy) to play a role he was playing at the time of an injury or unhappy moment in his life, regardless of when it was, and to try to rekindle the complex pattern of emotional issues present at the occasion. He maximizes all expression without fear of overstating or falsifying the issues. The emphasis is entirely upon "action insight," not upon verbalizing insights or "meaning" sessions, although postaction sharing may occur between the participants and the group observing. The idea is that the individual who plays himself in the midst of a group is better able to see himself as he responds to things than he can as an isolated individual. As Moreno puts it, "The function of the role is to enter the unconscious from the social world and bring shape and order into it."[11] And in addition the individual is better able to affirm himself, or accept the role he has played, when he performs the role in the supportive presence of a group.

Moreno stresses the importance of spontaneity in the discovery of the self, because the self is dynamic and not static.[12] We learn something significant about ourselves when we are placed in partly recognizable situations and are then permitted to improvise. The group around us becomes our mirror, and we see *how* we improvise, how we develop from one situation to another.

There are several techniques for varying the approach in these therapy sessions. Zerka T. Moreno, in a monograph entitled *Psychodramatic Roles, Techniques and Adjunctive Methods*,[13] lists a few of them: soliloquy (the actor talks only to himself); self-presentation (the actor "presents" himself, his father, mother, minister, professor, other persons, taking each role in turn and carrying on a conversation); self-realization (the actor, with the aid of some auxiliary egos, plays out the things he would really like to do in life, as opposed to the things he may be doing); the double (an auxiliary ego is asked to repeat everything the actor does or says, so that he sees himself imitated); multiple double (same technique, only with several alter-egos); role-reversal (actor exchanges roles with another person, perhaps his mother or father or some professional person, and each behaves as if he were the other); future projection (the actor portrays himself as he believes he will be at some time in the future); etc. Some therapists have reported striking effects from the use of projected imaginary death, in which the actor pretends to be dead, the lights are dimmed, and a funereal air is cast over the scene. The actor tries to describe what it is like not to exist any longer as a person. Auxiliaries may take the parts of Mephisto or St. Peter, and the dialogue may be carried on at some length about a life beyond the grave.[14]

There is something both intoxicating and potentially threatening about this kind of personal drama, and care must be taken not to let it move beyond the boundaries of potential control. The presence of a director skilled in counseling or therapy, while not absolutely required, is desirable and recommended.

An extension of psychodrama into a collective or group form, called *sociodrama*, is also useful, particularly for sensitizing members of one social group to the special problems, such as prejudice, neglect, or deprivation, involved in being a member of another group. This kind of role-playing has proved fruitful in numerous civic centers, churches, and therapy groups as a means of uncovering and coping with racial tension at the emotional level. J. L. Moreno has also experimented with what he calls "dramatized or living newspaper technique," in which persons read items from the morning newspaper and then assume the roles of the people in the accounts. Because the news items are world-wide in origin, the participants are thus required to assume various cultural and intercultural roles, sometimes playing Russians, Danes, English, Chinese, and Congolese all on the same day.[15]

The possibilities for incorporating the insights of personalized drama into Christian liturgy are limited only by our imagination and our willingness to engage in unconventional forms of worship. To employ such forms admittedly places a great deal of emphasis on the human in worship, and may appear thereby to detract from the adoration of the deity which is supposed to lie at the center of our purpose. But it may be that we cannot any longer recognize the relevance of the cosmic drama of salvation until we have begun with the finite drama of our own personal situations and worked out from it to the discovery that the two are really intimately related. As Dominic Cirincione, one of the contributors to *Multi-Media Worship*, complains,

> Each pew defines a person's place, and places him under arrest until his hour of observation is over. A booklet or hymnal further separates him from everyone around him while he is invited to

rejoice and celebrate the community of Christian brotherhood. The Sunday worshiper commemorates the history of Israel and the Lord's Supper with bowed head and somber isolation, but never is asked to celebrate the history of his own life and the supper of his own pain and passion in the world.[16]

One reason we have not structured liturgy in such a way as to provide for a more personal celebration of pain and passion— I am prepared to be corrected if I am wrong—is that we have not actually trusted worshipers to identify their suppers of pain and passion with Christ's. We have usurped their priestly prerogatives, and have done for them what we believed needed to be done. And consequently they have found the supper of Christ remote and unintelligible, with a significance only faintly recognizable from where they sit in the pew. Unable to begin where they are and extend their dissolving perspectives to the point where they are intercepted by the fact and meaning of Christ, so that Christ comes to them as a *discovery,* they experience the mystery of redemption as mere mystification, as only another factor of confusion amidst their disassembled values and beliefs.

I am thinking of a worship service in which the liturgist *did* trust the congregation to discover the mystery in their own suppers of pain and passion. After some excellent jazz hymns, which helped people to relax and come to a point of openness in their relationship to each other, he announced that *they,* the congregation, were going to provide the remainder of the worship. At his bidding, they formed circles of eight to a dozen persons. "Now," he said, "we are going to explore what we have brought to this hour with us. First, the secret fears and problems. Maybe you have not even realized what yours are. But now, in the group, in the body of Christ, you are able to articulate them to yourselves, and then to the brothers and sisters in Christ around you. Let's take about five minutes to share these."

It was a risk; perhaps these persons, who did not know each other well, would be unwilling to open themselves so easily to

their groups. For thirty seconds there was ominous silence in
the room.

Then, over on the left side of the room, a whisper began. It
was soon followed by a low voice on the other side. Then the
whole room seemed to burst into subdued noises. People afterwards expressed amazement at the ease with which they had
told things they had never before admitted to anyone; some
said they recognized constellations of feelings in themselves
they had been completely unaware of until that moment.

"Now," said the liturgist, when he finally got the congregation's attention again, "we are going to play a little support
game. This is the body of Christ. We want to bear one another's
burdens. And we want somehow to symbolize this, to say it
meaningfully, to one another." What he asked, in short, was that
everybody stand and, beginning with the last person who spoke
in the group, pass each person around the group, supporting
him at the shoulders while his feet remained on the floor in the
center.

Many persons had smiles of relaxation and happiness on their
faces as they were "handed" around the group. Even many who
were unable to relax and enjoy it confessed afterwards that it
was an act of great meaning to them.

"Finally," said the liturgist when they were all seated again,
"there is the matter of sharing our hopes. We have more to give
each other than our fears and problems." For the next five or
ten minutes, people eagerly spoke of the little excitements in
their lives—the people they loved, the ideas that meant a lot to
them, the words and memories they cherished. And, while they
talked, they passed around bowls of raisins and nuts and fed one
another with them. "Remember," the liturgist had said, "we are
feeding on Christ; we feed on him every day."

"We are going to take one more minute," said the liturgist.
"It is your minute to do what you want with . . . whatever you
feel like doing." It was an unforgettable moment. People began
to reach out and touch each other. Some hugged each other,

patted each other, kissed each other. Some just wept. Near the end of the minute, one group joined hands, stood, raised their hands aloft, and began softly and deliberately to sing the Doxology. By the time they had reached the second or third phrase, everyone in the room had joined in. It was an extremely moving experience.

"Well," said the liturgist, "there you are. You have preached the sermon by sharing Christ with one another, and those you preached it to will not forget it for a long time."

For a while, at least, their personal suppers of pain and passion had found their connection in the supper of Christ's pain and passion, and they would be able to deal with the conflicting values and illusions of life more easily than they had before.

This kind of sharing service is almost so antidramatic that it ought not to be called drama at all. It stands at the other end of the spectrum from traditional drama, in which actors on the stage do nearly everything for those who sit in the audience. Yet it may be the most important dramatic form of our time, for it involves everyone as a participant with a role of his own. It may in fact represent a return to pretheatrical times when entire communities performed the tribal rituals and specialized priests and actors had not been chosen to do it for them.

The overall effect of the use of drama is amazingly the same, however, whatever form it takes and wherever it occurs: men are restored to their sense of finitude and humanness; reminded of the illusoriness of all living, they nevertheless rediscover which roles are meaningful to them in the midst of it, and are enabled to celebrate the reinforcement of those roles; they gain a clear vision of the game again and rejoice in being able to commit themselves to it more fully than before; in other words, they recover the myths that make life real to them, and revalidate those myths in the very process of enacting them again: they learn to *live* by acting.

Story

ROBERT NEALE insists, in *In Praise of Play,* that man's psychic harmony requires design of his experience as well as discharge of his energy. Religiously speaking, "The sacred is always manifest as form as well as power; awareness of the sacred is awareness of *powerful form.* "[1] Myth and ritual, in other words, are interactive. "The full living out of myth creates a ritualistic life, and the full living out of ritual creates a mythical life."[2]

We have been talking thus far of ritual—of the methods by which we act out our designs and discharge energy. It is time to address the other side of the question by talking about myth. Or, in the language of play, we have dealt with games, now we must consider story. For, as Neale assures us, "Performance of ritual that is not grounded in story is not really performance but only going through the motions."[3]

Neale has cited an interesting example of ritual in which the myth is either truncated, confused, or missing, Samuel Beckett's play *Waiting for Godot.* "What is so disturbing about many modern stories in print and on stage," he says, "is not that they have negative conclusions to their tales, but no conclusions at all. The difference between *Othello* and *Waiting for Godot* reflects the condition of modern man—the man without a story."[4]

That is true, in a sense. There is almost no action of any consequence in *Waiting for Godot.* There are many small actions—dances, pratfalls, word games, identity games, etc.—but they are not united by any major action. If they are held together even loosely, for the purposes of the play, it is by the idea that someone possibly named Godot has promised to meet the characters at some ill-defined time in some rather uncertain place. The universal theme of the play, which by virtue of audience consensus overrides the author's own claims about it, appears to be the frustration of man at the failure of his own apocalyptic expectations, or, in other words, the collapse of myth.

The mythologists—those who study the structures of our experience in terms of the stories we use to explain it—have done much since the beginning of this century to give us a perspective on ourselves and the way we formulate, employ, and discard myths. What they have helped us to see, primarily, is that, contrary to the former notion that myth is extrinsic to society's experience (i.e., fables, fairy stories, untrue tales), it is actually intrinsic to experience. It "participates" in the real, to use Tillich's expression, and does not merely represent or symbolize the real. It arises from man's encounter with the world and this attempt to give shape to the way he experiences the world. Just as Moreno said the individual injects a role into the chaos of his being to produce a workable semblance of order there, the projection of myth into the chaos of his external realm brings about a sense of order in the universe. Myth cannot be divorced from the lives of those who live by it.

The contribution which C. J. Jung brought to the study of myth was the notion that myth is not really dependent on the historical repetition of sacred rites embodying it, as we had thought, but is a part of the racial memory or collective unconscious. It is part of our inherited, subliminal character, in other words: it is there whether the individual is exposed to specific external mythological sources or not.

The beauty of this theory, or one beauty of it, is that it helps to explain the repetitive character of myths around the world, in widely diverse cultures, and the delight which even adults take in various folk tales and fairy stories which are actually fragmented myths.

Jung spoke of "motifs," "archetypes," "prototypes," and "primordial images," which appear to perdure through all generations and cultures, suggesting that each individual has certain basic ingredients already inside him which, if he can only integrate them properly, will lead to psychic harmony and health. Until he can enact these bits of myth and bring them into harmonious relationship, he is in bondage to them. They frustrate and disable him. Once he has discovered their unity, however, they become the style of the man and enable him to act forcibly on his environment.

One of the most persistent symbols in the religions and mythologies of mankind, said Jung, is the *mandala,* the quartered circle which represents the totality of the four seasons, the elements of the universe, and the parts of man's own being. When the parts are in harmonious relationship, the whole is a compact geometrical unit. Famous instances of Christian adaptation of the *mandala,* as Alan Watts points out in his book *Myth and Ritual in Christianity,* are the widely used rose windows in cathedrals and the description of God in Dante's *Paradiso.*[5]

Jung noted that healthy persons or patients in the final stages of psychotherapy who were achieving a sense of well-being and integration tended to produce in their dreams or fantasies the image of the circle or *mandala* in prolific and enormously varied forms, suggesting that there is far more than a merely casual relationship between mythical ideas and symbols in the world's religions, on one hand, and the innate sense of health and normalcy in individuals on the other hand.

Derivatively this suggests that the efficacy of Christianity as a personal religion relies upon the same principles that are operative in other religions of even widely variant times and cultures, and that the accuracy with which we discern what the

E

Christian mythological structure is, precisely, depends in part upon our viewing that structure *vis-à-vis* the other, non-Christian structures. Only in this manner can we truly evaluate emphases within the Hebraic-Christian religion and decide which ones are structurally more significant than others.

There is a curious continuity among the world's mythologies, a persistent rhythm of emphases which suggests a general agreement upon four main categories of myth, in this order: creation, fall, trial, and restoration. The vocabulary differs slightly from religion to religion, but the emphases are similar and assume the same order and relationship to one another.

What follows is an arbitrary outline of these themes with various attendant subthemes, signalized in the language which, though capable of some neutrality, is really expressive of their associations in the Hebraic-Christian tradition.

CREATION: world, order out of chaos; paradise; rain; rivers, verdancy; plants and animals; man (Adam and Eve); concord; simplicity; fullness; awareness; love; joy; life (*period we have never actually known*)

FALL: failure; return of chaos; exile from paradise; barren ground; desiccation; confusion; frustration; discord; envy; complexity; misery; callousness; hiding; death (*period we are always in*)

TRIAL: the Hero (Savior); unusual birth; obscure childhood; initiation (temptation) and rebirth; magical occurrences; suffering; faithfulness or endurance; struggle to the death; true man[6] (*period we are always in*)

RESTORATION: endurance, success, or resurrection; redressing of alien forces; return of order, paradise, verdancy, etc.; life force unimpeded (*period we experience only in token or by expectancy*)

Various observations may be offered on the basis of such an outline, especially as the outline bears upon the mythological emphases in liturgy.

First, we have never actually known either the earliest state of creation or the restored state of creation in any full or realistic sense. We have always lived in exile. The mood of worship, then, should be exilic. It should frankly recognize the condition of the world we live in, and declare or celebrate any hope that is declared or celebrated in accordance with that condition. Any pretension that "all is right with the world" or "this is the best of all possible worlds" is mythically out of place.

Second, it is patently obvious, or nearly so, that we are in the state of fallenness. It is pointless to belabor this truth in worship, as the Puritans often did and as some liberal analysts still do. We can acknowledge the fact in brief and simple ways, but do not need to dwell on it. Dwelling on it only adds to the sense of misery we are already in.

Third, by deduction, our accent should fall on matters of trial and restoration, always remembering that restoration is possible only through trial and is not to be realized fully by even the most saintly among us. That is, our mood should be positive, affirmative, hopeful, and yet cautious and realistic.

Fourth, the extraction and magnification of subthemes without recognition of the major theme whose parts they are can lead to misemphasis and even misrepresentation. To deal with the unusual birth, for example, apart from the entire notion of the Hero, or even to deal with the death-struggle apart from it, can result in false judgments and assumptions as to their meaning. Similarly, to treat the Resurrection as a self-contained subject matter, without reference to the total pattern of restoration from fallenness, is a dangerous misemphasis. The difficulty many ministers face in composing a sermon for Easter each year stems precisely from the tendency to ignore the *Gestalt* of restoration for the fable of the empty tomb and appearances.

Fifth, restoration in this *schema* is both personal and societal in its dimensions, and the two emphases cannot be separated. The psyche or soul is sustained by the whole nexus of associations, and its health is never guaranteed by a *mere* personal conversion. For this reason, attention must be paid in liturgy to a proper balance between the necessary therapy for the individual and a redressing of society's problems, all the way from the dyadic or family unit to the community, state, and world levels. The two must be seen by worshipers as being mutually interrelated and interdependent.

Sixth, restoration, inasmuch as it is never complete within our lifetime, ought nevertheless to be represented in such token or partial fashion as to suggest motivation and incentive to worshipers to desire it and strive for it, finding their proximate wholeness in the same battle which the Hero undertook. An example of this in liturgy is the use, in one church's Easter celebration, of the witness of a man who had been cured of drug addiction. The traditional scriptures were read and the traditional hymns sung. But in place of a sermon filled with hyperbole and intimations of mystery, there was this simple, hardly dramatic recounting of a struggle against addiction, the help of friends and community agents, and victory. It was not final restoration, not even for the former addict—he still had other human problems to cope with. But it was a beginning, a symbol, *pars pro toto*—and it had an electrifying effect on many in the congregation.

If we may now go back for a moment to *Waiting for Godot,* we can observe that the problem of the characters in that play is that mythology for them has broken down somewhere in the Fall or Trial stages, perhaps slightly into the latter, and they lack the insight to pull themselves together and go forward. They are in exile with no real memory of Creation and no real hope of Restoration. The way Beckett has used fragments of the Mass, unrecognized by the characters throughout the play, underlines the significance of this. Waiting is the single exilic theme they know.

Why has waiting become so bereft of hope in the modern world? Apparently, if we follow Beckett in his several novels and plays, and think also of his early masters Joyce and Proust, it is because we know history. We have seen the cycle of exile-waiting-return-exile once too often. We have grown weary of penultimate satisfactions. It isn't that we have no myth to work with, but that we have too many We are in despair over a plethora of myths which never seem to get us out of the Fall or Trial epochs of existence.

This would explain the prevalence of the illusion theme in so many modern writings. Like either characters or audience in a play by Genet or in the movie based on John Fowles' *The Magus*, we are never quite sure whether myth is real or fabricated, whether it is helpful or demonic. The reason is that it never comes out anywhere. We are conscious of the presence of myth, in a way the primitives were not, and therefore we keep studying our situation to see where myth begins and ends, and where "reality" takes over. But the more real the myth becomes, the more it participates in our experience, the more difficulty we have in extricating it from "reality." Then, because we are sophisticated moderns and not superstitious primitives, we begin to feel that we are being victimized by the "illusoriness" of our time.

As far as the church is concerned, all this only says that religion in the Western world in our day has failed to carry its mythological emphases convincingly beyond the Trial motif so that men are able to believe in any meaningful form of Restoration. We have broken down in the wasteland and have difficulty cranking up the spirit to get out of it again. Therefore we become despondent and even cynical about either the first or the fourth phase of myth, Creation or Restoration, and begin to speak of "the death of God" or "the demise of Christianity." We fall into what Stanley Edgar Hyman in *The Armed Vision* calls the "baroque" period in myth, when, because we appear to be at the end of the line as far as any vital sense of myth is concerned, we concentrate on numerous small and insignificant myths.[7]

The error of concentrating on the resurrection motif, which I have mentioned, out of the total pattern of Restoration myth, is one example of this breakdown. Most intelligent ministers and laymen have real difficulty today assimilating the Empty Tomb motif to their contemporary scientific consciousness. Consequently many ministers embarrass both themselves and their congregations on Easter Day by trying to accomplish fideistic handsprings and other acrobatics for which they are no longer fit or suited. They behave like little puppy dogs who try to make it across wide streams by running themselves into a lather before making the leap and then feel guilty and surprised when they land only midway to the other bank. Unless Easter can be seen as part of a larger picture, so that it becomes an acceptable *poetic* statement of a Restoration myth which is real in many more prosaic ways, it is only an exercise in futility.

I recently asked a class of young ministers shortly before Holy Week what they were planning—or able—to preach on Easter Sunday. Only one or two confessed to be dealing with the Empty Tomb motif. Most of them were in a quandary about what to do. They said they could not in conscience treat the more traditional, expected emphases, and did not know what they would preach. They had all been through a period in their ministries when they would have agreed with James Stewart of Scotland that "Whoso says Christianity says Resurrection!" but they weren't sure in what sense this was so or how it should be interpreted today. One man suggested that if he were a truck driver awakened at 5 A.M. to attend a sunrise service with his wife, he would be damned if he would listen to any sentimental homily about Easter lilies and garden tombs!

Jung may have helped us more than we have yet realized. If myth is indeed psychological in nature, conforming outwardly to the inward rhythms and requirements of the individual psyche, so that it is possible, as Harry Levin points out, that each of us has lived through the world's major myths in embryo,[8] then the answer to our dilemma may lie in translation or transmission of the ancient story-myth into more and more tangible terms of human integration and wholeness. It is significant how the major therapists of our age, from Freud and Rank and Jung to Fromm and Jones and others, have utilized story-myth as a tool for understanding and dramatizing the functioning of the psyche. The correspondence is too functionally successful to be dismissed as chance or coincidence.

As Bishop Robinson said in *Honest to God*, it is no longer cosmologically possible for the enlightened Christian to conceive of God "out there"—Tillich's respatializing of the locus of God along the lines of depth psychology, so that he is thought of as being found "in there," in the recesses of man's own person, is much more palatable. The old mythical symbol of the *axis mundi*—a mountain or tree or totem occupying the "center of the earth" and connecting earth and heaven—must now be reconceived as standing at the center of each man's individual being. The idea that "the Kingdom of God is within you" is actually truer than men in earlier ages were able to see.

Campbell, in *The Hero with a Thousand Faces*, speaks of this "shifting" of "the center of gravity." "For the primitive hunting peoples of those remotest human milleniums when the saber-tooth tiger, the mammoth, and the lesser presences of the animal kingdom were the primary manifestations of what was alien," he says, "the great human problem was to become linked psychologically to the task of sharing the wilderness with these beings." Therefore man imitated the animals, invented stories about conquering the wilderness, and generally pitted himself against the mysteries of the forest and the sea.

Today all of these mysteries have lost their force; their symbols no longer interest our psyche. The notion of a cosmic law, which all existence serves and to which man himself must bend, has long since passed through the preliminary mystical stages represented in the old astrology, and is now simply accepted in mechanical terms as a matter of course. The descent of the Occidental sciences from the heavens to the earth (from seventeenth-century astronomy to nineteenth-century biology), and their concentration today, at last, on man himself (in twentieth-century anthropology and psychology), mark the path of a prodigious transfer of the focal point of human wonder. Not the animal world, not the plant world, not the miracle of the spheres, but man himself is now the crucial figure.[9]

This is a profound revolution in the need and purpose of mythologizing. The effect of it, as Campbell puts it, is that "the hero-deed to be wrought is not today what it was in the century of Galileo. Where then there was darkness, now there is light; but also, where light was, there now is darkness. The modern hero-deed must be that of questing to bring light again to the lost Atlantis of the co-ordinated soul."[10]

Does this strike chords of familiarity? How often the contemporary preacher takes his text from ancient scripture and then treats Jesus as a modern hero trying to bring light again to the co-ordinated soul. We are already *unconsciously* adapting to the necessity of treating our myths as psychological and integrative. It is time we became aware of the process and so were able to expedite and augment it, employing it consciously to make Restoration credible and feasible again in our congregations.

This kind of transference, sensitively made, will enable worshipers to believe once more in the totality of the mythical structure on the basis of limited or partly achieved goals. Each step toward integration and wholeness of the personality becomes encouragement to reaccept the myth of ultimate or complete Restoration, even though the person making the step does not *literally* expect to achieve total Restoration himself. He is able to live in exile, and to participate meaningfully in the Trial, because he sees the earnest of a more complete redemption. The *process* of redemption is thus remythologized for him, and he understands innately that this is more important than any kind of literal assurance that the process can ever be consummated. Consummation is important only for the wholeness or completeness of the myth, not for the realization of the believer. Faith thus becomes credible at the same time that it is incredible, and both the credibility and incredibility are seen to be necessary and interdependent. Celebration becomes possible even under the worst of conditions, for the soul is learning to find the object of its search by turning inward and not outward, in the integration of self with the emotions which we now know to correspond in this obverse way to the former integration of the self to the wilderness or external world.

Thus the Theology of Hope, with its emphasis on the Christ-event as earnest and its mood of expectancy and anticipation, is on the right track. What is needed in the church and its liturgy is the kind of affirmation in which life can flower and come to maturity more easily. If this sense of affirmation is present, then the function of myth and ritual is being fulfilled. Whatever helps men to find the grace they require to accept themselves and the way things are, and then to work consciously to come to a fuller realization of their potential, is serving the purpose of Christ in producing more abundant life.

As Campbell saw, it is difficult from a rational position to take myth as anything more than penultimate.[11] The ultimate is the openness, the void, the totality—whatever we call it—into which the soul is finally released and dissolved. And the important thing in Christian liturgy is to reproduce the mythical journey, the pilgrimage from Creation to Restoration, in such a way that the pilgrim "gets in sight of home." Otherwise it can only result in further frustration and dis-ease.

In practical terms, we must bend every effort to translate the liturgies we already have, or to design the ones we don't have, into sensible and acceptable terms of self, world, and society. As Mark Schorer said in his great study of *William Blake: The Politics of Vision,* our whole civilization today appears to be struggling toward a myth that will be explicitly ethical and political. This is not new, of course; the Greek city-state, on a smaller scale, was the apogee of such a myth in an earlier era. But it is the shape of things in a world where the control of life now necessarily transcends geographical and political borders,

and where the probability of exponentially multiplied popula-
tions will require some kind of centralized direction. How to be
a citizen in this brave new society is a major challenge facing
the Christian worshiper. And unless the liturgy rehearses him
regularly in the kind of mythic structures which will prepare
him to understand himself and the world he lives in, he must
fumble through on his own and grow ever more despondent
over the futility of worship.

Conveniently, our sacraments probably continue to exert the
proper emphases about persons and their development. Baptism, as a tribal symbol of initiation and rebirth, and Communion, as a symbol of union and sharing, are major opportunities
for dramatizing in public ways the partial realization of the
Restoration or Fulfillment.

The death of Christ as Hero, preserved in the Eucharist by
a conservative church which often loses sight of the mythic
significance of the act, remains the one thing capable of galvanizing and focusing the imagination in an age of illusion and
absurdity. It is the only motif serious enough, and absurd
enough in its own way, to challenge the contending idiocies of
the age and marshal them into some conceivable order. For this
reason there is no doubt that the Eucharist must still remain
fundamentally at the center of Christian worship.

The Hero may be regarded differently today than he was five
hundred years ago. Instead of being seen as a magician who
battled the powers of evil and was finally brought by mere force
to his death on Golgotha, he may be viewed as a man who knew
basically who he was and what life is about, so that he was able,
where other men fail, to reconcile the opposing forces in his
own nature and live freely and normally, willing finally to pay
the price of confrontation which must always be paid when
freedom clashes with tradition and insecurity. His leadership, in
other words, may be regarded as being more in terms of model,
catalyst, or wise man, than in terms of the now-difficult-to-con-
ceive *homo-ousion* controversy of an earlier age. But he is still

the Hero, and confidence in the Hero never fails to keep alive the sense of transcendence—and of the presence of God.

Modern literature speaks of a myth of the antihero in our time—the little chap who cannot cope with a baffling, overwhelming world. The sensitive liturgy will reflect this feeling, for it is the mood of fallenness and trial. But it will also set us in the presence of one who, sharing the attributes of the little chap, yet lived heroically and meaningfully, so that even the barren place where he died became associated with legends of fountains and greenery.

This vision, of the potency of barren places, is essentially what men need to keep them alive in barren places. And it is mainly what myth is all about.

Language

IT IS IRONICAL that in the very day when we talk about the way words were once identical with things and actions, ours aren't; that in an era when we have developed the most sophisticated philosophies of language men have ever known, we have the most trouble with it. The problem is, as Iris Murdoch noted in her book *Sartre: Romantic Rationalist,* that we have become too conscious of it. Our very consciousness has tended to make it dry and brittle. It becomes an obstacle to communication instead of a vehicle. Like persons who have become aware that they are looking at the world through a glass, and are therefore preoccupied with the glass, we find it increasingly difficult to use language freely and naturally.

At the end of what McLuhan called the Gutenberg or print-oriented age, the incommunicability of language became a major concern to poets and novelists. T. S. Eliot complained in *Burnt Norton* of the way words strain and slip and sometimes perish under the burden of meaning, of the way they "decay with imprecision" and "will not stay in place." Hemingway said in *A Farewell to Arms* that the meaning has evaporated from all the great words like honor, courage, and probity; now only the names of streets and numbers of roads have true significance. In *Death in the Afternoon* he reports a conversation in which he stopped himself abruptly while speaking with an old lady and admitted that he was only talking horse manure. And

Antonin Artaud once stated categorically that all writing is pig manure.[1] In each instance there seems to have been a despair about language.

What many users of profane language have obviously felt in recent years is that the real profanity or obscenity is not in scatological or erotic vocabulary at all but in traditional language which has ceased to be transparent to its former meanings, particularly as that language is employed by governments, business corporations, churches, and other institutional bodies which have been known to pander to public interest and piety for the sake of their own welfare. Any excessive manipulation of language is suspect. Because words are charged with emotional content, they are highly susceptible of misuse by both demagogues and saints, tyrants and evangelists. Linguistic profanity can therefore appear as a kind of iconoclasm, performing the thankless task of opposing the use of deteriorated and demonically infused rhetoric to influence the masses.

There are many persons who either openly or secretly feel today that there is a kind of reversed profanity about the traditional language spoken in the prayers, hymns, and sermons of the church. "The words no longer refer to the experience of the people," it is said. "Therefore there is something gross or obscene about their continued usage. Stained-glass vocabulary is not a real language. It is dead, archaic. Its perpetuation constitutes a bondage for the average churchman. Because he is uncritical in any conscious way, he lives under the tension of the pull between the real world outside and the artificial world of the sanctuary. And because he is critical in an unconscious way, feeling something awry though he cannot put his finger on it, it becomes a debilitating experience. Instead of freeing him to live more fully, as religion ought to, the church encumbers him with idioms and thought-styles which are alien and burdensome to him. He cannot on any account enter the past; but this manner of operation prevents his entering the present or the future."

The problem is of course related to the matter of myth. Words cannot sustain myth, as Protestantism has generally attempted to make them do over the past four centuries. They derive their vitality from the vitality of myth, not the other way around. As Wolfgang Schanze has said, "The mystery of language acquires an acute gravity when the church understands herself to be the Church not of words, but of the Word."[2] When the sense of experience is strong, there is no problem of words; then they come easily, freely, freshly imbued with meaning. It is in periods when the experience is only a historical memory that words become difficult; then they are noticed for their precision, their root relationships, their own history of associations. Or, to use the analogy of playing, there are no great conversational difficulties during the excitement of the game itself, or even in the first flush of feeling when the game is over; it is when the game becomes past history, when its events begin to lose their incandescence, that the players notice the awkwardness of being together, of having to generate speech, of having to make something of the fact that they find themselves together with nothing to do.

It is an obvious difficulty, if not an impossibility, for people to worship in a church where nothing is going on, where there is no sense of involvement in conflict, either local or cosmic. The removal from the actual time of Christ, two thousand years ago, becomes more real and apparent than it actually is. There is nothing happening to abrogate the linear quality of history and gather up past, present, and future into the experience of sacred time, or time out of time. Archaisms in both practice and language become especially apparent. They are like love-motions where there is no love. They are caricatures, pantomimes, exaggerated actions. Their reality-quotient is extremely low. People tend to awaken as from a dream, and find themselves in awkward, unnatural poses, wearing ridiculous costumes and performing strange minuets, and they ask themselves, "What in the world am I doing here? This is not me."

And thus they "spin off" from the church, wondering how they ever got caught up in the dream in the first place.

It is pointless to talk to such people about the nature of God, the meaning of Christ, the baptism of the Holy Spirit, and all the other wonders we are wont to speak of in the church. Such talk is only rabbinical, once the experience is missing. Then is when it becomes profanity. As William Hordern says in *Speaking of God,*

> Without the experience of mystery the meaning of the word "God" is distorted. Without mystery God is thought of in terms of the supreme manipulator of the universe, or he is considered to be a hypothesis no longer necessary to explain the universe. The proofs of God have lost their persuasiveness, not because men today can see their logical flaws more clearly than before, but because men have lost the sense of mystery.[3]

Others ages, says Hordern, have faced the possibility that God-language is either true or false; ours faces the possibility that it simply has no meaning at all.[4] Paul Van Buren has testified to this very possibility. We cannot even understand the Nietzschean cry that "God is dead!" he says; what is dead for us is the word God itself.[5] To continue prattling of God in a congregation where there has been no ongoing experience of God or his conflict with the powers of evil and resistance in the world becomes thus foolish and occult, without any power to shape the style of men's lives or their perspectives on their environment. It is an act out of time, in the worst sense, because it is an antiquarian or merely imitative act in which people have insuperable difficulty in participating. It is much more meaningful in some modern congregations to speak instead, as Geddes MacGregor has suggested, of the absence of God, not the presence, as a major biblical and Christian theme.[6]

The problem, most of us are convinced, has little to do with whether God is actually present or absent; it has to do instead with our ability to discern his presence or absence. It has to do, in other words, with the style according to which we perceive the world and what is happening in it. The traditionalist, taught to look for God in certain ways of acting by which he has become known in previous generations, scans the horizon and, seeing none of the telltale marks, concludes that this is a period of desolation. The more open or inventive mind, however, supposes that, revelation being what it is, it is not likely to occur in familiar forms. He poises himself therefore to watch for new signs, for new indications of power or presence. It is a precarious game. He can easily become excited about the wrong things, because he has set himself in an excitable mood. He can invest in the wrong stocks, so to speak, and undergo sudden losses and setbacks. But he is, on the other hand, predisposed to miracle when it occurs. He is on the scene and ready to go.

The difference between the staid and the exciting congregations in Christendom appears to be marked by these very qualities today. The former are oriented toward the past, rehearsing the great deeds and epochs of the faith, attempting to create the present and the future mainly out of the events which have already occurred in our historical consciousness. The latter are primarily present- and future-oriented, validating the experience of the past according to whatever new interpretations of it can be afforded from more immediate and accessible experiences.

And language itself seems to follow the two patterns. In the congregations with heavy emphasis on the past, language tends to be traditional, creedal, and repetitive. Hymns tend to rehearse the historical occurrences, particularly of biblical events. Sermons are often devoted to explanations of terminology and attempts to make relevant words and ideas which obviously emerged in other times and other cultures. In congregations with more accent on the present and the future, language is more likely to be exploratory, tenuous, precise, disposable. Its validation is in facilitating new experience, not in renewing or ravamping the old experience.

We cannot totally dismiss the old language out of hand, of course. It is never so dead as we sometimes suppose it to be. Words are symbols, and sometimes symbols become dormant. They can be ineffective for years, even centuries, and suddenly spring to life with a vigor and vitality that is simply astounding. It is probable that there is such a latent power in most of the words and symbols that have been discarded through the ages.

And not only that, but words undoubtedly have a way of carrying enormous unconscious and associative meaning for us even when we confess that they mean little or nothing to us cognitively. It is hardly out of the question that we have a racial memory for words in the same way that we have a racial memory for myth or story. If language and myth are as inextricably intertwined as Ernst Cassirer and Max Müller and others have suggested, then it is impossible to believe otherwise.

James Joyce depended heavily on this process of unconscious or subliminal association in his use of the "portmanteau" word or phrase, particularly in *Finnegans Wake*, wherein he strove to combine words or elements of words so that their literal meaning would be transcended and a mood or sense of something else achieved. His process of composition was to write slowly, perhaps two lines a day, and to revise continuously, working in words and sounds until he had quite obscured the text visually. An extremely simple and uncomplicated example of this is the brief line, "Missus, be good and don' fol in the say!" As A. Walton Litz annotates it, " 'Missus' suggests 'Mississippi', the Fol is a Turkish river, while 'say' reminds one of the Seine and is the Irish pronunciation of 'sea.' "[7] Or consider the word "papacocopotl," in which Litz discerns at least four major components:

papa (Joyce's hero, HCE, is all fathers)

Popocatepetl (HCE is identified with all mountains)

coco ("cocoa": In the *Wake* this is the body of the god and suggests HCE in his sacramental role)

pot (A vulgar reminder of HCE's indiscretion in Phoenix
Park. The entire word "papacocopotl"
suggests his guilt stammer)[8]

And Litz apparently failed to note that "coco" is suggestive of
the French colloquialism "caca," which is a childish word for
excrement and is therefore closely related to the syllable "pot."
As one critic (I believe it was Joseph Frank) said of Joyce, he
cannot be read, only reread. His method of compression packs
so many associations into every word and syllable that we can
approach them numberless times and still find new suggestions
and relationships in them.

In the same way that Joyce counted on the presence of primordial images or subliminal mythic structures to "unpack" the
levels of meaning in his language, any user of words may be
assured that there are various levels of communication either
latent or active in the vocabulary with which he establishes
contact with other persons. And in the church there is no doubt
that certain of the so-called "great" words and phrases in the
old liturgies still have a certain value and meaning even when
their denotative or cognitive value appears to have been
eroded by time and circumstance. This does not justify their
indiscriminate perpetuation, of course, or the habit of some
traditionalists of insisting that everyone venerate them. But it
does suggest that one can say only with great tentativeness and
hesitance that God-talk is no longer possible, even in situations
where men are most aware of the sense of the divine absence.

One curious instance of the carry-over of innate power when
words have become barren in their normal usage is to be found
in the phenomenon of cursing and obscenity. As Renatus Har-
togs has amply demonstrated in his book *Four-Letter Word
Games*,[9] the language of profanity is largely dependent on the
language of holiness for its vocabulary. It is when words have
ceased to be held sacred that they become most eligible for
common usage as profanity. And then it is the very words which
were most unspeakable, because of their intimacy to sacred

things, that become most powerful in a profane or obscene
sense. The names of the deities become coupled with the most
degrading verbs and modifiers. Sacralization has been inverted,
but the power of expression still depends on notions derived
from it.

One of the best discussions yet to appear on the subject of the
way we use or abuse words in the act of worship is Daniel B.
Stevick's book *Language in Worship.* "It is not just the words
that change," says Stevick, "but also the way they go together.
No one now converses like Samuel Johnson, writes letters like
Horace Walpole, or makes public addresses like Edmund Burke
—though at one time many people did, or wished they could.
Thus, language is like Heraclitus' river, and no two generations
ever speak the same language."[10] For a while, people don't
notice that language has changed, and so the language of worship tends to remain static. Then one day they wake up, and are
generations away from it. Significantly, Stevick's book is subti-
tled *Reflections on a Crisis;* many people are waking up today
to the fact that religious language is no longer the language of
their everyday life.

"We know what prayer sounds like in the language and for
the world of Spenser and Shakespeare," says Stevick. "But what
should prayer sound like in the language and for the world of
Randall Jarrell, Paul Goodman, James Dickey, LeRoi Jones, or
Samuel Beckett? Insofar as such spokesmen for the contemporary spirit tell me something about myself and my world, what
should prayer sound like for me?"[11]

When he examines the imagery of biblical thought, which
informed the language of worship throughout the Middle Ages
and in the major liturgical formulations of the Reformation,
Stevick concludes that it polarizes around two concepts: the
kingship of God and the relation between a shepherd and the
sheep. The reasons for this polarization in the biblical origins
are obvious. Monarchy was the one form of government known
to all the people. They lived in essentially rural conditions, even

in the larger cities of the day. The rhythms of nature, the importance of water and bread, of grass and grain, the meaning of
fortification, protection, shelter, and so on, were known to all
people. The imagery of kingship and the shepherd and his
sheep was pregnant with associations for anyone who heard it
or read it.

But now what is the situation? Monarchy is simply unknown
to many people. Even totalitarian regimes depend in part upon
propaganda and the sense that power is being vested in the
central government for the good of the people. Some people
have never walked on a green field in the countryside, or stood
by a gurgling brook. There are children in ghetto areas of New
York and Detroit and London and Tokyo who have never seen
a cow or a goat. The whole imagistic framework is invalidated.
Kings and shepherds are storybook characters, not vital, everyday providers; ward politicians and welfare workers are much
more familiar to many persons.

It is therefore necessary, concludes Stevick, to do some trans-
lating whenever the old imagery is used in liturgy. Either the
worshipers must do it for themselves, trying to enter the mind-
set of the ancients and recreate the original experiences, or the
poets and makers of liturgy in each generation must do it, saving the worshipers the trouble.

Once translation by the liturgists is agreed upon, there is not
really any place to draw a line and prevent innovation. Translation itself is a matter of creating, even though the existence of
a body of material to be translated imposes some limitation.
One thinks, for example, of the increasing freedom assumed by
translators—especially private or individual translators—of the
scriptures themselves. From the free, idiomatic version of J. B.
Phillips it was but a natural step to the pointed, sometimes racy
translations of the Cotton Patch Version of the scriptures by
Clarence Jordan, which are actually a rewriting of certain biblical books transposed into a rural, down-South, American setting. The Cotton Patch Version often brings out the truth of a

passage in ways that are more daring than polite translators·
would ever dream of employing. The man who fell among
thieves, in the parable of Jesus, is ministered to, not by a Samari-
tan, but by a Negro! It is obvious, on the other hand, that such
utter freedom in the handling of the text eventually leads to the
replacement of the original text with another text whose overall
tone and emphasis are doubtless different from those of the
original.

Suppose that a free hand is granted to develop new imagery
for contemporary liturgies, and that it is no longer necessary to
bootleg new understandings·in via the old imagery What is the
source of the new imagery? Stevick is surely correct when he
says that we cannot merely invent it. If myth and language are
related, and come about in the same way, then we can no more
invent the language of worship out of our heads than we can
invent new myths that way. Both must be plucked naturally like
ripe fruit from the tree. They must derive from the common
experience of the people. Otherwise they are not true symbols
and do not really participate in reality.

Stevick suggests that we turn to "the artists, writers, social
analysts, popular songwriters, and dramatists of our time."[12]
This seems to be a particularly viable alternative to translation.
There are recurrent themes and images which become obvious
on even the most cursory perusal of the arts in our time—
alienation, desiccation, the belief in creativity, the desire for
wholeness, the fear of technocracy, interest in dreams and the
unconscious, care for the individual as a person, loss of religious
meaning, discovery of the global village, the celebration of discrete objects in the creation, etc.

What we must do, it appears, is to be open to this imagery—
open in such a way that it is constantly informing what we do
in worship and facilitating those systole-disastole, expansion-
contraction movements by which the gospel and the world
interact in such a way as to make meaning of our faith. It is not
all new imagery. There is rarely any imagery, in fact, for which

we could not discover prototypes in another era. And it may be that we can expand upon the meaning of the contemporary imagery we do discover by finding analogues in other ages which shed light upon the current situation, latent symbols which are able, under the heat of contemporary pressures, to spring to life again. But the posture of openness, of readiness, of sensitivity, is extremely important. It has much to do with the atmosphere of credibility in religion. It fosters a sense of expectancy and aliveness. It means that faith need not feed upon itself, but may be constantly derived from the interaction between belief and environment.

We are speaking, in other words, of the freedom to use language creatively. This means the freedom to use old language as well as new. It means the freedom to use silence when we feel that words are inadequate. It means the freedom to use language playfully—as poetry, as fantasy, as dream object, as antilanguage—in any way that helps us to come to wholeness and relationship, and to find God in the newness of being we experience.

The freedom to use old language as well as new. Ironically, there is often as much prejudice among advocates of the modern emphasis as there is among those who wish to maintain the status quo. In their desire to make all things new, they are prone to overlook the significant and even valuable qualities in the old way, and, even if they don't throw out the baby with the bath water, to sling away maybe a good bar of soap or a silver teething ring. The old words and phrases do appear to have become clichés and barren symbols in the liturgy; but it is also true, as I have tried to suggest, that they are still the bearers of considerable historical investment, of meanings and symbolisms we cannot chuck away without serious loss. They belong to us, in a very real sense, even though we did not make them and do not thoroughly understand them any longer. They are part of our past, and, as such, part of us. They ought to remain in our possession, not as tyrannical things but as bits of furniture which connect us to our heritage. To press the furniture analogy a bit further, they should not be gigantic heirlooms beclouding our existence with their saturnine presence, but mementoes eliciting wholesome memories of who our forebears were, of whence we have come, of what life once was like.

One of the remarkable observations to be made about the liturgical service in Ann Arbor which formed the nucleus of experience for the various essays in Bloy's *Multi-Media Worship* is that surrounding the traditional Communion service with an antiwar mime show, contemporary music, and slide projections illumined the Communion in unexpected ways. That is, the modern paraphernalia revealed the truly mythical possibilities still latent in the conventional rite. Without the modern trappings, the service might indeed have been tepid and ordinary. With them, its richness of symbolism began to become apparent, so that people found various things about it at different levels to which they could honestly respond.

We have been taught by the arts in recent years that juxtaposition is often a powerful boon to communication, revealing new aspects of meaning and interpretation in things which it had been assumed were thoroughly known and explored. The same is true in liturgy. What had seemed barren and unproductive language can often come alive within a new frame of reference. Words that were thought to be utterly depleted can, in a new context, reveal depth upon depth. Phraseology which had even come to be regarded as demonic, because it had become so twisted and perverted through wrong emphasis, can suddenly resonate with very contemporary meaning.

Examples of this are the dramatic use of relevant scriptural passages in the middle of a rock concert, the combination of a traditional prayer of confession with a rhythmical drumbeat or the amplified sound of a heartbeat, the simultaneous use of an old Communion liturgy and a troupe of liturgical dancers, and the employment of Negro songs, with their ordinarily primitive

evangelical understandings, in an otherwise modern and sophisticated setting.

The important thing is the sense of freedom within which
language can become the impulse leading to new experience
and enlargement of the self. It is not enough to use old language
for its own sake, because it is old or traditional or venerable. It
must be transformed in the very act of using it. It must be
susceptible of new content. Instead of suggesting that the worshiper be playing some kind of game, it must be conducive to
the worshiper's abandoning himself and *really* playing a game,
playing it in such a way that he forgets he is playing, or, in other
words, in such a way that the playing becomes reality.

*The freedom to use silence when we feel that words are inade-
quate.* The usage of old words I have been describing is a playful, creative usage. And there are times, in real play, when one
refuses to speak, finding silence more articulate or responsive
than mere words.

The fact that Protestantism has billed itself so exclusively as
a religion of the Word may say something about its psychological stance. What is it that most of us fear about the pause, the
lapse in speech, the inarticulate moment? There appears to be
real evidence that we have overtalked religion, overrational-
ized it, oververbalized it, so that the cartoon portrait of the
minister as a dreary, hallucinative man surrounded by words-
words-words, in all sizes and apparently at all levels of vocal
intensity, is a defensible caricature not merely of what we look
like but of what we *are.* Does this illustrate some compulsive
need to possess our religion by explaining it? Why do we find
it so difficult to accept it, to dance to it, to exult in it, without
pulverizing it and de-animating it?

Suppose that many people today are bothered by a sense of
the deity's absence. How should we respond to that liturgically?
We know how most Protestant ministers responded to the news
when Altizer and Hamilton made it a matter of public concern:
they talked and talked and talked about it. It must be true, as

Robert Funk has said, that "When God is silent, man becomes a gossip; when God speaks and man hears, kerygmatic language is born and gospel is preached."[13] Silence—creative brooding, to use Robert Raines' phrase—might be a more apt response to silence in the heavens. Listening is communication too. Sometimes, maybe even in whole periods of time, we need to be still, to wait, to let the silence grow and become pregnant with meaning. It is usually more eloquent than words.

Who was it—Ionesco?—who said that "there are no words for the deepest experience"? Therefore his plays are moving images, attempts to create the experience without dependence on the words as normally used. The Hebrews must have understood something of this, in that they did not freely use the name of Jahweh. They lived in an animistic time, a time when men were sensitive to their own presence as intruders in the world, living stealthily, conscious of everything around them. There is evidence that we are coming into such an era again. The huge sense of alienation in our literature, from Melville to the existentialists to the absurdists, is suggestive of this very thing. Camus' whole philosophy of life, of being the stranger, evolved out of his experience as the fatherless child of a deaf mother; he lived in a world of silence. The nonsensicality of language in the Theater of the Absurd, especially in Ionesco and Arrabal and N. F. Simpson and Adamov, and the use of silence, particularly by Beckett and Pinter, indicate that it is widely suspected that we are astraddle of forces too monstrous or chaotic for words and logic, so that traditional speech is mere twaddle, mere chatter, mere gossip. We complain of the death of God in our time, and cite the absurdists in evidence, but it may be that they are testifying to just the opposite, to the birth of God, or at least to God's transcending the petty images of him we had settled for, and doing it, first of all, by making nonsense of our speech.

Here is a summary of our ororverbalized situation by literary critic George Steiner:

I am not saying that writers should stop writing. This would be fatuous. I am asking whether they are not writing too much, whether the deluge of print in which we seek our deafened way is not itself a subversion of meaning. "A civilization of words is a civilization distraught." It is one in which the constant inflation of verbal counters has so devalued the once numinous act of written communication that there is almost no way for the valid and the genuinely new to make themselves heard. Each month must produce its masterpiece and so the press hounds mediocrity into momentary, fake splendor. The scientists tell us that libraries will soon have to be placed in orbit, circling the earth and subject to electronic scanning as needed. The proliferation of verbiage in humanistic scholarship, the trivia decked out as erudition or critical re-assessment, threatens to obliterate the work of art itself and the exacting freshness of personal encounter on which true criticism depends. We also speak far too much, far too easily, making common what was private, arresting into the clichés of false certitude that which was provisional, personal, and therefore alive on the shadow-side of speech. We live in a tunnel which is, increasingly, a wind-tunnel of gossip; gossip that reaches from theology and politics to an unprecedented noising of private concerns (the psychoanalytic process is the high rhetoric of gossip). This world will end neither with a bang nor a whimper, but with a headline, a slogan, a pulp novel larger than the cedars of Lebanon. In how much of what is now pouring forth do words become word—and where is the silence needed if we are to hear that metamorphosis?[14]

It is time we had more silence in the language of Christian liturgy—silence to listen to God, silence to hear the neighbor, silence to detect our own breathing, silence to hear the great Nothing, the Void, the Emptiness, lashing its cold waves against the shorelines of our being. It is the one thing the Quakers have had—the drowned sea of all their symbolism—and we know it has preserved a kind of health in them while words were both serving and failing us.

We must learn to use silence—not as emptiness, but as com

munication. We are embarrassed by it, we fidget and twist and squirm in our too-tight mental underwear, because we have never learned its properties and possibilities. We have always lived with a fear of gaps. We carry an odd-bucket of assorted hems and haws, ah-wells and you-sees, to stuff up any draughty chinks we find in conversations or speeches. But we need to be reminded that silences are the cracks in the dome of eternity, whence wisdom can seep through. We need, in the church, to come to the place where we can be silent in the courageous manner of John Cage's *4 '33"*, whose obvious silence, in actual performances, is always filled with the remote noises of things people had forgotten to listen to—dogs barking, sirens bleating, jet planes taking off, children laughing, birds singing, etc.

What would it do for a scripture passage or a quotation from some secular work or a single sentence from the minister to surround it by a puddle of silence, say for even a minute on either side? What would it mean to a prayer to be quiet for thirty seconds between each phrase or petition? What would it do to our normal sensibilities to proceed through an entire service without any sound at all, but only with pantomime and gesture, the way it is on every occasion for the deaf?

Our world is so oriented toward sound and noise, everything from air-hammers and traffic to television and discothèques, that the rhetorical possibilities of silence are greater today than they have ever been. Again, it is a matter of freedom—freedom to employ both sound and silence as building blocks, as ingredients in an experience we are fashioning, partly consciously and partly as a happening which goes beyond our control.

The freedom to use language playfully. This is what it all comes down to in the end. It is what the Dadaists and Surrealists, who were so acutely aware of the linguistic crisis, saw as the way of restoration. Realizing that words and myths are at bottom interrelated, and that man today exists in profound confusion about himself and his myths, they insisted on the right of poets to compose automatically or unconsciously, without any attempt to coerce language or grammar, allowing the words to assemble themselves out of the unconscious of the artist and thus provide some clue as to what men now are really like, not just on the surface but in their depths. To an utterly serious public, especially in the Protestant city of Zurich, where Dadaism had its inception, such "compositions" were considered decadent, irresponsible, and even blasphemous. But the great artists of our times have seen otherwise. They have recognized that this may be the only real way out for a society which has become highly technological, analytical, and prosaic. If man has worked his way into a corner, into a narrow place, then this may be his way of freeing himself. And we have gained enough perspective on our culture to realize the truth of this. We have seen the deadliness of scientific jargon and sociological prose. We know that language was meant for much more than this complicated asthenia, that it is really the music of the human species, that it is the voice with which our spirits soar and delight and worship. And playfulness, experimentation, juxtaposition, are the means by which we put ourselves in the way of allowing that to happen. There is magic in words—there always has been—but we cannot release it when we hold a dictionary of approved usages in one hand and a philologists' manual in the other. The real magic, the delight, in words comes when speech is childlike, when it is untrammelled and uncluttered with adult precision, unfettered by adult convention. It must be able to gambol and frolic, to turn and bend, to run and stop, to leap and collapse—in short, it must exist always on the verge of becoming something else, of renewing itself by masquerading as what it is not, of finding release and leaving us gaping after it.

There is a place, of course, for what Stevick calls "Huntley-Brinkley" language in our dealings with each other, even in the liturgy of the church. There are times when we choose to be prosaic, to speak straightforwardly, to convey meaning as precisely and undramatically as possible. But there is room also, much room, for inventiveness, novelty, spriteliness, and surprise.

There is an analogy, I think, in the experience of Wallace Stevens, the Hartford insurance executive and poet whose way of seeing reality was changed at an exhibit of modern art. The fluidity of modern painting, the sense of unresolvedness in it, which permits the viewer to see much more than he could in a merely factual representation of objects, suggested to Stevens that it might be possible for the poet as well to capture not specific objects but a whole range of experiences, so that the reader might find more in a poem than a discrete item. When we enter a room or particular area of space there is a split second during which the eye becomes accustomed to the new environment and separates the various objects presented to the sight. The artist or poet traditionally presents us with a fixed view of those objects in their separated or individuated states. But what of the perception during the split second? Is it any less real? Stevens thereafter concentrated on reproducing the sense of reality in its indeterminate state. The person attempting to read his poems for their literal and explicit representations finds them hopelessly abstruse and difficult. But the reader who is willing to free-float, to wait upon the images, to let them form in his mind without forcing them into overprecise configurations or entirely recognizable shapes, rejoices in discovering levels of reality which he has indeed experienced but has been unable to reduce to a statement.

If we have been impatient with liturgical language, and in fact with religion itself, it may be because in a rationalistic age we have wished to reduce everything too quickly to its component forms and to call that reality. Reality exists instead in ourselves and in the way we apprehend our environment. If our reality has been drab and prosaic, inhospitable to gods and magic, it may well be because we have insisted on its being too fixed and precise. If we now wish it to become once more expansive and charged with excitement, then we must be willing to use language playfully again, trusting that the dreams and fantasies it evokes thereby are as worthy of our investing our being with them as the scientific mind-set where we had previously invested it. If we are fearful and unwilling to do this, if we insist on being literalistic, then worship will go on as it has— gradually becoming more and more effete and incapable of supporting a world-view. If we will but gamble a bit, and lend ourselves to the experimentation, we will discover the true nature of language, as a magical, incantatory, and rejuvenating factor in human existence.

As an example of what I am talking about, I have in mind the playful, synesthetic, sometimes improbable language of Norman Habel's litany entitled "Dreams for Celebration":

L. Today the Lord steps into the air once more to taste its color and feel its songs. He inhales the thoughts of children, the breath of yesterday, the fantasies of tomorrow, and he wonders whether his children are too old to celebrate their dreams.

R. Let us spin him our dreams.

L. Someday soon people will celebrate life every day.

R. But we would like to do it now, wet and wild and risen with our Lord.

L. Someday soon people will send up balloons in church

R. Turn tired old cathedrals into cafeterias

L. Paint gravestones as bright as the sun

R. Know they are beautiful, black, red, or white

L. Glimpse the face of God in their patient parents

R. Use the eyes of friends in place of mirrors

L. Bounce through the mountains on beachballs

R. Write their Christian names in the sunset

L. Become as free as that man called Jesus the Christ

R. Play kickball with cripples in the park

L. Sing for their supper in asylums

R. Sink their teeth into politics for peace

L. Airlift food and life to the starving

R. Have senses in their soul as sharp as radar

L. Love a man because he is a man
R. Grow flowers in their garbage can
L. Cover their cars with foam rubber
R. Turn all bombs into boomerangs
L. All bullets into blanks
R. And switchblades into tubes of finger paint
L. Slow down and wait for God
R. Run through the White House with muddy feet
L. Laugh with the falling spring leaves
R. Dance in the falling summer snow
L. Baptize their babies with love before birth
R. Celebrate Easter as angels do below
L. And hang Christmas banners from the moon.
R. Yes, someday soon people will live like that, but we plan to start right now.
L. Right now, Lord. Right now.
R. Amen, Lord, right now.[15]

Literally much of this is nonsensical. Yet the imagery speaks to us. It has a paradoxical quality which we have found to be innate in the Christian faith itself. It affirms the world where we live at the same time that it denies the existing structures of human logic and rationality. It springs out of, suggests, and beckons us to a world-view which is strong on restoration and redemption, which is entirely consonant with what we know as a resurrection faith. It may represent the true mood of Christianity much more accurately than the old creedal formulations or "Huntley-Brinkley" English are able to, for it mocks language at the same time that it employs it, and reminds us of human finitude and the measure of the mystery over against which we act out our little drama.

Robert Funk has written pertinently of this matter in an essay entitled "Myth and the Literal/Non-Literal." He says:

The messiah is crucified whenever the word he brings is reduced to its literal meaning. The inference to be drawn is that the messiah is risen from the dead whenever his word is given free play, allowed to strike like lightning, heard as the disclosure of the really real. . . .

The pristine grammar of the church is the parable, the similitude, the aphorism—a secular, literal non-literal language, comic in mode. The essentially comic quality of the language of Jesus has been obscured by an avalanche of moralizing commentary which, significantly enough, has never been able to make much of the resurrection, except to invoke it as the literal sanction of the pious life.[16]

This is the insight of a host of modern writers, especially from Kafka to Beckett, that creation occurs within a comic framework, not within a framework of seriousness and tragic thought. It is an insight much closer to the ancient spirit of the Hebrew poet than most of those we have had in the interim—the poet who could picture God laughing in the heavens and mocking the world he had made. There is tragedy in such a world, to be sure; but it becomes fullest tragedy, most unrelieved tragedy, when the comic framework is ignored. It will surely be an anomaly if the secular world has learned this truth and is able to laugh, while the church labors on in its stilted, mock-serious way, refusing to see the humor or join in the fun. It is, after all, the pedestrian spirit that is unable to see the wit in things.

What we are left with is the fact that words will not produce faith. They simply cannot. They may appear to substitute for it at times, though without great success when brought under fire. But they cannot generate an attitude of faith, a sense of being in God, a feeling that the world is good. This is why Stevick questions the reality of prayer as we have traditionally used it in worship. When the sense of faith has gone, prayers are only words, nothing more. They are hollow and ineffective. They echo and reecho with unreality.

What words *can* do is to represent a faith-mood, to catch it in its dance and merriment, or even in its moments of sadness, and create a certain tune in resonance with it. The tune then becomes a key to others, who may not have discovered the mood, as to how to set themselves for it. This is not the same thing as creating faith. Words in this instance depend upon faith, not the other way around. There is life in the words because they have been filled with the faith. They are not in-flated with meaning beyond their ability to carry meaning. They have not become great repositories to be studied and examined with meticulous care through the ages. They are like the branch the.bird lights on. He may choose another the next time. But while he is there they bounce to his touch and vibrate to his tune. They are, in a manner of speaking, disposable. They are used, not for their exquisiteness or exactness or potential longevity, but for their instantaneous ability to bear the weight of meaning for a moment and then give it up to another bearer.

To call this play-language is not to suggest that it is nonserious in a final sense, or that it is merely flippant. As David L. Miller suggests in his book *Gods and Games,* nonseriousness may really be the highest seriousness, and purposelessness the high-est purpose.[17] The person who is serious and purposeful, in the unimaginative denotation of those words, projects his own vi-sion of what the world and his life should be and then strives to conform to that. The self-limitation of such a procedure or way of functioning is obvious. Man never leaps higher than the mark he has set for himself. But the playful man, on the other hand, the man who greets the world as a playground where all kinds of exciting things can happen to him, is open to more serious and purposeful visions than his own; and his mood of openness is a kind of nonseriousness and purposelessness. Play-language, by such terms, is the only language suitable to wor-ship, for it is the only language which does not imply a closed-circuit, creedalistic faith-world.

Professor Stevick, in *Language in Worship,* suggests almost in passing the danger in changing from ancient imagistic mod-els to modern ones—that our theology will be changed in the bargain.[18] It will! We cannot change languages without chang-ing selves. Our sensibilities are invariably altered when we ex-

F

change one country of the mind for another, just as they are
when we literally move from one continent to another. And the
beauty and danger implicit together in play-language is that our
minds are always up for change. We remember that real playfulness carries us away from thoughts of the price we must pay
for being reckless. It robs us of caution. And the real question
for most of us in the church today is whether we are willing to
take the risks involved. It is possible to lose everything this way
—all those serious doctrinal and creedal and rationalistic advances that the church has made over the centuries. But it is
also possible that we lose them by standing still, by doing nothing, by taking no risk. They may have been disposable, only we
didn't know it. Are paper plates worth the saving? Maybe we
have everything to gain by playing, and nothing to lose.

Blasphemy

THERE ARE MANY things about contemporary liturgies that seem shocking or outrageous to the conservative religious mind. An act of absolution which consists of the flushing of a commode by a liturgist draped in a toilet-paper stole is liable to appear not only distasteful but sacrilegious.[1] The use of a prayer which begins "Damn, God, damn, God, God damn"[2] or of a hymn with the refrain "It's God they ought to crucify"[3] may seem only rebellious and blasphemous. A Communion meditation which interprets the pale-Victorian-Christ-with-winsome-come-hither-outstretched-palm in a Tiffany chancel window as "Jesus-giving-us-the-finger"[4] may actually constitute a rape of the imagination. How can one possibly justify such brazen acts and language in the worship of God?

The radical mind, on the other hand, asks how one can possibly justify the *traditional* acts and language—the prayer-book absolution and the pious meditation and the tepid hymnody.

The clue to the thinking of the radical mind on this question is the way it suspects even the most spiritual and transcendental of religions of degenerating into idolatry once it has ceased to question its own formal principles. There is a strong feeling, especially among artists, that religion must either be continually rearranging, recharging, and repudiating the patterns it has assumed or else obscure the very truths about life they were intended to reveal. Man forgets that the symbolism he has elected is only penultimate and not ultimate, and then he is liable to sacrifice the thing symbolized for the symbol itself. More dangerous yet, perhaps, idolatry gives way imperceptibly to ethnolatry, which Gabriel Vahanian has described as "the reduction of a particular civilization and the religion identifying it to the characteristics of a race and the idolization of its idiosyncrasy."[5] Then religion sanctions, or appears to sanction, lynchings, pogroms, and other forms of crucifixion.

It is very important then, to the radical mind, to mock and satirize the forms which have become too familiar and too well accepted in the church. The notion that God is a white-bearded, avuncular old gentleman unable to bear uncleanliness or dirty words must be subverted by the occasional use of profanity or insubordination. The idea that the church is an antiseptic fellowship of prim little old ladies and genteel little men who deal in antiques must be dispelled by the reminder that its members sometimes think salacious thoughts and behave unscrupulously toward one another. The picture of Jesus as an ineffective, well-meaning, essentially manipulable religious "fairy" must be replaced by an occasional glimpse of his robust, iconoclastic, and "Watch-out-Mac-the-house-is-falling-in" attitude toward the falsely pious. Otherwise the forms become too important in themselves, too distorted by false impressions, and thereby demonic and antispiritual.

Consider Robert W. Castle, Jr.'s famous "Litany from the Underground," with its radical prayer:

> O God, who hangs on street corners, who tastes the grace
>   of cheap wine and the sting of the needle,
>   Help us to know you.
> O God, who can't write or read, who is on welfare, and
>   who is treated like garbage,
>   Help us to know you.
> O God, who lives and no one knows his name and
>   who knows that he is nobody,
>   Help us to know you.

O God, whose name is spik, nigger, ginny, and kike,
  Help us to know you.

  .   .   .   .   .

O God, who sleeps in bed with his four brothers
  and sisters, and who cries and no one hears him,
    Help us to touch you.

  .   .   .   .   .

O God, who is tired of his church and its ministers
  and priests, irrelevant and unbloody,
    Help us to join you.
Etc.[6]

Many orthodox Christians have resented the liberties taken by Castle in this prayer and have protested that it is nothing short of sacrilegious. What Castle has done, however, is to identify God with the disenfranchised and dispirited, which is a bona fide New Testament emphasis ("Inasmuch as you have done it unto one of the least of these. . . ."), and overturn our ethnolatries and sociolatries, our identifications of God with our positions of privilege and status. Of course God is not a rummy or a black or a whore or a child in bed with half-a-dozen siblings; but neither is he a banker or a city councilman or a doctor or a reverend; and the very outrageousness of the identification in the first instances reminds us of our tendency to identify him with the structures and patterns of the second ones. Such poetry—for that is what it is—disturbs us in our too-easy assumptions that God is the preserver of the middle-class American way of life. If he is the preserver he is also, like Vishnu, the destroyer, and we do not worship him truly until we are reminded of that and made to tremble.

As Howard Moody, minister of the famous Judson Memorial Church in New York City, has said,

Worship as confrontation, though theologically and biblically correct, runs against the grain of our present concept of the meaning of worship. The atmosphere, arrangement, architecture, lighting, and music of our services today remove the worshiper from the world, its cares, troubles, and tragedy. At worst these services are pure escapism and at best soothers of the ruffled psyches of the people. The cultic-act worship, however, ought to be the place of honest confrontation of *ourselves,* with all our embarrassments and ambiguities, and *our world* with its inhumanity and tragedy. We can escape ourselves in words (especially if they are archaic enough) and cover up our "sick and bent world" (like Linus' security blanket) with prayers and music. Rituals and ceremonies can lie about us and our world and what God demands, but an authentic ritual is one where Reality is wrestled with like Jacob by the river Jabbok, struggling for the naked truth about himself and his place in the world.[7]

Iconoclasm, in other words, is a vital and necessary part of the ritual of worship. We must be constantly repudiating the very forms which once helped us to worship, lest they become idolatrous and permit us to escape the world they were supposed to help us be reconciled to and become agents of reconciliation in.

Sandra Archer, director of the San Francisco Mime Troupe which participated in the experimental liturgy of the University of Michigan's Canterbury House, says that the more beautiful and sublime an experience of worship is the more likely it is to be absorbed and forgotten by the worshipers. Her model for true worship, accordingly, is revolution. "We need to be disturbed," she says, "not fulfilled."

> The religious experience that is complete in itself, that demands only to be experienced, does not make people change their lives. It is immediately isolated from life; placed in a special category of "beautiful experience," it is consumed. We need forms which cannot be swallowed, which are open in a revolutionary direction and demand completion by the witnesses themselves.[8]

The same charge can usually be made against revolutionists that is made against arch-conservatives, that they are deficient in humor and the ability to look at themselves truly. Yet there is something very persuasive about these words. We *do* need "forms which cannot be swallowed" or dismissed, but require the total involvement of those worshiping, so that worship is a beginning, not an end in itself. Liturgy ought to confront us with our dullness, our blindness, our obtuseness, our carelessness, and make us see and feel again—not just who we are but who those around us are, and what the world is like. And it ought to provide us with a mode, not of transcending the world, or escaping it, but of entering it and becoming Christ in it. If it does not, then it must inevitably become antispiritual, for it deadens the consciousness by seeming to provide a form of confrontation it does not actually provide. Our spirits are lulled into complacency, and the world wheels on its merry, tragic way.

One of my students, Mrs. Ann Denham, has created a special drama-liturgy for "freeing" God from the conceptions commonly held about him. Three actors, who are dressed in liturgical garments and are preparing to lead a service of worship, begin to complain of the phoniness of what they are doing. They decide that they have been trying to manipulate God. What they will do in this service is try to set him free. Doffing their robes, they pass among the congregation, collecting slips of paper on which the worshipers have written the formulas by which they understand God. They read these formulas aloud—phrases like "God is the Holy Trinity, three persons in one substance," "God is the Father of our Lord and Savior, Jesus Christ"—and drop them into a brazier. At the height of the service, they ignite the slips and begin to move to the beat of the Fifth Dimension's rock version of "People Got to Be Free." The congregation is urged to join them. A second recording is introduced, blending with the first and then overcoming it. This is the Malcolm Dodd Singers in a swinging version of "He's Got the Whole World in His Hands." It builds to a frenzied conclusion, leaving the dancers spent and free, with arms stretched upward and heads thrown back. Quietly, the entire group joins hands in a circle, and one of the actors intones, as a benediction, e.e. cummings' lines,

—all nothing's only our hugest home;
the most who die, the more we live.

What is the total effect of all this? Does God really *need* to be set free in liturgy? Can we actually affect him in any way by what we do in worship? Of course the answer is no. Whatever God is, he is surely not subordinate to us or to the vagaries of the liturgical consciousness. But the point is that *we* are affected by what we do in worship, and a service in which we participate in the freeing of God does something to the narrow, routinized visions we have had of him. The end result, if the service is successful, is that *we* are set free, liberated from our inadequate conceptions, or that we are at least made to recognize our bondage, and in that to gain a measure of power over it.

The same can be said for the two or three occasions I have heard of when congregations conducted "funerals" for God, following the Nietzsche-Altizer-Hamilton announcement of the "death" of God by appropriate expressions of sympathy, grief, and rage, a eulogy in the sanctury over an empty coffin, and a decent burial in a graveyard or nearby field. What was symbolized was the congregation's attempt to bury or lay to rest their outdated, premodern ideas of who God is and how he acts in the world—an attempt, in other words, to come to terms with God as he is, or at least God as he may be known by a contemporary congregation trying to respond authentically to revelation in its own day.

If the acts bore an undertone of frivolity or playfulness, this may have expressed a facet of the revelation. That is, the modern consciousness may behold in the deity a sense of humor enabling him to respond joyfully and positively to any occasion on which Christians make an honest effort to transcend their own limited viewpoints and modify their sensibilities with regard to religious matters. The sacrilegiousness, or whatever sacrilegiousness there was in such an act, may have been mainly in the eye of the beholder.

Rudolf Otto, in *The Idea of the Holy*, noted the ambivalence with which most people regard the sacred, so that they are simultaneously drawn to it and repelled by it. He also suggested, in a few paragraphs on the "indirect means" by which people experience the *mysterium tremendum et fascinans,*[9] the possibility of arriving at the *sensus numinis* or the mystery of divine presence not by frontal assault but by some other, less conspicuous route. Émile Durkheim and others have enlarged upon this insight or opening by exploring the notion that even sacrilege can become a viable approach to the sacred. The conclusion of Durkheim was that the sacrilegious, because of its qualitative similarity to the sacred, can more easily be transformed into the holy than acts which are, because of their routinization or overuse, religiously neutral.[10] The one simply passes over into, and is absorbed by, the other.

The consequences of such an insight have not escaped the attention of many contemporary artists. Dostoevsky saw in crime and destruction a technique for provoking a profoundly religious sensibility and converting it, through an ordeal of fire and suffering, into something remarkably pure and good. Melville achieved an extraordinary sense of the numinous in *Moby Dick* by exploiting the diabolical signs and omens through which Ahab passes to reach the mammal from primeval depths. The English romantics, especially Wordsworth and Coleridge and Byron, generated a feeling for the supernatural through acts of desecration or indecency. An exhibition of paintings by the Dadaists Arp, Baargeld, and Ernst in Cologne in 1920 could be reached only via a public urinal, and on opening day a young girl in a Communion dress stood and recited obscene poetry. The playwright Fernando Arrabal has a little piece entitled *Solemn Communion* in which a girl similarly attired symbolically murders the man (or men) in her future life. The effect of combining purity and guilt, innocence and experience, in such a drastic image is theatrically exciting. The entire tradition of the *poètes maudits* or *poetes manqués,* the poets who glorify evil, from Baudelaire and Rimbaud and Mallarmé to Jean Genet and LeRoi Jones, is electric with the sense of the forbidden and the holy. And so is the tradition of what R. W. B. Lewis has called "the picaresque saint"—debauched or unholy protagonists who unwittingly and uncourageously do the will of God while outraging the community of "decent, law-abiding folk."[11] What the artists among us have seen is that life is never so orderly or predictable as most of us assume, that, as G. K. Chesterton once put it, "a wildness lies in wait" and the ways of God are not always to be traced along paths entirely familiar or expected.

Jean Genet, who has received enormous attention from the critics in recent years, is an interesting study in the ambiguity of holiness. A lifelong inhabitant of the great European prisons which were once monasteries and churches, Genet began at some point of his career to imagine that the criminals shuffling through the corridors of the prisons were the actual counterparts of clerics performing their duties to God. The characters in his first novel, *Our Lady of the Flowers,* a putrescent, macabre narrative of pimps, whores, homosexuals, thieves, and murderers, are named Our Lady, Divine, First Communion, Archangel Gabriel, etc. Crime is hallowed and criminals are idolized. The whole religious schema, the one we had become accustomed to, is inverted. The same is true of all of Genet's works. As Sartre says, Genet makes us look at the "whirligig"; he confuses us, spins us around until the landmarks themselves seem to be spinning, so that we have no sure notion about what reality is.

Sartre, in an elaborately contrived and monumental study of Genet entitled *Saint Genet: Actor and Martyr,* has identified Genet's intentionality as basically a religious one. Genet, he contends, has personally accepted vilification, has *chosen* it, and has elaborated on his criminal identity, for the purpose of being a scapegoat for ordinary society; he has grimly *intended* to be a thief and an outcast in order to gather into himself and mirror back to us our own evil and error. This is what Sartre means by calling him a martyr and bestowing on him the unexpected title of saint. He has sacrificed himself in order to reveal our vanities and crimes.

What Genet accomplishes, claims Sartre, is an experience of the sacred. Through the filthy, the sordid, and the unnatural, he makes us aware of their opposites; and the very contradiction constitutes a revelation of the sacred.

> Genet, a strange phenomenon in the universe, sees the universe as strange. Experience reveals to him in every object, in every event, the presence of *something else;* he senses the *supernatural.* And is it not precisely the sacred which thus manifests itself through the profane without ever letting itself be touched? The world is sacred because it gives an inkling of a meaning that escapes us. And Genet, an enigma that requires a solution, is himself sacred in a sacred world.[12]

Richard Coe presses the matter again.

> All Genet's crimes belong to a greater or lesser degree to the category of sacrilege—it is we, the readers, who acknowledge this whenever we shudder with nausea at Genet's perversions, obscenity or cynicism. Yet there *can* be no sacrilege unless there is something sacred: we, the readers, are affirming this when we shut the book in anger; and Genet, by stating that, through sacrilege, his characters penetrate into the realm of the sacred, is merely confirming a fact that we have already, by implication, admitted.[13]

"There can be no sacrilege unless there is something sacred"—that is the point. Genet invokes the sense of the holy again and again in his plays and novels precisely through his portrayals of the unholy. In a day when the *sensus numinis* was all but gone from the theater, or from contemporary theater at any rate, he managed its return by the manipulation of its inverted form, the *sensus profanus.*

Now what does this say about worship? That we must institute Black Masses, as Genet does in his plays, and consciously strive to irritate and outrage the conservative mind? That we must glorify evil and sing praises to the devil and have a soloist intone operatically, as Arrabal has a character in one of his plays do, "Defecate on God; defecate on his divine image; defecate on his omnipresence"?[14]

Hardly.

What it does say is that the sense of the numinous is almost always related to a feeling of danger. There is a strongly existential quality about it, as though we were poised on the brink of disaster and the only ultimate safety lay in leaping into the void, not in inching our way back towards temporary security. The experience of God is not for fainthearted people. It is for fools and saints and heretics, for adventurers and lunatics and diehards. It is for people who are ready and willing to make mistakes if only there is a chance that they will succeed beyond most men's dreams. It is for those who are daring enough to use the wrong forms as well as the right ones in addressing the deity, who will risk hell and its perils for the sake of a single glimpse of his face, a momentary assurance of his presence.

The trouble with most of Christianity, as Richard Coe says, is that it has "destroyed our power to touch and experience the sacred through limited and controlled transgression."[15] It has manifested identically the fault it has so consistently polemicized against in Judaism, namely an unshakable preoccupation with legalistic righteousness. It has swallowed up Jesus at a bound and has come down heavily on the side of the scribes and the Pharisees. Consequently it has only rarely known that swaggering sense of grace and freedom so easily found, once one knows how to watch for it, in the person of its nominal Lord. It has not been able to "sin boldly," as Luther advised, or to live with *élan* and imagination as the artists have. It has existed in mortal fear of desecrating the sanctuary or phrasing a prayer in improper grammar or spilling the Communion wine on its Sunday bib and tucker. It has, in short, given up its claims on the sacred in favor of its predilection for safety and caution. It has renounced *das ganz Andere*, the Wholly Other, in favor of More-of-the-Same.

It is important in the church therefore—imperative, even!—always to be including in liturgy what Robert Bellah has called "not merely the religiously neutral but the consciously profane."[16] The acids of contemporaneity must always be allowed to work upon the old structures, threatening them and dissolving them, so that nothing about them becomes sacrosanct in itself and thus, pretending to be spiritual, antispiritual. The God who is supposed to be a jealous God—an epithet full of passion and specificity—is hard to find in stagnant places. His element is really, as the epithet implies, *passion* and *specificity*. He is found where the static occurs whenever the sacred and profane begin to clash, to come into conflict and, in the resolution, pass over and into one another.

The truth is—and in this Judaeo-Christianity differs from many primitive religions—that the sacred is only where God is, not that God is where the sacred is. When he has moved on, the place where he was is no longer truly sacred. Whatever is holy about unused temples or cathedrals, superseded prayer books, and hocked communionware is so only by virtue of the humanity invested in them, not by virtue of any residual divinity. There is an obsolescence about everything he uses and every place he inhabits. The holy is always in process of becoming the profane.

The profane, on the other hand, is always becoming holy. When it has become most empty of God, most barren of presence, it is most in the way of being a bearer of grace, a vessel of the divine. What was "without form and void" becomes a world. What was "uncomely and not to be desired" becomes the Messiah. What was motley, untutored, and subject to ridicule becomes the church.

The language and the acts which at first sight appear blasphemous and sacrilegious are seen on further examination to hold real possibilities as the words and deeds of worship!

Sermon

WHAT JOSEPH SITTLER says in his book *The Anguish of Preaching* is doubtless true, that "the act of preaching is so ecologically imbedded in the total reflection and witness of the community that the sermon as a particular act cannot be separated out for very useful discussion."[1] Nevertheless, the sermon (homily, reflection, meditation, comment, or other surrogate) is still ordinarily an important part of worship, and a word ought to be said about it.

There is no question about the old-style, nineteenth-century sermon's being out today. It is! Not that there would be no room for a Spurgeon or a Robertson or a Maclaren today if he were around; there are always traditionally oriented congregations clamoring for "good preaching." But the style is simply no longer consonant with our total life-style—with who we are and how we think and what worship is becoming. This is not really the time for men like Melville's Father Mapple, the minister in *Moby Dick* who climbed into a pulpit shaped like a ship's prow and hauled his ladder in after him, symbolizing his separation from the congregation, his elevation of office, his responsibility for prophecy. The preacher who has that attitude becomes more and more remote, and people pay less and less attention to him. They may still honor him with titles and teas, an honorary membership in the country club, and an occasional clerical reduction on the price of a suit of clothes or a railroad ticket.

But that is on the polite level. On the impolite level, they don't listen to him any more. They have written him off. As a communicator he is like a man trying to address the crowd at a cocktail party while the chattering grows louder and louder, until he is shouting and still no one notices him.

But this does not mean that preaching is through. On the contrary, there is more possibility for it today than there ever has been. As one of my colleagues has put it, "The sermon is out; preaching is in." What is out is the highly rhetorical, stylized homiletical effort of an earlier era—not the communication of the gospel. This is an age of communication, more than any other before it. There is more dialogue, more touching, more beaming of messages today than at any other time in history. People obviously believe in communication. Our whole economy turns on it. What they don't believe in is some functionary paid to wear a black robe and stand behind a funny old desk and bore them with truisms, clichés, and platitudes about beauty, life, and truth while they twiddle their thumbs and squirm for the hour to be over so they can get to the golf course or the picnic grounds or the televised ball game.[2] What they do believe in is somebody who is clearly struggling with life and its issues and bothers to phrase his discoveries (or even his questions) in such a way as to speak to their own conscious and unconscious concerns about the same things. He may do it all at once, in twenty minutes on Sunday morning, or in installments around the community during the week, but that—the form—is no longer so important. What is important is that it be real and not some canned, artificial, or useless junk assembled by the minister as partial fulfillment for the requirements of his role. In the words of David Randolph, "preaching is being rejected as a habit and affirmed as a happening."[3]

Reuel Howe, director of the Institute for Advanced Pastoral Studies, is right in his books (especially *The Miracle of Dialogue* and *Partners in Preaching*) to underline the importance of *listening* as part of a sermon. It is isolation that kills most sermons

—isolation from persons, isolation from their fears and problems, isolation from their aspirations, isolation from the world that is pressing in on them and demanding to be dealt with all the time. If ministers would only listen to people more they might be able to agree with Hans Karl Bühl, the former soldier in Hofmannsthal's comedy *Der Schwierige,* who says, "I understand myself much less well when I speak than when I am silent." In fact, they might find that they even understand *others* less well when they speak than when they are silent.

The preacher, in an age of comparative enlightenment, when many of the persons he addresses in the congregation are as intelligent and as well-educated as he, and when they are accustomed to hearing, via television and community lecture halls, many speakers even more intelligent than he, cannot hope to be relevant as a voice of authority, a bearer of *the* Word, or an ultimate source of wisdom and understanding. He cannot even pretend to carry off his act as an expert in the scriptures or theological inquiry, for, unless there is far more than that in his portfolio to manifest the importance of his opinions, most people today will not be interested: the Bible and theology are becoming daily more peripheral in their existence.

What he must be satisfied to be—and *will* be satisfied to be, for it is unspeakably fulfilling—is a man, a sensitive, creative, poetic figure, grappling with the problems of being human and secular and whole in our time, and sharing both the quest and its results with other individuals around him. This is finally the only justification for his being paid a salary to be a minister. He is freed from the demands of a nine-to-five position in order to circulate among the persons of the congregation, to ask questions about their living, their style of existence, to reflect on them and the sum of knowledge he has acquired and is still in the process of acquiring from books, teachers, and other resources, to share the results of this process, and then to work with them to correct his own interpretations of the results. He is their freed man, in other words, their freed mind, their freed heart, their freed conscience, their freed dreamer, their freed critic, their freed believer. And unless he and they both have some agreement on this principle, then they are both likely to be disappointed in their relationship.

The preacher, in the act of preaching, is thus symbolic of the entire congregation itself struggling with the issues of life and death and banality and transcendence. Dialogue preaching is an extension of the same principle: it is *more than one person* struggling in behalf of the congregation. Congregational preaching, in which the congregation dissolves into buzz groups for the purpose of discussing a text or theme, is a further extension: it is *all of the people* struggling together. Even if the preacher alone is visibly engaged in the act of preaching, the evidence that he has listened to the congregation, that the objects of his concern are actually theirs corporately, symbolizes the participation of the whole congregation. The sermon is thus an integral part of worship and is not to be defined as something appended or antithetical to the liturgy.

If McLuhan is right in saying that this is an era of cool, low-definition media which require maximal participation of viewers and hearers, then this concept of preaching is doubly important. The average person has simply outgrown the situation his forebears were in, of being *told* what the world was like and how they were to act and think in it. Now more than ever he must himself enter into the task of defining the world and his relationship to it. His *Weltbilt*, his view of things, must be arrived at partly by his own efforts, so that it is intimately his. Paradoxically, though this is in many ways an age of vanishing privacy, it is also an age of great intimacy. Men feel that they must cooperate in the decisions that affect them. They may still be manipulated and controlled without their being aware of it. But most of them are like the child in the advertisement who says, "I want to do it myself."

The theology which a homiletics of dialogue operates under

is flatly and unabashedly different from the traditional Theology of the Word. It does not regard the Word which became incarnate in Jesus of Nazareth as having been solely confined to him. On the contrary, it assumes that the same Word is in a sense incarnate in all of us, although it is normally fragmented, confused, and thwarted in us until the Word in Jesus addresses the Word in us and helps it to become what it is, namely Word or *Logos* or Order. The sermon time in the liturgy, that is to say, is not a time for introducing some new thing or idea which is alien to us, but for subtly regarding the *Logos* in Jesus and seeing how that enables us to rearrange the pieces of our own patterns so that *Logos* or Word prevails in us. More simply put, we try to reorder our existence in the presence of his. Although there is a mystical feeling which occurs when this attempt is successful, there is nothing magical or supernatural about it. We have the equipment for the converted or rearranged life all the time. We merely need the template, the pattern, for realigning it. And our relationship to Jesus, then, becomes one of gratitude, affection, and loyalty, the very qualities provoked by anyone who does an exceptionally meaningful thing for us. It is even quite possible, in such an attitude, to speak of being "in Christ" as the Apostle did: one feels that he is indeed the mystical and titular head of those who have found life through him and his Word.

This has marked implications for the relationship of the Bible and preaching. Biblical preaching is still vital and meaningful, but not in the sense that we once understood what biblical preaching is. The center of gravity is not in the Bible but in the contemporary congregation. The generations are not enslaved to a particular era or to a series of letters and pamphlets for what they potentially say to the present age, and it is possible that they will be *freed* by them. This does not rule out revelation from other sources—from poetry, drama, movies, discussions, paintings, a thousand things. It does indicate agreement that where there was so much heat, even a couple of thousand years ago, there was also obviously some light, and that that light, if it can be focused on the present in a suitable way, is still able to introduce order and understanding into men's lives. The preacher must turn to the Bible, in other words, not as a book whose authority is *ipso facto* in itself, but as a clue—indeed, an impressive clue—to the meaning of human existence. The authority will not underlie every word in it, or even every idea. It will evince itself wherever sense from the scriptures and the sense of the reader or hearer intersect, wherever validation occurs by virtue of the reader or hearer's own confirmation from experience, wherever the reader or hearer suddenly says, "That's it! That's what I needed to hear! That's what I wasn't seeing clearly until now."

Harry Emerson Fosdick may not have inaugurated a new age in preaching, but he was certainly a manifestation of it. He urged that nobody but the preacher still proceeds upon the notion that people come to church breathlessly awaiting word of what happened to the ancient Jebusites, and that the least the preacher can do in learning to preach effectively is to begin his sermon in New York or Seattle or Indianapolis and not in Jerusalem or Jericho or Ramoth-Gilead. It is easy enough, once the preacher has begun with the people where they are, to make an excursion to the Bible lands to pick up some information or aid of one kind or another. It is impossible for some preachers, on the other hand, ever to make their way from the biblical setting to where their congregations are idly and absent-mindedly despairing of their return. As Sittler puts it in his inimitable way: "Biblical reportage of mighty events remains a sort of verbal iconography, a celebration of godly vitality that remains unpunctured for explosion into presence."[4] The action is now, and that is where the accent of the sermon must be.

The important thing, says Sittler, discussing what he calls "the anguish of Christology," is the sense in which Christ is alive to us today.

He means—and no repetition of past meanings is equivalent to present requirements; he intends—and no celebration of the purity and force of his historically experienced intentions is equivalent to what he now intends. Nor does ardor in reporting the past provide a substitute for depth and clarity in specifying Christly intentions for the world now. By the *anguish of Christology*, then, I mean the heart always restless and the mind always asking what the disclosure and concretion of the holy in the event of Jesus Christ means for the life of the world.[5]

The restlessness and the inquisitiveness—those are indispensable properties of the man who would really attempt to preach, to "pull it off" in the congregation. He knows, if he is honest with himself, that he doesn't have the answers in a sealed envelope, or a sealed Bible—that he has got to dig for them, and scratch for them, and claw for them, and sometimes admit to his congregation that he hasn't found them at all, that they are elusive, or that he is thickheaded, and that they simply wouldn't come for him. He has got hints—or thinks he has. He is almost never without those. But woe unto him if he preaches them as more than hints, turning toothpicks into pillars and pebbles into foundation stones. He will have immediately switched off his audience—perhaps indefinitely.

The frustration and confusion of much traditional preaching is clearly seen in the attempts to deal with the matter of the Resurrection. Even the most benighted minister can guess that there is something of central significance about the Resurrection for the early church's experience and witness. The impact of Christ's being raised from the dead lay somehow at the very heart of New Testament life and faith. But how does the average preacher today approach the subject of Resurrection in his sermons? Simple research indicates that it is rarely approached at all, except by limited allusion or reference in sermons on other topics. Most preachers attempt to preach on it on Easter Day, primarily because it is expected, and they feel that there is a better climate of acceptance for it then. These sermons indicate a general embarrassment over the miraculous aspects of all the Resurrection accounts, and attempt to deal with the embarrassment by adducing "proof" from the physical sciences, from analogies, or even from romantic rhetoric, for the historicity of the occurrence. In short, the preachers spend their time trying to convince the congregation—and perhaps themselves in the bargain—that the Bible is not exaggerating, that Jesus was (*could have been?*) literally raised from the grave and that *somehow* it makes a difference. Most of them are like the contemporary preacher described by David Randolph in *The Renewal of Preaching,* who "labors under the delusion that it is his job to *prove* the truth of Christianity. He seems to try to 'make a case,' to 'argue the point'—and too often he seems like a second-rate lawyer arguing a case in which he does not really believe. He is a kind of Perry Mason of the pulpit who differs from his television counterpart in that he *loses* all the time."[6]

The problem is that they start at the wrong end. They assume, being Christian ministers at Easter, that they must begin with the more obvious Easter texts and work forward to validate them to congregations living in the twentieth century; while the truth is that they ought to begin with their congregations in the twentieth century, asking what possible forms restoration would take among them, and then examine the biblical materials (along with others) for insights as to how that restoration might be achieved. The church is a resurrection fellowship, it is true; but even on the crassest level of hope in an afterlife, far more confidence in the survival beyond death springs from a quality of intensity of life here and now than ever sprang from mere trumped-up "historical" proofs for the resurrection of Jesus. Survival in the first instance has to do with being, with density, with emotion; in the second, with idea, with doctrine, with propaganda. And people are no longer to be convinced of the historicity or significance of resurrection on the basis of argument. The only appeal is on the ground of psychological and sociological integration, of wholeness for the person and wholeness for his world. The question is not, then, "Did Jesus come back from the dead?" but "In what way is his coming back, and what happened among the disciples, relevant and analogous to what we desire to take place in our midst?"

The most effective preachers are those who are able to establish a therapeutic context for their congregations by reminding them of the signs of life *presently* to be seen in particular persons or movements or ideas. The preaching of Frederick Buechner and Norman Vincent Peale, to name two ministers of very different styles, is evidence of this. There is a *hopefulness* about their sermons because they constantly allude to individuals they know who have reached new levels of integration, identity, and understanding. Resurrection in their preaching, instead of being an obtrusive doctrinal formulation, is a particular, tangible kind of fact: it is going on in men's lives today. And when that is happening there is no need for an apologetics to substantiate the resurrection of Jesus. Men recognize, out of their own positive feeling, their own sense of restoration, the validity of the early church's teaching about it. They say, "Yes, isn't it wonderful! That is what it feels like!"

In the church, then, as the community of Restoration, the preacher is not called on to be an orator or public advocate. He is instead a listener, a mediator, a friend, a fellow, a catalyst. And he is all of these primarily as a man among men who is always seeking more and more wholeness for himself and is never inhibited about saying this to his congregation. It is the church itself, the entire congregation, that is responsible for the sense of Restoration, and, by that token, for the preaching of the church as well. The preaching, or witness, is a congregational function. The minister may be the focus of this function, but he is by no means the whole of it. The sermon is the church's sermon, and the responsibility for communicating a feeling of Restoration is incumbent on everyone.

One of the hardest stereotypes among young ministers to

break—indeed, *the* stereotype which must be broken if they
are to be human beings in the ministry—is that of the preacher
as *performer*. It has been the bane of both clergy and congregation for well over a century, at least. Reuel Howe says that it
induces in preachers one of two effects: it either paralyzes them
with fear that they cannot perform acceptably, and thus turns
them into exhausted, anxious, and self-despising men, or it
makes exhibitionists of them, so that they exploit the dramatic
possibilities of the gospel without real regard for people's welfare or spiritual being.[7] Either way, the performer image dehu-
manizes them, so that they are disabled for being what they
need most to be in the congregation, models of wholeness and
freedom.

The point where most ministers are hung up on the matter
is over the question of authority. "If I don't keep up the preten-
sions," they say, "if I don't bluff my way through, then people
won't listen to me." This says a great deal about the security
needs of most ministers. Actually the majority of parishioners
gave up the notion of the preacher's infallible authority a long
time ago—if indeed they ever held it. The real authority for
preaching has always been *in the listeners* themselves. They
choose to hear or not to hear. They decide on the person in
whom they will vest authority; they grant it to the one in whom
they have confidence. And most of them will eventually invest
it in the minister who is "restless" and "inquisitive" about the
right things, to use Sittler's terms; who stays doggedly on the
trail of a deeper sense of humanity and a kind of Restoration
which they can recognize as meaningful in terms of their daily
existence.

Once the preacher realizes this—realizes it at an ontological
level—an exhilarating sense of freedom begins to suffuse his
entire person. He is freed to be human, to take himself less
seriously. He is freed to listen and interact. He is freed to be
playful in his language, because he knows that words cannot
precisely capture the deepest things of the spirit, that, as Aaron

Copland says,[8] even a composer of music only approximates his ideas, and can never render them exactly. He is freed to be brief, to be discursive, to speak in parables.[9] He is freed, as Howe says, "to preach out of the weakness of his understanding of the gospel and of life as well as out of his strengths."[10] He is freed to do "oblique" sermons,[11] fragment sermons, dialogue sermons, interview sermons, poetic sermons, ironic sermons, demonstration sermons, sermons using slides, posters, and other multi-media aids—in fact, almost any kind of sermon imaginable, even the reading of a Jonathan Edwards "horror" sermon. No longer under obligation to do something self-contained, a high-wire act for the entertainment of the congregation, he is able to see the sermon as part of the total orchestration of worship, and as something the congregation helps to do. He is able to step to the pulpit on a Sunday morning and say, as one of my student-friends did on a recent occasion, "I have worked and worked to prepare a sermon for you this morning, but it just wouldn't come. Now you are going to have to help. If there is to be a sermon this morning, it will be *our* sermon." He can regard the sermon as a moment in the liturgy when the playing is briefly stopped in order that he and the others who are involved with him may clarify what is going on, how the people are playing, and what is the meaning of the playing, enabling them, at the end, to resume their playing with even more fullness and freedom.

What is the preacher's role in the service then? Kierkegaard's analogy has been used so often that it is almost hackneyed now, but it is difficult to improve upon: the preacher is the prompter offstage who feeds cue lines to the congregation onstage for their performance before the living God in the audience. I tried to think of other images. Some musician once said that a conductor is a man who dances while the orchestra plays; that has some applicability. LeRoi Jones reminds us that the Negro preacher was originally a singer, responding antiphonally with his congregation;[12] that too may be relevant. Martin Marty likes to call the minister a "player-coach." And the group leader in a sensitivity training session may also provide a useful analogy. But Kierkegaard's picture is still hard to beat, especially as it involves a sense of drama appropriate to liturgical action.

I did recall one unforgettable vignette of a preacher I had read in the *Christian Century* some months ago, and went scrambling back through old copies to find it again. It was in an article by Richard L. Stanger, chaplain of MacMurray College in Illinois, about the visit of San Francisco poet William Everson, now Brother Antoninus, to the MacMurray campus. Apparently the strange, towering guest made a staggering impact on students and faculty alike. On the final Friday night of his visit the chapel was filled despite such normal weekend competition as the showing of the film *Candy* at a local movie house. What the audience beheld was an ursine, middle-aged Dominican in flowing white robe who "glided, clawed, bolted across the chancel" while reading poems, reflecting on the tattered ends of his life, watching those assembled, and generally reacting to whatever stimulated him at the moment. It was such a moving experience, such a genuine experience, that everyone was reluctant to leave when it was over. One girl, without waiting for the crowds to disperse, even came to the front as though there had been an altar call.

Stanger said that this impelling, sobering occasion made all his previous attempts at relevance—"jazz liturgies, folk hymns, upbeat confessions and the like"—seem suddenly pallid and flat in comparison. Why? What was there about Brother Antoninus's appearance that should have had this effect? "I think," said Stanger,

> it was the "becoming" quality of the man and the event. Brother Antoninus had little idea where the evening would go. Certainly he had some intention, emerging from his vocational commitment, to risk a radical openness with his audience that some might be led to an awareness of the living God who moves amid the

"horrors" of the human heart. But the outcome was not laid out in advance. Nor was his life! One had the sense that here was an unfinished product—a life still writhing, still struggling, still becoming.

How often our worship in the church is flat and sterile precisely for a lack of this quality. We are confronted with a "polished" liturgy, a "finished" theology, an "answer" to the "angst" of existence. And the smell of death meets our nostrils as worshipers because life just isn't like that! . . .

We came as a campus, sensing that here was a man "on to something"; a man of Christlike bearing. And, in the end, all there was was a man—struggling! And that was the refreshing glory of it all.[13]

"A man—struggling." This is one of the most beautiful and moving portraits I have ever seen of what preaching might look like if done in freedom and high playfulness. It has to do with creating order out of chaos, with finding a design for life that is more meaningful and more orderly—*together*. It has to do with finding refreshment and restoration—*together*. Always together. For that is what the Christian community is about.

A group of Presbyterian clergymen in the San Francisco area have put the matter succinctly in their thoughtful summary of *The Church at Worship in an Urban Age.* They say: "In the sermon the minister is communicating his own personality. If he is a free man and if this freedom is expressed in and through the styles he uses, he will have the effect of setting other people free."[14] That is the secret of true preaching.

Music

"THE REAL POWER of music," says Suzanne Langer, "lies in the fact that it can be 'true' to the life of feeling in a way that language cannot; for its significant forms have that ambivalence of content which words cannot have."[1]

In the past, unfortunately, this ambivalence has often been regarded in the church with suspicion and distrust. Anything with the capacity to address the inner self nonverbally, with more accuracy than language, is a potential subverter of language and therefore of doctrine as well. The report of the Archbishops' Committee for the Church of England in 1951 was not untypical: "Music that is in keeping with the spirit of the liturgy will be characterized by qualities of nobility and restraint; by freedom from sensationalism or mawkishness, and from all suggestions of secularity."[2]

Today, however, there appears to be a remarkable change in the general attitude of church people toward music. There is far more openness than there was a decade ago. The fear of what George Steiner has called "a deeper, more numinous code"[3] is less prevalent. People are willing to submit themselves to other tunes and other voices, regardless of the church's doctrines and dogmas.

A fascinating case study of this change can be made by examining the writings of hymnologist Erik Routley from the early fifties through the late sixties. Routley, a Congregationalist minister in England, is a widely recognized authority on theology and church music. His book *Hymns and Human Life*, published in 1952, is an informed, intelligent, and eminently readable examination of the church's hymnody; but it is obviously traditional in scope and opinion. It speaks of hymns as "the folk-song of the church militant" and suggests that Christian theology is often soundest in eras when the church's culture and music are most defective.

Church Music and Theology, issued in 1959, reveals a growing awareness of musical "legalism"—the tendency of trained church musicians to interpret texts strictly and without regard for the congregations involved—and registers an important identification between the Christian's awareness of *newness of life* and the theological requirement, therefore, of *newness in church music* (more on this later). But the same book speaks somewhat disparagingly of Fr. Geoffrey Beaumont's *Folk Mass*, which had recently appeared, for its "music hall" idiom and "misconceived" notion of evangelism. Father Beaumont, wrote Routley,

> has not sufficiently considered how far this music deliberately partakes of the corruption of the world out of which he would redeem people, and how far transcends it. To most ears it appears to be positively tainted with that corruption—the corruption of arrogance, carelessness, impatience and even fear. Its characteristic obsessions with short phrases alternating with abrupt changes to new phrases, its hypnotic rhythms which are not rhythms but metrical patterns . . . these things do not suggest redemption. They suggest acceptance where the church should be saying "No." The Folk Mass brings back quite starkly the question of evangelism in the form, "How far may the church go to meet the people?"[4]

Next, in 1964, came *Twentieth Century Church Music*. Dr. Routley was still chiding Father Beaumont, though more mildly than before, with reminders of the New Testament's concern lest Christians in their singing and ecstasy give way to "drunk-

enness and the dissipation that goes with it" (Eph. 5:18 NEB).
But now he was praising the "holy worldliness" of François
Poulenc's music, which he said was full of "sacred laughter,"
and was taking more than a little interest in the folk songs of
Sydney Carter, of which he cited especially "Lord of the
Dance" and "Friday Morning." The latter is an obviously bitter,
satirical piece of music, sung as though it were the thoughts of
one of the malefactors put to death with Christ. The refrain
after each verse says:

> It's God they ought to crucify,
> Instead of you and me.

Routley noted the appropriateness of such satire in an era
which had just seen the birth of the B.B.C. program "That Was
The Week That Was," and opined that "one doubts now
whether 'When I Survey the Wondrous Cross' makes the Crucifixion any more real to a modern believer" than "Friday
Morning" does.[5]

Finally, in 1968, appeared *Words, Music, and the Church,*
which is probably the finest book-length statement of the case
for freedom and experimentalism in church music we have
seen. The old hesitance about jazz is gone. It is the "modern
puritan" who is opposed to jazz, says Routley, because with his
work ethic he is uncomfortable around relaxation and improvisation, and with his sexual hang-ups he fears the *eros* implicit
in jazz.[6] A citation from another author is endorsed which notes
a relationship between medieval plainsong and the singing of
blues.[7] Because the Christian is a free man, and Christianity a
religion of freedom, there must be a corresponding freedom in
the church to use jazz, electronic, twelve-tone, or even "pop"
music.[8] Such freedom is far more important than any "funda-
mentalist" attitude arising either among the musical purists on
one side or the theologically and practically conservative
church members on the other. It is expressive of who we are
and what has happened to us in the church.

Basically, these changes in Routley's position reflect muta-
tions in the mood of the church itself. In the fifties, the church
was beleaguered and weary; there was dissatisfaction everywhere with the clichés of hymnody, the tired formulas of evangelism, and the emptiness of church routine and ritual. Statisti-
cal reports on its programmatic vigor and energy to the contrary, it was known to be dying of hardening of the arteries.
Then, in the early sixties, came Bishop Robinson's *Honest to
God* and the atheistic confessions of Altizer and Hamilton and
Van Buren—the end of Christianity seemed suddenly to have
heaved into view. But, paradoxically, the end of something was
also the beginning of something. Many Christians breathed a
sigh of relief. The sense of the numinous was felt more surely
amidst declarations of agnosticism than it had been felt for
years. Harvey Cox's *The Secular City* put us onto a whole new
way of thinking and talking about the church in the modern
world. Everybody reread Bonhoeffer on the necessity of sec-
ularizing the gospel. We began to realize it was a new era.
Confidence came back, and we felt like celebrating. Theologies
of hope suddenly began to spring up, as though hidden away
until that moment, and this time were more generous to
worldly cultures than eschatological theologies had ever been
before.

And this is essentially where we are now. The freedom Routley speaks of in *Words, Music, and the Church* is the freedom
to be men in our time, to live in our culture, at the same time
that we acknowledge a worthy heritage in the faith. It is a
freedom from thinking and composing and singing in a precon-
ceived "Christian" manner, a freedom to appropriate everything in the world, to commandeer it in the name of Christ the
Redeemer. W. H. Auden, in an essay in *The Dyer's Hand*, laughs
at the notion of a "Christian" art. "There can no more be a
'Christian' art than there can be a Christian science or a Christian diet."[9] Similarly, we are prompted to inquire whether
there is any such thing as a "Christian" style of music. Bach and

Handel, who stand high with most churchmen today as Christian composers, freely adapted tunes from dance music and
other secular sources. Was their music less "holy" for this?
"There are many practical problems in church music," says
Routley, "whose solutions must wait until it has been generally
recognized that musicians and Christians are all men."[10]

I have mentioned Routley's early emphasis (in *Church Music
and Theology*) on "newness" in the church and its music. He
refers to the aesthetician J. E. Barton's requirement of newness
as an ingredient in all art. Then he examines an old hymn tune,
St. Crispin, by G. J. Elvey, and finds it to be less than Christian
because of the composer's dependence on dull and traditional
compositions. "The 'newness' which J. E. Barton required of
good art," he says,

> corresponds with the "newness" in the biblical expression "Be-
> hold, I make all things new" (Rev. 21:5) or in "a new creation" (II
> Cor. 5:17). Church music should manifest this "newness," and that
> hymn tune, like so many, fails to do so. It is important to note that
> at the time of its composition it failed here; it is not that it has been
> obscured by a large number of imitations. This kind of "newness"
> does not, as a matter of fact, tarnish in this way; imitations never
> obscure it. In the beginning its composer was too ready to accept
> what he had been given in the way of conventional music and
> conventional religion. He said "Yes" too often: and the result was
> a "No" in his music. Much of this kind of music is world-denying
> and in the end faith-denying because it relies too much on
> security.[11]

This is, in my opinion, a vitally important viewpoint with
regard to music in the church. The experience of the Christian
is an experience of recreation, of newness, of novelty. To limit
the musical expression of that experience to traditional, approved, orthodox music is to saddle it immediately with a
weight it cannot continue to bear; it must inevitably develop a
lameness, and end in total paralysis. The experience itself will
be productive of new modes and techniques. It will spawn them

as the spinning stone strikes sparks. And they in turn will keep the experience fresh and vital.

Language and theology cannot be allowed to crimp the inventiveness of the composer. That is to get the order reversed, and to submit the subtler art to the grosser, the greater to the lesser. If Mrs. Langer was right, that ambivalence is part of the genius of good music, then music ought not to be restrained. The linguist and theologian should be made to listen to it—truly listen—for instruction in their own realms. The people should sing and dance and THEN the creeds should be written; not the other way around.

Sam Keen has said, in *To a Dancing God*, that "a graceful future"—i.e., the future which is full of God's grace—"is one open to psychological, political, and ontological novelty. It emerges naturally from a life-style which centers in awareness of the vibrant present."[12] This is essentially the witness we have from Routley: that the true Christian posture is not one which regards all the great epochs of faith as lying in the past, so that memory is the only function to be exercised in song and proclamation, but one which is open to the newness of life in every moment, to the novel possibilities resident in every situation. In the latter case it is *hope*, not memory, that is most significant. Life is oriented toward its present potentialities. The world is being constantly restored.

And this is to say, with regard to my earlier categorization of universal mythology into the motifs of Creation/Fall/Trial/Restoration, that only an attitude of openness and innovation in liturgical music is truly expressive of the sense of Restoration, and so finally proper to the Christian service of worship. We are too often, in our singing as in our preaching, stuck in the Fall and Trial categories. These are necessary parts of our ritual, but they are incomplete and tend to become wearisome without the natural complement of an emphasis on the new world achieved by the Hero and his imitators. It is natural, in the situation of exile and trial, to develop stereotypic songs. Work songs, the songs of slavery, are exemplary of this. They require a certain rhythm, a certain kind of refrain, a certain mood, so that all the workers can join in at appropriate intervals and unite their singing and their labor. But the stage of Restoration is something else. It signifies effulgence, completion, super-fluity, overflow, lilt, playfulness—all the opposites of spareness, discipline, hardship, and seriousness. And the music for this mood will reflect the former qualities. It will not be restrained by convention or memory or tradition. It will seem to break out everywhere with new energy, taking unheard-of patterns and configurations. It is important that Christians be able to use this kind of music more than they normally do now, lest they in fact mistranslate the faith to which they give mental or verbal assent.

If a Restoration faith is truly operative in the church, then what we will feel with regard to the music we engage in may be basically characterized as freedom: freedom to use new music, freedom to use secular music, freedom to use sensual music, even freedom to use traditional music.

Freedom to use new music. This is essential. We become neurotic, narcissistic, and ethnolatrous in periods when we feed only upon conventional idioms, whether in music or philosophy or anything else.

I have previously cited Aaron Copland's Norton Lectures at Harvard University in 1951–52, in which he spoke of the unfortunate preponderance of old music on the programs of most secular concerts.[13] One cannot help sensing in that particularly vivid passage the horror with which Copland viewed the current musical scene: the old scores not only dominate the concert halls, they actually hamper and forbid the appearance of new scores. And the horror is easily transposed to the scene of church music. Constant repetition of old favorites, of hymns, anthems, and cantatas out of the past, out of the "classic" age of Christianity, forbids the emergence of our contemporary character in its encounter with spiritual realities. Young musi-

G

cians come to associate the church with dullness and repetition and anachronism; they do not find in its music a sense of the invigorating venturesomeness of the faith, which would draw them to make their own new songs to God.

Without rhythms and melodies attuned to our own environment, to the world of nylon and plastic, saturation advertising, computerized production, and electronic communication media, we have a very difficult time knowing who we really are. As Eric Salzman says in discussing the new musical possibilities today, "In this music, we rediscover ourselves, our ways of experiencing, perceiving and knowing, altered and extended right up to the constantly expanding, redefined limits of our capacities."[14] If we are not free to experiment with various kinds of music, we are not finally free to uncover our identities today.

The artist knows, more surely than most churchmen, how important it is to be radical, to carry things too far. As Michel Seuphor expresses it, "The world would stand still if no one ventured beyond the limits of the familiar."[15] In this sense the artist has an even stronger sense of grace than the average churchman. He is confident that no matter what he does to distort reality, reality will resist, will remain, will stand still. But he, the artist, learns from his distortions. Playing with sounds or colors or shapes, he gets the feel of the world. He knows the meaning of humility. He stands in awe of the creation. What does it matter if he makes mistakes? Aaron Copland speaks of "the immemorial right of the artist to be wrong." "A creator often learns as much from his miscalculations as he does from his successes," he says.[16] The trouble with the orthodoxist, the legalist, is that he never learns anything. He is so inflexible in his adherence to the code book that he never makes mistakes, or at least not any large enough to be noticeable. Ironically, of course, he makes the most fatal mistake of all: he is never free enough to get any kind of perspective on who he is and what he is like in his Pharisaism.

Most legalists in church music have so little understanding of
the history of music that they do not know that the piano and
organ are actually newcomers to the church sanctuary, that
choirs in Protestant churches are carry-overs from the monks
who sang the holy offices in the medieval church, that poly-
phony is a relatively modern invention, that the drum was
probably the original and basic instrument used in religious
rites, or that many psalm tunes were once dances and still
require to be played as such if they are to make sense musically.
They will insist on doing things according to a specified tradition without ever realizing that the tradition is really one of
innovation, of adapting new modes and techniques to the service of God. Far from representing the sense of grace or restoration in the church, they represent the spirit of bondage and
slavery.

The real spirit of restoration is served far more by the talent
and inventiveness of, say, John Cage than it is by most of the
tedious musicians produced by schools of church music. Cage's
defiance of "information structure" in his music, his willingness
for sounds to be sounds without carrying any further burden,
reveals an undeniable feeling for grace in the world. Yet most
church musicians would probably react violently to a performance of Cage's music. They are accustomed to treating music
as purely functional, as being subservient to a "message." They
have not learned to listen without listening for meaning—at
least not while they are in the sanctuary. And they have certainly not trained their congregations to listen. Consequently
many Christians are exactly like Von Ogden Vogt, who in his
book *Art and Religion* said with no apparent embarrassment
that music in a service "should fill the chinks and make the
transitions."[17] At best, they regard music as a conditioner to
prepare men for hearing the gospel from a preacher or to induce them to respond to it once it has been proclaimed. They
have never realized that salvation can be found in sound itself,
sound without any logical verbalizing, sound that establishes a

resonance in people's bodies and helps them, even below the level of consciousness, to discover wholeness and joy.

It is a healthy thing to be hearing guitars and drums and zithers and flutes and trumpets again in the sanctuary, and to be hearing, in addition, the indescribable productions of electronic synthesizers. Suddenly we realize that we have ears, that we have been cut off from many forms of sound in worship, that God can be known and worshiped in ways that may at first seem novel and unusual to us. Ed Summerlin, a composer and musician who frequently collaborates with Roger Ortmayer in arranging contemporary liturgies, is fond of using the mouthpiece of his saxophone for improvisation in a service. In some of the choir numbers he has written, human voices are employed to imitate the sounds normally produced by instruments and machines. There is a sense of liberation that pervades a congregation when he is present, as though the bonds of musical taste and usage were opened and people were released to feel new feelings, think new thoughts, and explore new worlds.

Until we have learned to do this regularly, to sing and make noises and generally experiment with sound in the sanctuary, there will be a kind of vulgarity about our musical efforts. And it will infect everything about us, including our theology, our morality, and our piety. We will perform our acts safely and securely; but we will miss the true idiom of the Christian faith, which has to do with exposure and discovery.

Freedom to use secular music. Properly speaking, of course, there ought to be no division made or inferred between church music and secular music, just as there is no definable difference between Christian art and non-Christian art. But some music does obviously originate outside the church—indeed, *most* music—and we need to speak of the freedom to borrow it for the liturgy without being accused of sensationalism.

What is involved in using a popular song like Bob Dylan's "A Hard Rain's a-Gonna Fall" or the Beatles' "She's Leaving Home"? They are hardly kerygmatic, to be sure; yet they are

informed by a Christian sense of value which is possibly more
acute than one sometimes finds in a particular church; it is
entirely possible, we reflect, that our bread cast upon the waters
is returning to us in some dimly recognizable form—that the
"Christianizing" of the West has produced numerous secular
prophets who, though they do not presume to speak from the
stance of the church, nevertheless bear an authentic spiritual
witness in our midst.

More important than this, possibly, is the fact that these songs
and others like them speak intimately from *the secular context
where we exist on a daily basis.* That is, they represent our
environment more accurately than we usually do in so-called
sacred music. The poetry of the secular song is more leisurely.
Its composer is less likely to be driven by the compulsion to "say
something profound." He toys with something—an idea, an
occasion, a relationship, a feeling—which more serious church
music would probably telescope into a generic phrase or even
a word. He explores the subtle terrain of our existence—the
unspoken fears or hopes, the limited ambitions, the erotic
desires, the whimsical thoughts. He presents the trivia of our
humanity, which Dennis Benson in *The Now Generation* says
are as important in understanding our culture as papyri fragments uncovered by archaeologists in ancient cities are in dis-
cerning those cultures.[18]

One of the signs of richness in the younger generation is
doubtless its care, its almost incredible care, for the details or
specifics of any situation. There is a great impatience with
generalities, with catch-all phrases or glorious, ineffective
moralities. Perhaps this is why high-school and college-age students appreciate hearing popular ballads and songs in religious
services—their banality, if they are banal, is small banality, not
large banality. They deal with simple, discrete, identifiable
emotions and events. They are in touch with reality of the
hardest kind, and do not deal in vague philosophies or senti-
ments which evaporate when the song is over.

Consider, for example, the way we are captured by Paul Simon's "The Sound of Silence," with its description of ten thousand people "talking without speaking" and "hearing without listening." Or Simon and Garfunkel's "7 O'clock News/Silent Night," which brings the sweet, melodious carol into harsh confrontation with the news of war and civil disturbance and other contemporary problems emanating from an evening newscast. Or the Beatles' "Eleanor Rigby," with its picture of Father McKenzie writing "the words of a sermon that no one will hear," of the poor girl who died and was buried in his church without any attendants at the funeral, and with its plaintive refrain about all the lonely people, asking where they come from and where they belong. The mystery of the appeal in these songs, if indeed it is a mystery, is the mystery of incarnation. They have caught who we are. They have said how we suffer, how we make mistakes, how we delude ourselves, how we long for companionship, how we are human.

Is it any wonder that people write to popular singers like Bob Dylan or Joan Baez and pour out their troubles and aspirations to them as if they were priests or counselors? People naturally resonate to these expressions of the way it is with them. They find such accurate representations of their emotions incredible, mystical, compelling. They *trust* those who capture them so convincingly. Why, if these songs fix us so completely, arrest us in flight, as it were, like the single frame of a bird photographed in motion, shouldn't they be used in worship to say who we are, to establish the identities of those who offer themselves to God and seek some resolution of the problems in those identities?

All music is arranged by human beings, says Igor Stravinsky; that is the most fundamental thing that can be said of it.[19] And we shall not be free in the church to be human, to find the meaning of our mortal identities, until we are free to use *any* music in the sanctuary, even the music which appears to yield nothing to our constant search for "religious" meaning and moral instruction.

Freedom to use sensual music. I have noted in an earlier chapter Alexander Lowen's warning that persons who ignore their bodies, or repress feelings about them, become schizoid and lose touch with the reality of their corporal selves. Place against this one of the interesting sidelights or serendipitous discoveries of the current black-white confrontation in America: the suspicion, among both whites and blacks, that the black man has a stronger sense of his identity today than the white man because he has been less untrue to his physical, visceral self. The reader finds the viewpoint in Eldridge Cleaver's *Soul on Ice* or William Melvin Kelly's *dem*, for example, that the white man is an inadequate lover because he lives in a false, puritanical society, and that many white women cannot help wondering what it would be like to be loved by a black man. There is no laboratory evidence of the Masters-Johnson variety to confirm such opinions, of course; but there is no doubt that they are widely held. There is something about the Negro—his slow, rhythmical, animal-like grace, his resistance and endurance, his sense of physical *presence*, his music—that seems to indicate an integration or unity between mind and body that is either missing or damaged in the American white man.

The music cannot be said to be responsible for this—we still cannot say whether the chicken or the egg came first—but it is at least part of the picture. It is an expression of the black's body/soul relationship, even if it is not the cause of the relationship, and there is little doubt that it is, minimally, part of the cause. The ring dances and shuffle dances, the intensely rhythmical movement during the singing of spirituals, the physical implications, unavoidable, of jazz and blues—these are somehow related to the physical health of a people who have less arterial sclerosis, fewer heart attacks, and fewer cases of asthma and allergenic aggravation than their white counterparts in society.

What is it with us? Why are we so afraid of *engagement* in our music? Is it because we are afraid of behaving like fools, of losing control over ourselves? It is the old pattern of mind-dominance, so strong in Western history during the centuries of rationalism. I observed, in a recent jazz service in a university chapel, that the students and younger professors felt much freer to express themselves through swaying, twisting, and jiggling their bodies than most of the older professors and visitors there. It was almost as if the rigidities of the disciplined mind would not permit the use of the body as a responsive instrument. I felt a little sad at the thought that one day many of those who had been free to react rhythmically would grow beyond doing so.

Our theology itself, says Sam Keen, must become more "visceral." It must incorporate again an appreciation for the carnal or else simply stop talking about incarnation. Part of our problem, in fact, lies in the way we are always *talking* about things and not *feeling* them. "It is the real, literal, carnal body which must be resensitized and educated to the sacredness which lies hidden in its feelings. Talk, gab, words (even words about 'the psychosomatic unity of man' or a visceral theology) are impotent to cure us in an age of propaganda."[20] If the church really believes that God somehow involved himself in human flesh in the person of Jesus of Nazareth, then it should become concerned for discovering ways of reawakening in men a reverence for the body and its rhythms.

It is already obvious from experiments with jazz and other "physical" forms of music that one significant path to this reawakening is through the use of sensual and stimulating music which will break down the worshiper's innate fear of self-exposure and get him out into the physical world inhabited by all the others in the congregation. Music with a strong beat helps him to overcome his hesitancies and inhibitions and bring his own physical presence as much as possible into the immediacy of the liturgy.

Jazz seems to offer particular advantages in that it is historically an outgrowth of a religious tradition and possesses marked similarities to the music of another oppressed people very central to the consciousness of our religion: the Jews. Routley says:

> As folk music, jazz is subject to all the organizational anarchy that folk music is content to bear. Its religious and social origins ensure that it becomes a folk music that is as near to prophetic ecstasy —typical yet escapist, earthy yet aspiring, crude yet haunting— as are the Negro spirituals in which it has its musical roots. The "inspirational" content of jazz has a close affinity with the singing and dancing of the ancient Israelite prophets—much closer than any it has with conventional European music.[21]

There is, moreover, a relationship of spirit between the improvisational technique of jazz and the sense of freedom I have spoken of in Christian worship at its best. There is a rubric, a rhythmic and harmonic framework from which to work, but there is also room for variation, for individuation, for private response and invention. The sense of freedom can actually be felt and embodied in the music. And there is the additional advantage, in an era of racial strife and resentment, of white men's employing rhythmical forms which have been the staple of the black men's culture for centuries—which owe much, in fact, to the Dark Continent from which they were first brought to these shores.

Whatever the kind of music used, however, it is important that the church find musical idioms which permit maximal participation of worshipers, physically as well as vocally and mentally. There is always a reciprocity between a culture and its music. If the music is folk music, with emphasis on tales, cleverness, irony, and rhythmic movement, it is a reflection of a society with folk virtues—home, history, heroes, humor, etc. If it is sophisticated orchestral music, then the reflection is of a highly genteel, economically established, and probably socially stratified society. And the same reciprocity is seen in the church at various epochs of its history. Medieval plainsong is usually related to a mystical, sacramental kind of Christianity; Calvinistic psalmody to a severe, methodical, rather dramatic kind; and revivalistic hymnody to a bourgeois, personalistic one. Now, in an age desperately trying to trace its way back—or forward—to the point where man's being was (is, will be) one, a unity of mind and body and spirit, in order to set him over against a technological environment which necessitates the clarification, the cultural requirement is for music which facilitates this recovery of unity. And the church ignores or repudiates this requirement at its own peril and the peril of its mission, which is to bring redemption within the cultural situation.

Sam Keen playfully suggests that the resurrection of the body the church needs to talk about today is the resurrection of the physical, carnal nature of man.[22] It is ironic to see the church even trying to conceive of the resurrection of the body along doctrinal lines when most of those entering most prominently into the discussion, the theologians and teachers and ministers, and perhaps most doctrinaire laymen, probably have least idea of what their bodies really are from an experiential standpoint. It is likely, on the other hand, that a congregation whose sensitivities to the body have been whetted by a serious investigation of the possibilities of a visceral theology, and which is able to sing, in the liturgy, the "Walking in Space" song from the musical *Hair*—the one hymning both body and soul—will easily and profoundly grasp the meaning of such a doctrine at a nonverbal and vastly more significant level.

Freedom to use traditional music. Now we are ready to suggest, as I did earlier in the chapter on language, that traditional expressions of the Christian faith are revalidated and given heightened meaning when set in the context of the new and contemporary, and that the freedom to employ them is part and parcel of the total freedom to be creative in the worship of God. Words, doctrines, and songs which would amount to no more than clichés now if their original contexts were preserved indefinitely in our midst, become piquant, arresting, and re-charged with significance when provided with contexts which are fresh, contemporary, and relevant.

Imagine, for example, the use of the Negro spiritual "Were You There" in a conventional service whose focus is the Cross and Resurrection of Jesus. It is surrounded with other popular old hymns (popular by *somebody's* measuring stick) such as "Beneath the Cross of Jesus," "There Is a Green Hill Far Away," and "Jesus Christ is Risen Today." The prayers, readings, and sermon all act unilaterally to direct the worshiper's attention back, back, back to the original object of Christian piety and devotion, becoming contemporary only to the extent that the worshiper himself, as a contemporary individual, is beckoned out of his current situation and into the ancient one, becoming united to the Christ of faith. Whatever merit there is in this, the result can be little more than a pietistic one, fortifying the believer for walking insularly in the world outside the sanctu-ary.

But contrast with that the use made of the same hymn, "Were You There," in an Easter liturgy designed by Kent Schneider of the Center for Contemporary Celebration. First, there is a "Liturgy of Death and Despair." There is silence, then a muffled drum roll. A solo voice sings "Were You There," accom-panied by the drum roll. The "Let him be crucified" passage is read from Mark's gospel, with the choir shouting the crowd voices. The community response is a litany, for which Schneider provides this example.

Men have shot out their hatred and killed man.
  (Short news account that documents the above statement.)
  He died for reducing the law to one commandment: Love.
Men murdered a man in angered confusion.
  (News account.)
  He chose the poor, the bums, the outcasts, and told
  the establishment that they were corrupt with lies.

Society released its race hatred and shot a man down.
(Referring to Martin Luther King, Jr.)
He died and we buried him in Atlanta.
A bullet pierced his head and a nation wondered "Why?"
(Referring to the killing of Senator Robert Kennedy)
He died and we buried him near his brother.
Men mocked him and spat on him and beat him.
He died and they buried him in Jerusalem.
Men convicted him and nailed him to a cross.
He died and they buried him in a borrowed tomb.[23]

It is not necessary to go into the succeeding "Liturgy of Announced Life" and "Liturgy of Becoming Life," I think, to
convey the difference in the two settings for the same hymn.
Here, in the latter case, the traditional spiritual becomes electrically related to the whole modern scene of frustration, political murder, and social involvement. The fact that it is a *black*
hymn becomes very important; the particularity of origin
heightens the universal effect of it. And the final stanza, "Were
you there when they raised him from the dead?" (which many
hymnal commissions have seen fit to omit from their printings
today), introduces an irony at the outset which will prove con-
trapuntal throughout the service and finally dominate the
service thematically, with the vision of resurrection and restoration.

As Routley has pointed out, the two pioneers of English musical dissent in the twentieth century, Ralph Vaughan Williams
and Gustav Holst, were as fully concerned for the development
of musical idioms in the past as they were for totally new or
innovative idioms.[24] They realized that the present is built on
the past, and that many modes and styles now apparently lost
to the past still hold latent power to stir people if the musician
can only unleash that power.

Freedom, whether for the artist or the Christian, is always
total, and involves this freedom to borrow from the past whatever will serve the vision of the present. The prejudiced liberal

mind, which cannot bear to hear or see what is traditional, is actually no more liberated than the prejudiced conservative mind that cannot tolerate what is novel or unconventional. The true liberal, the free man in Christ, ranges easily through time (past and present) and space (secular and holy) for whatever materials he requires for his celebration. There are no boundaries; every wall has been broken down.

The sum of the matter is that music itself is freed when we are freed, when we operate out of a sense of man's gathering wholeness, of the restoration of creation among the people of God. We need no longer be "fundamentalists" or "purists" in our approach. We can see that all instruments have been developed as accompaniment to the human voice—and concentrate on singing and whistling and offering rhythmic response. We can accept noise as sound—clapping, clacking, tapping on hymnals. We can see the possibilities of jazz and blues and "pop." We can reject certain formal or poor pieces of music as being "less human" than others. We can let music be what it is—the "deeper, more numinous code"—not "chink-fillers" or "transition pieces" but "the prime expression of human life." We can move to a beat, and abandon ourselves in the feeling of grace. Hopefully we can recover our unity and integrity as persons. As Routley says, "the church's business at worship is to show the whole man to himself, and to call forth the gifts and the responses of the whole man."[25]

The free approach reminds us always that theology, the science of man's thinking about God and revelation and related matters, is itself a very tenuous matter, limited by numerous factors of the human situation, and that the sacrifice of a wholeness in music to some limited perspective of doctrine is an inversion of the proper relationship. Religion is sung, whistled, stamped, danced, clapped, more than it is *thought*. There should exist a precarious balance between the two, of course; but it is essential that thought not prevail always over the ability to vent the emotions rhythmically. When it does the sense of

God becomes dry, brittle, chimerical, not because he is dry and brittle but because we are. As Suzanne Langer has said, music permits us to express ourselves biologically as well as psychologically and mentally.[26] Its wholeness goes beyond that of traditional theology, which has been far more philosophical than biological.

The insistence on an attitude of freedom as an overall principle will likewise govern us in the many small matters raised with regard to music and worship.

The question of congregational ability? A free congregation can happily practice new music *as part of its worship*. Why should practice be relegated to preservice warm-ups or Wednesday night choir sessions? Isn't it part of what the congregation does for God? Ed Summerlin, whom I have mentioned before, is marvelously free and relaxed in leading congregational singing. He will often stop the singing after a verse or two and chide, "Aw, now, you're not doing that very well; let's go back and practice it a minute." And the informality is refreshing after the pseudo-formalism most Protestant congregations have let themselves get boxed into during the years. It is a bit like an orchestra or ensemble's pausing to tune its instruments in the midst of a performance—it is a thoroughly human touch in the middle of everything, a reminder that these are human beings doing something, not machines. Conceivably a leader of music might even take a congregation through a "method" course occasionally, asking the worshipers, using the voice alone and no verbalization, to express sorrow—anger—love—longing—tenderness—strength, etc. It would loosen up personalities for fuller expression—and that too is a part of worship.

The question of solo performers and choirs? Well, again we are free. What is natural in the group and contributes to the overall or comprehensive picture of the worship? Even primitive societies had their superstar dancers and singers who were spotlighted in moments of tribal ceremony—although usually the tribe was doing something at the same time to keep the rhythm going—humming, clapping, swaying, or drumming. Study the audience participation pattern at a popular concert sometime, especially when the audience is young and the performer is an idol: something really passes between the performer and the crowd, something as electric and real as it is indefinable. Again, we are free, and must judge each situation for its contribution to the sense of wholeness among the worshipers participating.

The question of balance between sacred and secular music? It could be depressing to sing and hear nothing but popular music reminding us of what is wrong with the world and how desperate we are to find something better, or music that is stuck precisely where so much church music is, in the motif-categories of fall and trial. Daniel Stevick is right to remind us that there is a kind of "vulgarity, cheapness, or sentimentality" about worship which does not begin and end in God.[27] But here again we are governed by the freedom of the whole. It is the sense of restoration or recovery that we are after, and the expression of fallenness and trial is a necessary part of the total picture. We cannot arrive at a true feeling of integrality until we have seriously addressed the problem of our fragmentation. Although the final mood ought to be one of restoration, there is freedom in the principle of balance and tension.

If we seek a formula as a guideline (and not as a mandate), perhaps this one will be helpful.

> *It is important that music be*
> more than creedal,
> more than functional,
> more than performance by special group
> or individual;
> *that it be*
> self-expression, as total as possible,

whereby
the self is joined to the group,
the group is joined to the world,
and the world is claimed once more as God's.

We recall the famous remark of the Negro matriarch Dilsey in Faulkner's novel *The Sound and the Fury* as she leaves the little church where she had a rapturous experience, that she has seen "de first en de last," the beginning and the end. This is what myth is about and how it works. It has to do with setting one's present condition in the perspective of both a beginning and an ending—of Creation and Restoration. And music, which is deeper and subtler in its effects than either language or logic, plays a vital role—perhaps the most vital single role—in accomplishing that end.

Time/Space

EGO₁: *Axis mundi.*

EGO₂: What's that?

E₁: *Axis mundi*—the center of the world.

E₂: Oh?

E₁: You know. They say that a sacred place, wherever men worship, always becomes the center of the world to them.

E₂: Who says?

E₁: Oh, Durkheim and Eliade and a lot of other people.

E₂: Do you suppose it's so?

E₁: I guess so.

E₂: Why?

E₁: Why what?

E₂: Why is that so? About the center, I mean.

E₁: Psychological. Something happens when you worship. Time and distance are null-and-voided. You are where it's at.

E₂: Run that by again, will you?

E₁: Time—you know, tempus fidgets and all that—time stops. Not only that, it is overcome. Everything is like now, telescoped into the present.

E₂: Like—

E₁: Like Creation, the Fall of Man, the Sufferings of the Faithful, the Trial of the Hero, His Overcoming, His Return in the Future—all of that.

E₂: I'll be darned.

E₁: And space is overcome too. Or at least it's reordered. All lines converge at the altar where the god is worshiped and thought to be present. That's why so many primitive peoples erected poles in worship—because they thought they were marking the center of the earth. Or the center of the universe even.

E₂: I'll be darned.

E₁: What's that?

E₂: Oh, I just said, "I'll be darned."

E$_1$: Why?

E$_2$: I was just thinking.

E$_1$: What about?

E$_2$: About the phrase "time of my life." When I'm having a good time, really enjoying myself, I'm not conscious of time either. How is that related to worship?

E$_1$: I don't know. Huizinga says in *Homo Ludens* that there are obvious similarities between play and ritual, and also between the playground and the holy spot. "The arena, the card-table, the magic circle, the temple, the stage, the screen, the tennis court, the court of justice, etc., are all in form and function play-grounds, i.e. forbidden spots, isolated, hedged round, hallowed, within which special rules obtain. All are temporary worlds within the ordinary world, dedicated to the performance of an act apart."[1]

E$_2$: In other words, I could be playing at worship.

E$_1$: Guardini said it, you didn't.

E$_2$: And there are lots of ways to make space special. Think of the motel where Martin King was shot, or the kitchen where Bobby Kennedy was struck down, or the old home place in the country, or the room where your baby took his first step, or the golf course where you made a hole-in-one, or—

E$_1$: Or Hemingway's Cantwell, in *Across the River and into the Trees,* tracing his way back to the exact spot in Italy where he had been wounded years ago and burying the medal he had received from the Italian government and then defecating on the place.

E₂: Yeah, that too. But that raises another question. What about acts of desecration? We don't really confine the word to the despoiling of sacred places. We use it to describe vandalism in our homes or an irreverent attitude in some public place like the grave of a hero or the halls of Congress.

E₁: Which only underlines the fact that the sacred and the secular are not so clearly separate as we sometimes suppose. The sacredness of a place has something to do with the amount of humanity invested in it. People will swear oaths by their mothers as readily as by altars.

E₂: I remember a statement from Richard Rubenstein's book *Morality and Eros:* "Paris has something no American city possesses, *sacred places.*"²

E₁: That sounds like a lot of bunk to me.

E₂: Me too. I know what he means. It has something to do with a deep sense of history. But I have felt something just as holy in a Shaker meetinghouse in Canterbury, New Hampshire, or in the Transcendentalist house in Harvard, Massachusetts, as anything I ever felt in Our Lady of Paris or St. Germain–des–Prés.

E₁: Right. It's a matter of humanity.

E₂: All life is shot through by the holy. Holiness is a matter of life-intensity.

E_1: That doesn't deter us, though, from designating some places for congregational worship and feeling that they are special because of the group investment there.

E_2: Of course not. Think of Westminster Abbey. It's both— a church and national museum.

E_1: Yes, it focuses the two together and provides a sense of national purpose that is also religious. The jealous theological mind would object to that, I suppose.

E_2: I must confess that something in me grates a bit at the thought of memorial windows and name plaques and the like in church buildings.

E_1: It may be your puritanical background.

E_2: I expect so. I don't like national flags in sanctuaries, either. But I will give the matter some more thought.

E_1: Maybe there is no single way. A Calvinistic purism is all right, but there is an antipurism that is all right too.

E_2: *Anti*purism?

E_1: It isn't a good word, but I mean clutteredness and mixedness. There is a place for the cluttered sanctuary in our society too. Certainly there are private homes of both kinds, some severe and some cluttered.

E_2: I suppose so. Pluralism is big these days. Justus Dahinden, in his book on church architecture, praises what he calls "a lively diversity within the global unity."[3]

E₁: I've read Dahinden.'I think he's a very sensible fellow.

E₂: So do I—especially in his insistence on the incorporation of local cultures and traditions in church buildings.

E₁: That is another way of saying what I said before: it is the amount of humanity invested in something that really makes it holy.

E₂: He is especially pleased with recent church architecture in Africa which annexes the shape of the native hut as a major design feature. And he also notes that it has reorganized the inner space of church buildings to make room for tribal dancing around the altar.

E₁: Beautiful! The memory of the worshipers must be twofold: it must recall both their past and the past of the Hebraic-Christian faith. The two must somehow be viewed as concentric, not as antithetical. Otherwise the people cannot "locate" themselves in time and space. They become schizoid, and their faith is something apart from life.

E₂: Sometimes I think that is what is wrong with Didi and Gogo in Beckett's *Waiting for Godot.* They can't locate themselves any more because they can't remember accurately. Many things they say are *reminiscent* of meaningful times and places, but so vaguely so that they cannot imbue the present time and place with significance or hope.

E₁: Right. Even the withered tree by the road is obviously descended from Ygdrasil or the Tree of Life, and is related to the Cross. But lacking the cultic memory, the tramps can't lay hold of this. They are locked in a recurrent present which is a kind of hell to them because it can make no use of the past or the future to break through to what Eliade calls "sacred time."

E_2: Sometimes I know how they feel. I have this sense of being caught in a "time between the times"—a time when the past is shut off to me and the future is too uncertain to mean anything.

E_1: What about your religion at such times?

E_2: That's the point. It doesn't help. I go to church and feel like some kind of intruder, an interloper who is unable to share the vision of the past it represents.

E_1: You're like Jake Barnes in *The Sun Also Rises?*

E_2: Sorry.

E_1: He went into a cathedral to pray and couldn't. He said he guessed he was just a "rotten Catholic." Actually it was the war The war had made the cathedral seem out of date or something. It didn't apply any more.

E_2: Yes. I share that inability to feel involved. The cruciform on the Communion table or chancel wall is as meaningless to me as Didi and Gogo's tree is to them.

E_1: What do you think would help?

E_2: I don't know. Sometimes I think a radically new kind of church building might improve things. One that didn't have CHURCH written all over it the way most of them do now, with their rectangular arrangement and orderly pews and predictable chancels and muted colors.

E₁: But that is the "past" you said Didi and Gogo need.

E₂: No, I don't think so. Not really That is one past, but it is a very limited past. The altar may be different. You can't go further back than an altar. Maybe what I want is a free situation where we start with the roots again— the indispensable altar—and work out from that with less responsibility to the other parts of our architectural traditions.

E₁: Aha! Now you are speaking like a modern architect. Reduced to its bare essentials, a church is "a building to house a congregation gathered round an altar."[4] "Table, space and walls make up the simplest church."[5] You are unhappy with the old arrangements of space. They do not help you to enter into sacred time.

E₂: What I think I would like is a church building designed like Saarinen's TWA terminal at Kennedy Airport in New York—on a more modest scale, of course. Something wildly expressive of today in its use of prestressed materials and plastic shaping of space, and at the same time reminiscent of the contours of caves and meadows and prehistoric natural settings.

E₁: Do you know the new churches of Europe?

E₂: Some of them. Corbusier's chapel at Ronchamp, the Kaiser Wilhelm Memorial Church in Berlin, Coventry Cathedral—

E₁: How do you feel in them?

E₂: It varies. Corbusier's chapel is wonderful. There is something about the way the light enters and intersects itself from those irregular windows that says to the visitor, "This is no ordinary place." You feel an instinctive excitement there. Still, it is a *pilgrimage* chapel. It adorns a hilltop. It is good for what it was meant for but it is almost *too* different from the world I live in at the bottom of the hill.

E₁: What of Coventry?

E₂: Coventry confuses me. Its details are often exquisite—the glass etchings at the entrance, the stunning window behind the rock font, the tapestry of the Pantocratic Christ, the Crown of Thorns chapel. But somehow it fails to integrate my feelings, to help me to be more whole.

E₁: Hammond, you know, says it is not really modern except in techniques. Its form is essentially that of a medieval cathedral.[6]

E₂: Yes, I can see that, and I think I agree. It is gorgeous, but it does not induce the kind of feeling of worship I need. I do react positively to the charred cross in the ruins of the old sanctuary, however; that is a remarkable symbol of the faith that triumphs through flames and bombs.

E₁: I believe it is Hammond also who points out that the great simplicity of many recent European church buildings was dictated in part by the relative poverty of the congregations after the war.[7] The people simply could not afford the costlier traditional forms.

E₂: Providential, I'd say. There is something out of character about big cathedrals in our day. People can regard the passing of the age of faith, which was usually identified with the erection of enormous, ornate buildings, as the onset of an era of spiritual and architectural inferiority. But I personally agree with Theodor Filthaut, who says that "simplicity is not a sign of impotency but of meaningful expression."[8]

E_1: That is what Hammond says. He views the chapels at Ronchamp and Eveux as being "two of the most completely satisfying churches built in any country since the war," and says that each is distinguished by a marked quality of "simplicity and silence and poverty."[9] And a little further on he identifies this as a sign of the renewed artistic integrity of church architecture.

E_2: Certainly that is what I have been talking about. Too many of our churches look as if the architect has been warned against the free play of his spirit in designing a building. Consequently, unless he is an independent person who will not be argued down in such matters, he compromises his integrity and turns out a bastard of a building which says nothing very meaningful about either the past or the present.

E_1: Will you forgive me one more reference to Hammond, and then I will promise not to refer to him again?

E_2: Of course.

E_1: He is so indispensable in these matters. He says: "Sacred art must do far more than provoke an aesthetic or emotional *frisson*. Its function is to make manifest under the form of sign and symbol the presence of the New Creation—that new order of reality which entered into the cosmos as the fruit of Christ's strange work. The decay of sacred art into religious art, a language of energetic symbols into a mawkish sentimentality, is symptomatic of a growing blindness: the transformation of contemplation and communion into aestheticism. As André Malraux has written: 'The great Christian art did not die because all possible forms had been used up: it died because faith was being transformed into piety.' "[10]

E_2: I—

E_1: One moment, I am almost through. To pour money and effort into the attempt to infuse new vitality into symbolic forms which have lost all meaning and reference, says Hammond, is a pathetic waste. If the church is a solid piece of good architectural design, the symbolism will take care of itself. Bad churches not only ruin our sense of aesthetics, they obscure the very nature of the church.[11]

E_2: I was just going to applaud what I seemed to be hearing about the relationship of Christianity to newness or novelty. It reminded me of what Erik Routley said about the music of the Billy Graham campaigns, which he calls "Sankey music"—it depends on clichés, both verbally and lyrically, to manipulate people, and does not engage in the true spirit of exploration and novelty which characterizes the ongoing New Creation of Christ in the world.[12] The same characterizations can be applied to architecture.

E_1: Yes, you are right, without doubt. But now let's take a slightly different tack. You have expressed your sense of discomfort or alienation in most traditional church buildings, and we have talked about what some of the figures in new church design are saying. Let's suppose for a moment that *you* were going to design a church. What kind of place would it be?

E₂: That's an embarrassing question. I'm no architect.

E₁: I realize that, and shall make allowances for it. But let your mind react freely, and just tell me what you are thinking.

E₂: I am thinking you're a son of a—

E₁: Seriously, now.

E₂: Well, I confess that I have thought of it some. But you will think my ideas foolish.

E₁: No, I promise.

E₂: What I have been thinking is that the old church architecture, with its spires and towers and vaulted ceilings and so on, was designed in response to a Ptolemaic universe in which heaven was up there over our heads. Now the emphasis is different. We don't even know where up is—it's all relative. The only directions now are inward and outward. Man himself is a symbol of these directions —he is introverted and he is extroverted. I think the symbolism of church building could embody this change.

E₁: The real currents to be symbolized would be centripetal and centrifugal, not up and down?

E₂: Yes, in a way. And I think the predominance might be given to the centripetal movement. We come to church to discover how to be integrated, to experience whole-ness, unity, oneness; then we are sent out to be the church in diaspora.

E₁: But what of the idea that we should come to church to *bring* our worship, not to *get* something?

E₂: I think that is a pietistic delusion. Nobody I have ever known really consistently went to church because he had enjoyed God's presence in the world and wanted to honor him by going to the place of worship—not for that reason only. But most of the persons I talk to say they go because they are looking for something. Maybe they are wrong to do this. I won't debate the theology or the spirituality of it. But that's the way it is.

E₁: I'm not sure I agree with you. But continue with your notion of a "centripetal" design. What would it look like?

E₂: Well, I have even thought that it might do just the oppo-site of what a traditional building does, which some poet whose name I can't recall described as "yearning for the sky." Space is limitless and, except for our sun, nondirec-tional. Our real direction then, on a radius with the sun, must be either toward the sun or away from it.

E₁: And—

E₂: And I think I would like to see a church designed in the shape of a hornet's nest or a cocoon, burrowing into the ground toward the center of the earth and the geograph-ical center of mankind.

E₁: In Freudian terms, that would suggest a womb.

E₂: Yes, I am aware of that, but do not regard that characterization negatively. Baptism itself is a womb symbol. We recover ourselves by retreating to the womb—rediscover who we are, what our sources are, and how we enter the world.

E₁: But aren't you disregarding the important symbolism of light that way? Bruggink and Schwarz have both observed that church architecture depends on Christ's characterizations of himself and his followers,[13] and the metaphor of light figures prominently in those characterizations.

E₂: Perhaps we must sacrifice one motif or metaphor for another. And remember that I am not designing *all* churches, but only one, and one for my own needs at that.

E₁: Continue.

E₂: I am not sure that daylight is that important to churches now. Perhaps it once was. But many persons now work in offices with only artificial light. It may be a romanticism to suppose that the worship of the church must be identified with sunlight. Besides, the early Christians at Rome worshiped in catacombs, and the medieval cathedrals were not designed to bring light in but to display colorful designs, which we can now do electrically.

E₁: I can see a similarity between your "burrowing church" and the catacombs.

E₂: Yes. And I do not think it beyond reason to say that it might be good for us to enter such a "womb," with its

plain, simple, stucco walls, and worship by candlelight.
There is something far more mystical about darkness
and candlelight than there is about bright lights.

E_1: Perhaps, though do not forget your characterization of
the light in the chapel at Ronchamp. But we have got
your geometrical design in mind now—and I concede
that it is somewhat appropriate as an apocalyptic or eschatological symbol in an age when mankind is threatened by nuclear and pollutive death. What would the
interior be like?

E_2: My mind is not settled about that. I only have some ideas.
For one thing, I would not like traditional pews, which
hamper the activity of the worshipers.

E_1: Hammond says they turn worship into a spectator
sport.[14]

E_2: You promised!

E_1: I'm sorry. I couldn't help it.

E_2: I wasn't serious. Maybe the center of the sanctuary could
be sunken, like a sunken living room, with succeeding
stages or tiers which, if carpeted, would be quite suitable
for seating. The table, or altar, could be in the very
center, in the most depressed area, with the congregation arranged conically around it.

E_1: What about the pulpit? You know, word *and* sacra-
ment?

E_2: I think it might be left out. The ministers could sit near

the table and speak when necessary. But their place-
ment *with* the congregation would say something basic
about our new theology of the ministry.

E₁: May I suggest an alternative to your seating provisions?

E₂: Surely.

E₁: I was thinking of the little Theatre Rochechouart in
Paris, which accommodates only 60 or 70 persons. The
size is immaterial to the design, however. The seats are
in the center, and revolve, with stages built all the way
around the room. The audience merely turns individu-
ally to concentrate on the part of the action it wants to
take in. It is a highly effective arrangement.

E₂: Yes, I can imagine its usefulness in a church which employed multimedia equipment as a regular part of its
worship. Maybe you saw the pictures of San Francisco's
Glide Memorial Church in *Holiday* magazine a few
months ago, with its specially equipped basement room
and projectors for flashing slides and movies on the walls
around the people lying on pillows in the center. That
offers some real possibilities. It is similar to what Milton
Cohen of the University of Michigan calls "Space
Theatre," whose heart or core is "a system of rotating,
adjustable mirrors and prisms that can project light,
slides, or motion picture images in any direction—either
onto a dome or onto screens surrounding and above the
spectators."¹⁵

E₁: Multimedia raises some real questions about the nature
of worship. Some people object to it as being manipulative in the way the old evangelism was.

E₂: I know. Harvey Cox has an interesting notion in *The Feast of Fools*, though. He says that there are similarities between the absolute plainness of the monk's cell and the sensory overload of combined film, light, and sound techniques today. Each is a way of blowing the mind.[16]

E₁: You're gonna kill me for this.

E₂: For what?

E₁: All this discussion about Glide Memorial and Space Theatre and blowing the mind keeps drawing me back to something else Hammond said.

E₂: What now?

E₁: Well, actually he didn't say it. He was quoting some principles of theater architecture laid down by Walter Gropius. One of them was that "there must be 'no separation between stage and auditorium.' The architect must use 'all possible spatial means capable of shaking the spectator out of his lethargy, of surprising and assaulting him and obliging him to take a real, living interest in the play.' "[17]

E₂: That sounds very much like the dramatic advice of Antonin Artaud, who insisted that every means possible be marshaled into the task of making the theater-goer respond and overcome the inertia binding him to habitual ways of seeing and hearing and thinking.

E₁: It is also like Brecht, although Brecht came later. But it is interesting to observe, isn't it, how the need for spatial

H

reconsiderations in both theater and church parallel the
need for theoretical reconception in both.

E_2: Yes. The contemporary dramatic sense demands the
shift from traditional proscenium-arch theater to thea-
ter-in-the-round, wrap-around theater, living theater,
environmental theater, etc.; and the contemporary religious consciousness requires a similar shift from the rectangular cathedral, where the "action" took place in
front, to a more intimate, circular arrangement bringing
people face to face and eliminating the nonparticipa-
tional aspects of the old method.

E_1: Some proponents of new church architecture don't advocate church-in-the-round, of course. I'm thinking
especially of Jean-Philippe Ramseyer's *Word and Image*,
in which he contends that the rectangle better symbolizes the church *on its way* to something because it is like
an autobus, with the pulpit and table along the way and
not at the end.

E_2: That's all right with me. I don't expect that everyone
should feel as I do about the form of the building. But I
can't escape the suspicion that you put us onto something significant by injecting the theater reference. I can
imagine my round sanctuary now with plain white walls
capable of receiving projected images or colors all
around and helping us to overcome our verbal impasse
in worship. I'm all for getting beyond our linguistic
hang-ups. I think we need a period of sensory stimulation just to help our bodies catch up with our minds
again, so that we worship as whole persons.

E_1: What do you think about using the sanctuary for purposes other than worship?

E₂: What do you mean?

E₁: Like the room at Canterbury House described in Bloy's *Multi-Media Worship*, which is not reserved for so-called sacred purposes at all. Sometimes it is used for marriages, sometimes for arguments, sometimes for poetry readings, sometimes for lunches, sometimes for dances. Howard Moody says it is the same at his church, Judson Memorial, in New York City: "In our own church the place where we worship is not a 'sanctuary' in the traditional Protestant, churchy sense, nor a place set aside and sanctified for religious rites and acts, but a place made holy by human happenings of every kind. It is a *meeting room* in the fullest and most extensive sense of that word."[18]

E₂: I have mixed emotions about that. Logically—with my mind—I agree with the principle. I believe that "human happenings" do sacralize space. One of us said as much in the beginning of this conversation. But there is something deep inside me, stemming from a sense of reverence I felt as a boy entering a sanctuary where nothing but worship was allowed, which still longs for that special regard for the place where the congregation assembles. I doubt if I will ever be able to work through this visceral reaction in such a way as never to feel it again, even though with my mind I agree that mere spatial reservation does not make a place of worship.

E₁: It is the Communion meal, not the table it sits on, that is important; and behind that it is Christ, not the meal, that is important.

E₂: Yes, there are levels of symbol. Yet we attach meaning

to each successively lower level because of our feeling for the one above it. I remember the sense of outrage I felt as a high-school student when I saw another student idly sitting on a Communion table, kicking his legs. He meant no harm, and I am sure it would not have occurred to him that he was desecrating anything holy. He really wasn't. But my concern for Christ and the meal had descended also to the table.

E₁: Which says that there is often a lot of emotional involvement in issues like this.

E₂: That's right. And it suggests the importance of iconoclasm, of always being critical of ourselves for the attachments our minds effect to things and forms, lest we end by revering objects and methods more than Christ and other persons.

E₁: We have spoken at some length of space in worship, and have paid only minimal attention to time. Is there more we should say about that?

E₂: Maybe we have said more about it than we realized.

E₁: How is that?

E₂: I mean, there is a sense in which the proper architecture permits men to enter the kind of temporary timelessness that is sacred time. You enter the sanctuary with a congregation, and it is a time apart, a time cut off from the flow of life, diverted, detoured, or what have you.

E₁: Yes, I can see that. But time is a matter of more than what happens in the sanctuary. You remember, Gregory

Dix, in his great book *The Shape of the Liturgy,* discussed the medieval system of hours and prayers as an elaborate attempt to sanctify time itself and make all of life holy for man.[19]

E₂: I see. You mean rhythm and cycle and things like that. The way sacred space helps to sanctify all space.

E₁: Right. I'm asking *when* we should come into the church, and how we should dispose ourselves toward time when we are *not* in the church, and that sort of thing.

E₂: Gosh, I don't know. There is so much involved. I do think there have been sensible suggestions to the effect that the whole calendar of Christian worship ought to be reconceived today allowing for the discrepancies between our way of life and that of our more rurally and agriculturally situated forebears.

E₁: Some people would never hear to that, would they?

E₂: I don't know. There is certainly precedent for such adaptation. The early Hebrews doubtless adjusted their special festivals to coincide with the seasonal celebrations of the Canaanites. And Christmas and Easter are both "accommodating" dates, marking the combination of Christian festivals with more primitive observances.

E₁: What sort of "rhythm" do you see in the life of technological man?

E₂: Well, for one thing, there are obvious differences in the length of his work week. If you have been on the freeway on a Friday or Sunday afternoon, you know what a tidal wave of humanity ebbs and flows by that pattern these days. When we go to a four-day work week, as we doubtless shall one of these days, many people will in effect have two half-weeks, one for work and the other for leisure.

E_1: That word leisure is deceptive.

E_2: Yes, it is. Most people exhaust themselves more "enjoying leisure" than they do working. What I was going to suggest is that there are, or will be, *two* beginnings each week, not one as in an agricultural situation—one to start the work-life and one to start the play-life.

E_1: Which means—

E_2: —that Sunday morning, which breaks into the play-life, may not be the most appropriate time to worship—not if worship celebrates and reinforces the rhythms of human existence.

E_1: I know a church that tried Sunday afternoon services, at 5:30, and found them very agreeable to most of the congregation.

E_2: That is the sort of change I had in mind. A congregation could operate on a Thursday-night/Sunday-afternoon axis and perhaps do more to sanctify the week's rhythm than it does now.

E_1: I seem to have gotten into the role of straight man here, but what does this do to the notion of a Sabbath Day or Lord's Day?

E_2: I'm not sure it matters. The Lord's Day was never a holiday for the early Christians anyway. The combina-

tion of Sabbath and Lord's Day was apparently a rather
late invention, and never really took hold in some parts
of Europe. And now even the puritanical Lord's Day/-
Sabbath has broken down as an institution. What really
matters in the cultic observance of a day of rest is that
the faithful enjoy the repose which enables them to con-
template God and renew themselves spiritually and
physically.

E₁: I get it. If the church does its job of reminding its members of the holiness of life *all* the time, they will rest as
they go and really sanctify time by remembering God
and their brothers.

E₂: That is essentially what I was driving at. Jesus was con-
temptuous of a legalistic sabbath. He understood what
the sanctification of time is about. It's about the sanctification of *life*. We are not stuck with a particular rhythm
of worship, but are free to adapt to the genuine rhythms
of life.

E₁: Good. If I can shake the straight man's image for a second, I'll make a contribution. I have just recalled seeing
a prepublication draft of the pamphlet called *The
Church at Worship in an Urban Age*,[20] and realize that
something which was omitted from the final publication
was an interesting calendar of Christian festivals based
on the rhythm of the secular year in our time. It outlined
someone's thinking about the principle seasonal modes
or undulations in our collective being—things like the
return to school in September, the preparations for
Christmas, the beginning of a new year, the paying of
federal taxes, and the coming of spring and summer.
Then it proposed that we observe the following festivals:
in September, a Festival of Learning; in December, a

Festival of Expectation and a Festival of Giving and Love; in January, a Festival of Discovery (corresponding with Epiphany); in February or March, a Festival of Honesty and Self-Examination; in April, a Festival of New Life; and in May, a Festival of Courage and Power.

E_2: That sounds exciting. And it would be a far more open representation of ourselves than we currently present in our festivals. Ministers now spend half their sermon time trying to explain how our festivals are related to the way we live and think.

E_1: It would be helpful, wouldn't it, to worship in contemporary structures according to the rhythms and patterns of contemporary life?

E_2: Indeed it would. Then maybe we could really play at worship and let ourselves go, without always stopping to think what the significance of this or that is, or how we translate from one liturgical milieu into another.

E_1: I thought of one other thing we haven't mentioned that pertains to our subject: vestments.

E_2: *Quoi?* I don't follow your thinking.

E_1: Clothing has always been of great significance to ritual and religion—the primitive mask, the painted face or body, the holy garment, the head-covering, the sacred belt or sash—

E_2: —and washing the hands or feet—

E_1: Yes, that too. But I'm thinking that a special garment— perhaps a simple stole—would enhance the feeling of "apartness" for a person entering a sanctuary or saying prayers in a special place.

E₂: You mean something for all the worshipers, and not just the ministers?

E₁: Yes. The farmer or laborer used to do something like this when he put on his "Sunday-go-to-meeting" clothes. Because he worked in simple clothing all week, this marked special occasions for him. Maybe we all need something symbolic to signal our preparation for worship.

E₂: *Sartor resartus* and all that.

E₁: *Sartor resartus?*

E₂: Yeah, you know. Carlyle. Clothes philosophy.

E₁: Oh.

E₂: And by the way—

E₁: Yes?

E₂: No more *axis mundi*. Okay?

Metaworship

ONE OF THE things made increasingly clear by the enormous changes in the world in the last twenty years is the fact that many of the religious truths we said we believed in are both less true and more true than we had thought. They are less true in that our understanding of them had been too narrowly and parochially defined. They are more true in that we now see them to be particular and necessarily distorted versions of truth that are universal and held in other particular and distorted forms by all men.

While it is impossible to say whether all faiths will ever evolve into a satisfactory unilateral expression to which believers everywhere can give common assent, it is not at all uncommon any more for theologians to hold, as Nels Ferré does in *The Universal Word*, that revelation is "not only interfaith but ahead of all faiths and traditions."[1] Hans Küng, perhaps the most famous Roman Catholic scholar in the world today, has vigorously denounced the ancient statement that "there is no salvation outside the Church,"[2] and the Constitution on the Church adopted by the second Vatican Council on November 21, 1964 explicitly states that God is not "far distant from those who in shadows and images seek the unknown God."[3] We are obviously approaching an era "beyond belief," to use Robert Bellah's words, when particularities of dogma and doctrine will no longer blind us so completely to the intrinsic value in all venerable religious systems.

One highly esteemed Protestant minister has put it this way in a recent book.

It comes as no surprise to you, I am sure, but I never did think my crowd of Christians would take over the world. Our leaders said we aimed to "win the world," but we never went at it as if we meant it, and besides: we were always too few, too poor, too local, and too easy to join. And now, thirty years out in some kind of service to the Christian faith, with an acquaintance among hundreds of pastors and a score of major denominations, I would say the same of any other crowd of Christians I know. We are all too local, too little, and too proud. It is not our day to rule or to win —not yet. And Christendom, with its present forms and frames, has about run out its string. In spite of the fact that Christendom never did look like, or represent, its great Christ too well, or for long, it still trails behind it clouds of iridescent beauty, sacrifice, noble intentions, beautiful martyrs, legends, liturgies, and memories of days when we almost took over some culture or other. And there are pockets of the faithful left to celebrate a day that never came, clusters of raisins dried on the vine, and waiting expectantly the new grapes that do not appear. But now we can see and say, with all that behind us: *something new is coming.* The makings of a new faith are all around us.[4]

Something new is coming! McLuhan's "global village" has caught up with us, and with a vengeance. Suddenly we find ourselves cheek-by-jowl with whole continents of people we could once ignore, and the pressures of their histories, cultures, and beliefs are upon us like the weight of an entire planet, threatening to break or crush everything we think or believe about human existence unless we listen to them too. No wonder some have shrieked and shivered and pulled the blankets tighter. Change is always threatening, especially when there is no way to avoid it.

But maybe it came just in time, when what we had—if those

broken bits of liturgy in *Waiting for Godot* are any kind of evidence at all—had become too remote and desiccated to save us from our boredom on one hand and our illusions on the other. Maybe the very thing that threatens to destroy us is also a way out of our destruction—a birth at the same time that it is a death.

Huston Smith, without saying as much, makes this point over and over again in *The Religions of Man.* Is Western man exhausted by his commitment to industry and technology, so that in the very moment when he has achieved the greatest physical comfort in the history of man he is moved to inquire, plaintively, "Is that all?"?

> This is the moment Hinduism has been waiting for. As long as a person is content with the prospects of pleasure, success, or dutiful living, the Hindu sage will not be likely to disturb him beyond offering some suggestions as to how to proceed toward these goals more effectively. The critical point in life comes when these things lose their original charm and one finds oneself wishing that life had something more to offer. Whether life does or does not hold more is probably the question which divides men more sharply than any other.
>
> The Indic answer to this question is unequivocal. Life definitely holds other possibilities.[5]

Our young, tutored in the Christianity of their fathers, have turned to the East for help; and what they have found is our own tradition of no-saying. "What shall it profit a man?" It was there all the time, of course, but we had ceased to notice it. It had not fully occurred to us, apparently, in this critical moment when our environment is about to become poisoned beyond our ability to continue in it, that we had the resources within our own religious background to say, "If that is the way it is, then we must repent and deny ourselves more automobiles and chemical plants and other instruments of pollution; we must decrease in order to make amends to the creation we have

offended." But finding a similar tradition of self-denial in Buddhism or Hinduism reinforces the memory of our own tradition
and restores our nerve.

Is Western man baffled by the illusory nature of human
existence? Is nothing what it seems? Kafka's world is unsettling to most of us, products of the plain, matter-of-fact Romanesque way of transacting business in the market place.
We simply do not know how to operate in a chimerical universe. We are practical people, and proud of it. But the
world is no longer always practical. And again our religion is
not always as helpful as we might wish it were, for we have
imparted our practicality to it. One reason we have been
able to develop elaborate theologies of the Word is that we
have trusted in words and reason. Only now words and reason seem to count for less; we are onto something deeper.

We turn to the East—to Tao and Ch'an and Zen, and the
traditions of waiting, musing, pondering. We remember
Chuang Tsu's story of the man who dreamed he was a butterfly and when he awoke didn't know whether he was a
man dreaming he was a butterfly or a butterfly dreaming he
was a man. We recall the great art of the Chinese, and how
some of the paintings were made a stroke at a time with
perhaps a stroke a day or a stroke a year, depending on how
long the artist had to wait to "know" how to make it. Man's
part in the vastness of the nature he paints is so small, as
Huston Smith says, that we have to look hard in the picture
to find him.

Usually he is climbing with his bundle, riding a buffalo, or poling a boat—man with his journey to make, his burden to carry,
his hill to climb, his glimpse of beauty through the parting
mists. He is not as formidable as a mountain; he does not live
as long as a pine; yet he too belongs in the scheme of things as
surely as the birds and the clouds. And through him as though
the rest of the world flows the rhythmic movement of *Tao*.[6]

Man is small and short-lived, but he is part of a harmonious whole. As the Zen master Joka put it:

> One moon, and one only
> Is reflected in all waters.
> All moons in the water
> Are one with the One moon.[7]

Illusion. *Maya* is the old Sanskrit word for it—much older than the Latin *ludus*, or "play," from which our word is derived. The East has lived with it longer.

Maybe the discovery of this will remind us again of the *Easternness* of our own backgrounds of faith—of the inscrutable Jew who, according to one story, knelt and dawdled in the sand when the Pharisees brought to him a woman taken in adultery, and who was dumb "like a lamb before his shearers is dumb" when they nailed him to a cross—and will enable us to find new levels, new depths of life and meaning, in our own heritage. It is possible that our Western activism has betrayed us into misjudgments and misunderstandings about the teachings of Christianity, and that "new light from the Orient" will help us to restudy and reinterpret our origins.

And as for the problem of God-language in our day, which has so exercised the philosophers and theologians and perplexed the average man, isn't the exhaustion of speech about the deity primarily the exhaustion of speech or logic itself when it comes to talking about the "really real" or the "ultimately ultimate"? What has happened to our sense of humor? The Zen fondness for *koans*, or problems, is to the point: What is the sound of one hand clapping? What is the meaning of zero? How far is out? The student of Zen meditates endlessly on these problems, coming frequently to check his answers with a master. The mind is freed to travel; mere rationalism is transcended. It is little wonder that a favorite saying among Zen masters is this one: "Those who say do not know; those who know do not say." Or, as it is expressed in Saraha's *Treasury of Songs:*

The whole world is tormented by words
And there is no one who does without words
But in so far as one is free from words
Does one really understand words.[8]

One senses here a freedom from the bonds of reason, a willingness to approach life as poetry, to allow the whole being of man
to contribute to intuitive solutions for the seemingly insoluble
problems. It does not negate the uses of logic, but it does remind
us that there are some things for which logic is unsuitable. And
Christians, who are prone to be dogmatic, need to be reminded.
We can learn from the antique East, where our brief history
glimmers like a tiny firefly at the edge of a deep forest.

All of which is to say that religion is never so effete as the
committed secularist has convinced himself that it is today.
Particular manifestations of it may appear barren, but the
sterility is likely to lie in the interpretation of them and not in
the religion itself. It is important for Christians to get beyond
their pride and ignorance to discover what Joseph Campbell
calls "the fundamental unity of the spiritual history of mankind."[9] Then the Christian experience, related as it already is
to the Indo-European basin and Judaism, Zoroastrianism, Islam,
and the Greek mystery cults, will absorb new life through its
own root system. We are far too inclined to treat it as one of the
class of parasites which feed ever outward to the air beyond
instead of as a religion with its origins imbedded solidly in the
fertile ground of past understanding and wisdom.

Many artists, writers, and psychologists of the West began as
much as a century ago to look to the East for the resuscitation
of our increasingly brittle and self-conscious civilization. Justus
Dahinden, in his book on architecture, notes that the same was
true with regard to Africa: "It is well known that Matisse, Klee
and Picasso were inspired by African fetishes and that Gauguin
chose for his subjects tropical motifs. Modigliani received many
ideas from naive primitive art of Cameroun, and Nolde saw

African figures of 'supreme beings' in his abstract images."[10] It was evident that the industrialized society of the West, superior as it was in technical advantages, carried in certain ways the seeds of its own destruction, and that one antidote, for many sensitive persons, was the recovery of something timeless from the cultures as yet untouched by the "blessings" of our way of life—or, as Melville liked to put it, of "snivelization." These persons realized instinctively that the end of an epoch does not in any wise mean the end of man. Civilizations flourished and fell in the East many centuries before Christ. The secret was to discover the unchanging below the surface of the changing, the permanent in the midst of the transitory.

It is a denial of our times, as well as of the spirit of God, to refuse the gifts of other cultures and religions to our own. One might almost call it a manifestation of the *Thanatos*-instinct—of the will to die, stubbornly and perversely, when life is at hand. Admittedly it is hard to exchange life-styles and move from a provincialism of the first magnitude to the idea of "one world" or "global village" overnight. Yet that is almost what is required. By the end of this century, those of us who are still alive will probably look back upon this present year as an age of great darkness and superstition. Events are rushing us along that swiftly.

Not that we shall convert to some huge monoreligion over-night. That is not the point. A true overview of cultures never works that way; it always results in a cherishing of the particular in the midst of the universal. The sensitive traveler savors what is unique in each locale. He compares it with what is unique in his own, carries home recipes, cloth, and garden hints, and in the end is more appreciative of the culture he knew in the beginning. When Noel King tells us of a lake in Ghana which is so holy to Akan fishermen that they will not set oars in it to propel their tree-trunk rafts, but paddle them with their hands and feet,[11] we do not suddenly give up oars and outboard motors. Instead, we feel a deeper sense of reverence for our own holy places, and remember with a sense of affection the high quotient of humanity involved in every religious discipline. "All we can do," says Huston Smith, "is try to listen, carefully and with full attention, to each voice in turn as it is raised to the divine."[12] That is our program, our agenda, already defined for us. It is a matter of a greater ecumenism—a larger household of God—than we have been accustomed to dealing with. It makes our more limited ecumenical efforts, our attempts to hear and understand one another within the Christian religion itself, appear a little feeble and laughable. But the promise of such an experience, if we can have it, is almost beyond our imaginations.

The promise for Christian worship is especially staggering. Consider some of the practices common to a number of religions other than our own which may either deepen our understanding for our own practices or represent febrile possibilities for innovative directions in liturgical development: circumambulation of the holy place, ceremonial cleansing, the wearing of special garments for worship, the presentation of highly personalized gifts, the use of bodily prostration as a sign of humility, extended meditation, reverence for the dead, making pilgrimages to hallowed places, etc. The world is full of rich and meaningful ways to express the humility of man, the wonder of the universe, the miracle of life, the care of God, and the relationship of the temporal to the eternal. There is no reason for Christian liturgy to exist in a self-created ghetto and not discover the resources for the imagination in other traditions.

I remember a friend's description once of the effect upon him of seeing a Zen monk in Japan standing, in the early morning hours, in a narrow gorge where a little waterfall descended. His feet were planted widely on a big stone and he was looking upward, receiving the torrent of icy water straight in the face. Others standing nearby testified that the monk had been there in that position all night. "Imagine how I feel now," said my friend, "when I go to church to pray and remember that fellow.

I think of him standing there in that chilly water all night, and then I think of myself and my halfhearted efforts at prayer and meditation. He really believed. He was really committed. And, what's more, I imagine that his whole way of life was integrated by that fact."

What if my friend were to carry over into his own religion something of the power of concentration he beheld in that monk? Even without the Zen philosophy it would be meaningful. I find it interesting that his own worship is now haunted by the vision of the monk. It is almost a symbolic confrontation between East and West, a token reminder of what we can learn from the East. Not that we don't have such things in our own past, for we do; there are obvious relationships between many of the great mystical writings of the Middle Ages, such as the anonymous *Cloud of Unknowing*, and the meditative philosophies of the Orient. But, as Winston King observes in *Buddhism and Christianity*, any kind of mystical tradition is essentially foreign to most Christians today, even their own.[13] And it may be a shorter road to the East today than it is to medieval history.

There are particularities in each tradition, as I have said, which obviously should not and cannot be overridden or elided. Rudolf Otto, after speaking of the "fundamental kinship" of all religions, warned us against mere "mingling and confusing" or "whittling away and artificial adjustments" among them. Despite all the analogies and resemblances among them, he said, "the parable of the prodigal son cannot be transliterated into the Gita, nor the Bhakti-Yoga into the Koran, nor the Fatiha into the New Testament without committing excruciating offences against style."[14]

But the other traditions do enlighten and enliven our understanding of our own and suggest ways of drawing more creatively on the unexploited resources we already have. As Robert Lawson Slater says, the man who looks upon the meeting of various religions today may well regard it as "a bewildering clash of opinions and folkways" of which he has already seen quite enough within the boundaries of his own faith.

But if he sees it as a coming together, not just of religions in the abstract, but of believers, each with his own partial testimony to that which constrains man to pursue the adventure of faith, he may be led to consider more deeply the terms of this same adventure in his own case, the strength of its call, the invitation to life in all its fullness, life bordered and invaded by Eternity and constantly challenged thereby to new vision, new resolution, new courage.[15]

If we need a special term for this new concept of religion and worship, we can perhaps coin one on the analogy of Lionel Abel's title for a book on drama[16] and call it *metaworship.* That is, it participates in all the old forms which previously characterized it, and yet, because of its awareness of other forms which impinge upon it from other religions and philosophies, subtly changing its consciousness, it is more than the old worship. It has gained an aesthetic distance on itself, a new perspective which is both inner and outer, that causes it to transcend itself and be both the same and more than it was.

The "more than it was" may have been caught by Dom Aelfred Graham in his absorbing book *Zen Catholicism,* which explores the real affinities between the two religions and the possibility of their being united in an individual worshiper.[17] Somewhat in advance of the current emphasis on a theology of play, Graham devoted an entire chapter to "The Importance of Not Being Earnest," and said, in effect, that one result of bridging two or more religions is the ability to be "in earnest" without being "earnest," to regard worship as something which man seriously plays at. We do not abandon our interest in particular forms of worship when we become aware of similar forms in other religions; on the contrary, we newly perceive them as mere forms, as humanly designed ways of demonstrating our concern for ultimate matters, and are thereby freed from concentration on the forms to concentrate on the thing they are trying to express. It is like the Buddhist saying about words, that one understands them only when he is freed from them. Worship assumes a new prospect and character for us when we have been liberated from the methods by which we had pursued it. We are finally enabled, harkening back to Guardini and Neale and the chapter above on "Games," to play before God.

The last word, I think, belongs to Huston Smith as he describes what it is like to live in "the strange new world" of our times and be religious there.

To borrow Nietzsche's image, we have all been summoned to become Cosmic Dancers who do not rest heavily in a single spot but lightly turn and leap from one position to another. We shall all have our own perspectives, but they can no longer be cast in the hard molds of oblivion to the rest. The Cosmic Dancer, the World Citizen, will be an authentic child of his parent culture but related closely to all. He will not identify his whole being with any one land however dear. Where he prides himself on his culture or nationality, as he well may, his will be an affirming pride borne of gratitude for the values he has gained, not a defensive pride whose only device for achieving the sense of superiority it pathetically needs is by grinding down others through invidious comparison. His roots in his family, his community, his civilization will be deep, but in that very depth he will strike the water table of man's common humanity and thus nourished will reach out in more active curiosity, more open vision, to discover and understand what others have seen. For is he not also man? If only he might see what has interested others, might it not interest him as well? It is an exciting prospect [18]

It is indeed!

Notes

INTRODUCTION
1. *The Art of Time* (New York: E. P. Dutton & Co., 1969), p. 26.

FORMS
1. Michel Seuphor, *Abstract Painting* (New York: Dell Publishing Co., 1964), p. 64.
2. Michael Kirby, *The Art of Time*, p. 51.
3. *New Think* (New York: Basic Books, 1968).
4. Seuphor, op. cit., p. 16.
5. Tom Stoppard, *Rosencrantz and Guildenstern Are Dead* (London: Faber & Faber, 1967), p. 61.
6. Aaron Copland, *Music and Imagination* (New York: Mentor Books, n.d.), p. 27.
7. Antonin Artaud, *The Theater and Its Double*, Mary C. Richards, trans. (New York: Grove Press, 1958), p. 77.
8. Harvey Cox, *The Feast of Fools* (Cambridge, Mass.: Harvard University Press, 1969), p. 95.

GAMES
1. *In Praise of Play* (New York: Harper & Row, 1969).
2. Ibid., p. 64.
3. Ibid., p. 146.
4. Johan Huizinga, *Homo Ludens: A Study of the Play-Element in Culture* (Boston: Beacon Press, 1968), p. 206.

DANCE
1. Neale, op. cit., p. 113.
2. Jane Harrison, *Themis: A Study of the Social Origins of Greek*

Religion (Cambridge, Eng.: The University Press, 1912), p. 125; R. R. Marett, *The Threshold of Religion* (London: Methuen & Co., 1900), p. 48; Huizinga, *Homo Ludens*, p. 15.

3. W. O. E. Oesterley, *The Sacred Dance: A Study in Comparative Folklore* (Cambridge, Eng.: The University Press, 1923).
4. Cited by Cox, *The Feast of Fools*, p. 53.
5. *Sacred and Profane Beauty: The Holy in Art*, David E. Green, trans. (New York: Holt, Rinehart & Winston, 1963), p. 36.
6. Cox, op. cit., p. 52.
7. *Blues People* (New York: William Morrow & Co., 1963), pp. 43–44.
8. *Risk*, V, no. 1 (1969), 42–44.
9. Op. cit., p. 12.
10. James Frazer, *The Golden Bough* (New York: Mentor Books, 1959), p. 350.

BODY

1. Alexander Lowen, *The Betrayal of the Body* (New York: Collier Books, 1967), pp. 1–18.
2. Arthur McGill, *Celebration of Flesh* (New York: Association Press, 1964), pp. 33–34.
3. Op. cit., p. 5.
4. Cited in Conrad Bonifazi, *A Theology of Things* (Philadelphia: J. B. Lippincott Co., 1967), pp. 32–33.
5. Op. cit., p. 6.
6. *Joy: Expanding Human Awareness* (New York: Grove Press, 1967), pp. 15 ff.
7. *The Varieties of Psychedelic Experience* (New York: Dell Publishing Co., 1967), pp. 11–12.
8. M. D. Herter Norton, trans. (New York: Capricorn Books, 1958), p. 14.
9. New York: New Directions, 1941, pp. 21–22.
10. Albert Camus, *The Myth of Sisyphus* (New York: Random House, 1959), p. 20.
11. Myron B. Bloy, Jr., ed., *Multi-Media Worship* (New York: Seabury Press, 1969), p. 8.
12. B. Z. Goldberg, *The Sacred Fire: The Story of Sex in Religion* (New York: University Books, 1958), p. 110.
13. Ibid., pp. 176–77.
14. "Studies in Worship Open New Horizons," *San Diego Evening Tribune*, October 26, 1968, p. A–5.

15. Compare, in the "theater-of-touch" movement, the staging of the *James Joyce Liquid Theatre* by The Company in Los Angeles. About twenty playgoers at a time, sitting in a circle, are instructed by a soft-spoken director to squeeze hands, each person squeezing his right hand as his own left hand is pressed. Then, after some "loosening-up exercises," the twenty pair off and sit cross-legged on the floor opposite each other. Taking turns, the participants close their eyes and, on command from the director, feel the eyebrows, eye sockets, nose, chin, cheekbones, and lips of the other person, mentally sculpting the person as they do it. After that, the twenty persons press close together on their sides and lie there quietly for a few minutes. Then each person is led by a guide of the opposite sex through a maze, receiving and returning caresses and kisses on the way. His hands are perfumed with honeysuckle. A piece of apple or a grape may be popped into his mouth. When he emerges from the maze, and the "play," he has an unusually acute sense of the tactile, and is strangely awakened to the appearances and feelings of other persons. *Vide* "Love Play in Braille," *Time*, February 23, 1970, p. 68.
16. New York: Collier Books, 1968.

PERSONS

1. *Joy*, pp. 117–186.
2. *A Time for Everything* (Waco, Tex.: Lake Shore Baptist Church, 1969), p. 12.
3. Ibid., pp. 18–19.
4. Ibid., pp. 22–23.

DRAMA

1. Richard B. Sewall, *The Vision of Tragedy* (New Haven: Yale University Press, 1959), p. 5.
2. Sam Keen, *To a Dancing God* (New York: Harper & Row, 1970), p. 99.
3. The next chapter will deal more carefully with the subject of myth. For the moment, of course, it should be borne in mind that drama and ritual can never be actually separated from the meaning and evolution of myth.
4. Cf. Al Hansen, *A Primer of Happenings & Time/Space Art* (New York: Something Else Press, 1965), p. 7: "The majority of happen-

ings are quite formal, are very carefully rehearsed, and do not invite any audience participation at all."

5. *TDR: The Drama Review*, XIII, no. 1 (Fall 1968), 93.
6. Op. cit., pp. 34–35.
7. Roger Ortmayer, "The Liturgical Scene," *Religion in Life*, XXXIX (Spring 1970), 18–27.
8. Lawrence Ferlinghetti, *Routines* (New York: New Directions, 1964), p. 52.
9. *The Impossible Theater: A Manifesto* (New York: Collier Books, 1965), p. 302.
10. At St. Clement's a priest, a paper bag over his head also, began the liturgy with this statement:

> I am a dead priest
> This is a dead mass
> The church is dead
> People are looking at us
> Because we are dead. . . .

(Cited by Ortmayer, op. cit., p. 24.)
11. J. L. Moreno, *New Introduction to Psychodrama*, Psychodrama and Group Psychotherapy Monograph no. 19 (New York: Beacon House, 1963), p. v.
12. One of J. L. Moreno's books is entitled *Theatre of Spontaneity* (New York: Beacon House, 1947).
13. Psychodrama and Group Psychotherapy Monograph no. 41 (New York: Beacon House, 1966).
14. See Robert W. Siroka and Gilbert A. Schloss, "The Death Scene in Psychodrama," *Group Psychotherapy*, XXI, no. 4 (December 1969), 202–205.
15. J. L. Moreno, *The Concept of Sociodrama*, Psychodrama and Group Psychotherapy Monograph no. 1 (New York: Beacon House, 1944), p. 7.
16. Myron B. Bloy, Jr., ed. (New York: Seabury Press, 1969), p. 117.

STORY
1. *In Praise of Play* (New York: Harper & Row, 1969), p. 126.
2. Ibid., p. 127.
3. Ibid., p. 129.
4. Ibid., p. 60.
5. *Myth and Ritual in Christianity* (New York: Grove Press, 1960), p. 12.

6. To set the Christian traditions regarding Jesus in perspective with the Hero tradition generally, see especially Lord Raglan, *The Hero: A Study in Tradition, Myth, and Drama* (London: Watts & Co., 1936) and Joseph Campbell, *The Hero with a Thousand Faces* (New York: World Publishing Co., 1956). Raglan offers the following summary of the Hero-pattern and then proceeds to "score" various figures on the basis of their conformity to it:

    (1) The hero's mother is a royal virgin;
    (2) His father is a king, and
    (3) Often a near relative of his mother, but
    (4) The circumstances of his conception are unusual, and
    (5) He is also reputed to be the son of a god.
    (6) At birth an attempt is made, usually by his father or his maternal grandfather, to kill him, but
    (7) He is spirited away, and
    (8) Reared by foster-parents in a far country.
    (9) We are told nothing of his childhood, but
    (10) On reaching manhood he returns or goes to his future kingdom.
    (11) After a victory over the king and/or a giant, dragon, or wild beast,
    (12) He marries a princess, often the daughter of his predecessor, and
    (13) Becomes king.
    (14) For a time he reigns uneventfully, and
    (15) Prescribes laws, but
    (16) Later he loses favour with the gods and/or his subjects, and
    (17) Is driven from the throne and city, after which
    (18) He meets with a mysterious death,
    (19) Often at the top of a hill.
    (20) His children, if any, do not succeed him.
    (21) His body is not buried, but nevertheless
    (22) He has one or more holy sepulchres.

7. *The Armed Vision* (New York: Vintage Books, 1955), p. 51.
8. "Some Meanings of Myth," *Myth and Mythmaking*, Henry A. Murray, ed. (Boston: Beacon Press, 1968), p. 111.
9. Campbell, op. cit., pp. 390–91.
10. Ibid., p. 388.
11. Ibid., p. 258.

LANGUAGE

1. *Antonin Artaud Anthology*, Jack Hirschman, ed. (San Francisco: City Lights Books, 1965), p. 38.
2. "The Language of the Liturgy," no. 7 in Documents Preparatory to the 1969 Meeting of Societas Liturgica, p. 1.
3. *Speaking of God* (New York: The Macmillan Co., 1964), p. 116.
4. Ibid., p. 14.
5. *The Secular Meaning of the Gospel* (New York: The Macmillan Co., 1963), p. 103.
6. Cf. *The Sense of Absence* (Philadelphia: J. B. Lippincott Co., 1968).
7. *The Art of James Joyce* (New York: Oxford University Press, 1964), p. 110.
8. Ibid., pp. 72–73.
9. New York: Dell Publishing Co., 1968.
10. Daniel B. Stevick, *Language in Worship* (New York: Seabury Press, 1970), p. 2.
11. Ibid., p. 145.
12. Ibid., pp. 59–60.
13. *Language, Hermeneutic, and Word of God* (New York: Harper & Row, 1966), p. 9.
14. George Steiner, *Language and Silence: Essays in Language, Literature, and the Inhuman* (New York: Atheneum, 1967), pp. 53–54.
15. Norman Habel, *Interrobang* (Philadelphia: Fortress Press, 1969), pp. 95–96.
16. In *Parable, Myth and Language*, Tony Stoneburner, ed. (Washington: The Church Society for College Work, 1968), p. 64.
17. *Gods and Games* (New York: World Publishing Co., 1969), pp. 139–42.
18. Stevick, op. cit., p. 68.

BLASPHEMY

1. Reported in Paul W Hoon, "Liturgy or Gamesmanship?," *Religion in Life*, XXXVIII, no. 4 (Winter 1969), 485.
2. By Dr. Hycel Taylor, then Dean of the Chapel, Fisk University, in a convocation service at Vanderbilt Divinity School on September 13, 1969.
3. "Friday Morning," by Sydney Carter.
4. By a female graduate student whose name I shall withhold.
5. *Wait Without Idols* (New York: George Braziller, 1964), p. 24.

6. In Malcolm Boyd, ed., *The Underground Church* (Baltimore: Pelican Books, 1969), pp. 62–69.
7. Myron B. Bloy, Jr., ed., *Multi-Media Worship* (New York: Seabury Press, 1969), pp. 96–97.
8. Ibid., p. 99.
9. *The Idea of the Holy* (London: Oxford University Press, 1957), pp. 61–65.
10. Émile Durkheim, *The Elementary Forms of the Religious Life*, Joseph W. Swain, trans. (New York: The Macmillan Co., n.d.), pp. 317–21.
11. Cf. R. W. B. Lewis, *The Picaresque Saint* (Philadelphia: J. B. Lippincott Co., 1961).
12. Jean-Paul Sartre, *Saint Genet: Actor and Martyr*, Bernard Frechtman, trans. (New York: George Braziller, 1963), p. 255.
13. Richard Coe, *The Vision of Jean Genet* (New York: Grove Press, 1968), pp. 37–38.
14. Fernando Arrabal, *L'Architecte et l'empereur d'Assyrie* (Paris: Christian Bourgois, 1967), p. 166.
15. Coe, op. cit., p. 38.
16. "The Dynamics of Worship," *Multi-Media Worship*, p. 57.

SERMON

1. Joseph Sittler, *The Anguish of Preaching* (Philadelphia: Fortress Press, 1966), p. v.
2. Cf. this passage from Arthur Herzog's *The Church Trap* (New York: The Macmillan Co., 1968), pp. 100–101: "Listen one Saturday or Sunday to a sermon of a typical rabbi or minister. The theme is all too likely to be a question to which everyone knows the answer in advance: 'Is God dead?' (No.) 'Are the Young without morality?' (This topic—the answer to which is also no—never fails to interest the predominantly older churchgoers.) 'Is there hope for mankind?' 'Can we live without God?' Such interrogatives are followed by a series of quotes pasted together, without a hint of discipline, from whatever sources happened to land on the minister's desk that week—an editorial or a news event, a scientific article, a line or two of poetry—followed by a biblical quote and the predictable conclusion. There is a complete and conspicuous absence of any *religious* insight. 'I try,' one minister told me, 'to give them a little of this and a little of that, a little uplift, a little scaring, a little food for thought.'"

3. David Randolph, *The Renewal of Preaching* (Philadelphia: Fortress Press, 1969), p. 1.
4. Sittler, op. cit., p. 5.
5. Ibid., p. 34.
6. Randolph, op. cit., p. 54.
7. *Partners in Preaching* (New York: Seabury Press, 1967), pp. 23–24.
8. *Music and Imagination* (New York: Mentor Books, n.d.), p. 59.
9. Gerhard Ebeling and Robert Funk, both New Testament scholars, have emphasized the significance of parabolic speech in the church. Roger Ortmayer's parables, which usually replace the sermon in liturgies where he is a participant, have a piquant, teasing, sacramental quality about them. With regard to brevity, it is interesting to note a movement in this direction among certain Protestant groups as they become more concerned for broader liturgical questions, at the same time that many Roman Catholics are laying new stress on the Word and providing more time for the sermon.
10. Howe, op. cit., p. 85.
11. The term is Edmund Steimle's, in *Renewal in the Pulpit* (Philadelphia: Fortress Press, 1966), p. x, referring to a sermon in that volume by John W. Vannorsdall, "Letter Home," cast in epistolary form for a congregation of college students and parents.
12. *Blues People* (New York: William Morrow & Co., 1968), p. 45.
13. Richard L. Stanger, "All There Was Was a Man—Struggling," *Christian Century,* October 1, 1969, pp. 1248–49.
14. Privately reproduced. Available from Celebration West, 2735 MacArthur Blvd., Oakland, Calif. 94602, at one dollar per copy.

MUSIC

1. *Philosophy in a New Key* (New York: Mentor Books, 1964), p. 206.
2. *Music in Church* (London: SPCK, 1951), p. 7; cited in Erik Routley, *Church Music and Theology* (Philadelphia: Muhlenberg Press, 1959), pp. 63–64.
3. George Steiner, *Language and Silence: Essays in Language, Literature and the Inhuman* (New York: Atheneum, 1967), p. 43.
4. Routley, op. cit., pp. 106–107.
5. *Twentieth Century Church Music* (New York: Oxford University Press, 1964), p. 187.
6. *Words, Music, and the Church* (Nashville, Tenn.: Abingdon Press, 1968), p. 111.
7. Ibid., p. 115.
8. Ibid., pp. 47–48.

9. *The Dyer's Hand and Other Essays* (New York: Random House, 1962), p. 458.
10. Routley, *Words, Music, and the Church*, p. 91.
11. Routley, *Church Music and Theology*, p. 71.
12. Sam Keen, *To a Dancing God* (New York: Harper & Row, 1970), p. 35.
13. See p. 12.
14. *The New American Arts*, Richard Kostelanetz, ed. (New York: Collier Books, 1965), p. 264.
15. *Abstract Painting* (New York: Dell Publishing Co., 1964), p. 16.
16. *Music and Imagination* (New York: Mentor Books, n.d.), p. 83.
17. *Art and Religion* (Boston: Beacon Press, 1948), p. 168.
18. *The Now Generation* (Richmond, Va.: John Knox Press, 1969), p. 20.
19. *Poetics of Music* (New York: Vintage Books, n.d.), p. 24.
20. Keen, op. cit., p. 159.
21. Routley, *Words, Music, and the Church*, p. 74.
22. Keen, op. cit., p. 157.
23. "The Peace of Christ: An Easter Celebration," *Christian Ministry*, March, 1970, p. 29.
24. Routley, *Twentieth Century Church Music*, p. 23.
25. Routley, *Words, Music, and the Church*, p. 173.
26. *Feeling and Form: A Theory of Art* (New York: Charles Scribner's Sons, 1953), p. 141.
27. *Language in Worship* (New York: Seabury Press, 1970), pp. 157–58.

TIME/SPACE

1. Johan Huizinga, *Homo Ludens* (Boston: Beacon Press, 1955), p. 10.
2. *Morality and Eros* (New York: McGraw-Hill, 1970), p. 168.
3. *New Trends in Church Architecture* (New York: Universe Books, 1967), p. 11.
4. Peter Hammond, *Liturgy and Architecture* (New York: Columbia University Press, 1961), p. 28.
5. Rudolf Schwarz, *The Church Incarnate*, Cynthia Harris, trans. (Chicago: Henry Regnery, 1958), p. 35.
6. Hammond, op. cit., pp. 6–7.
7. Ibid., p. 2.
8. *Church Architecture and Liturgical Reform*, Gregory Roettger, trans. (Baltimore and Dublin: Helicon Press, 1966), p. 40.
9. Hammond, op. cit., p. 158.

10. Quoted ibid., pp. 160–61.
11. Ibid., pp. 164–67.
12. Routley, *Twentieth Century Church Music*, pp. 200–02.
13. Donald J. Bruggink and Carl H. Droppers, *Christ and Architecture* (Grand Rapids, Mich.: William B. Eerdmans Publishing Co., 1965); Schwarz, op. cit.
14. Hammond, op. cit., p. 47.
15. Michael Kirby, *The Art of Time* (New York: E. P. Dutton & Co., 1969), p. 119.
16. *The Feast of Fools* (Cambridge, Mass.: Harvard University Press, 1969), p. 109.
17. Hammond, op. cit., p. 42.
18. Myron Bloy, Jr., ed., *Multi-Media Worship* (New York: Seabury Press, 1969), p. 90.
19. *The Shape of the Liturgy* (London: Dacre Press, 1945), pp. 303 ff.
20. See n. 14 under "Sermon."

METAWORSHIP

1. *The Universal Word* (Philadelphia: Westminster Press, 1969), p. 18.
2. Hans Küng, "The World Religions in God's Plan of Salvation," in Josef Neuner, ed., *Christian Revelation and World Religions* (London: Burns & Oates, 1967), pp. 27–28.
3. The full paragraph from the Constitution of the Church reads: "Nor is God far distant from those who in shadows and images seek the unknown God, for he gives all men life and breath and all things (cf. Acts 17:25–28), and as Saviour wants all men to be saved (cf. I Tim. 2:4). Those who through no fault of theirs are still ignorant of the Gospel of Christ and of his Church yet sincerely seek God and, with the help of divine grace, strive to do his will as known to them through the voice of their conscience, those men can attain to eternal salvation."
4. Carlyle Marney, *The Coming Faith* (Nashville, Tenn.: Abingdon Press, 1970), pp. 29–30.
5. Huston Smith, *The Religions of Man* (New York: Harper & Row, 1958), p. 23.
6. Ibid., p. 186.
7. Quoted in Thomas Ohm, *Asia Looks at Western Christianity*, Irene Marinoff, trans. (New York: Herder & Herder, 1959), p. 32.
8. *Buddhist Scriptures*, Edward Conze, trans. (Harmondsworth, Eng.: Penguin Books, 1959), p. 177.
9. *Myth and Mythmaking*, Henry A. Murray, ed. (Boston: Beacon Press, 1968), p. 21.

10. *New Trends in Church Architecture* (New York: Universe Books, 1967), p. 44.
11. Noel Q. King, *Religions of Africa* (New York: Harper & Row, 1970), p. 10.
12. Smith, op. cit., p. 2.
13. *Buddhism and Christianity* (Philadelphia: Westminster Press, 1962), pp. 32–33.
14. *Religious Essays*, Brian Lunn, trans. (London: Oxford University Press, 1931),.p. 116.
15. *Can Christians Learn from Other Religions?* (New York: Seabury Press, 1963), p. 85.
16. *Metatheatre: A New View of Dramatic Form* (New York: Hill & Wang, 1963).
17. New York: Harcourt, Brace & World, 1963.
18. Smith, op. cit., p. 7.